# QUICK ESCAPES®
# PHILADELPHIA

"Born and raised in Philadelphia—and I didn't realize there was so much, so close. Marilyn provides great ideas."

—Steve Levy, News Anchor, *NBC-10* (Philadelphia)

D1153569

## Help Us Keep This Guide Up to Date

Every effort has been made by the author and editors to make this guide as accurate and useful as possible. However, many things can change after a guide is published—establishments close, phone numbers change, facilities come under new management, etc.

We would love to hear from you concerning your experiences with this guide and how you feel it could be improved and be kept up to date. Though we may not be able to respond to all comments and suggestions, we'll take them to heart, and we'll also make certain to share them with the author. Please send your comments and suggestions to the following address:

The Globe Pequot Press
Reader Response/Editorial Department
P.O. Box 480
Guilford, CT 06437

Or you may e-mail us at:

editorial@globe-pequot.com

Thanks for your input, and happy travels!

# QUICK ESCAPES®
# PHILADELPHIA

### 24 WEEKEND GETAWAYS
### FROM THE CITY OF BROTHERLY LOVE

BY

**MARILYN ODESSER-TORPEY**

The
Globe
Pequot
Press

**GUILFORD, CONNECTICUT**

Copyright © 1999 by The Globe Pequot Press

**Photo credits:**

P. 1: photo by Michelle Mykowski; p. 11: courtesy Bethlehem Muskifest Association; p. 23: courtesy Carbon County Tourist Promotion Agency; pp. 34, 47: courtesy Pocono Mountains Vacation Bureau; p. 60: photo by Donna M. Traylor; p. 73: courtesy Endless Mountains Visitors Bureau; pp. 91, 141: photos by Cindy Turnstall, courtesy Maryland Office of Tourism Development; p. 131: photo by Tom Darden, courtesy Maryland Office of Tourism Development; p. 248: courtesy Maryland Office of Tourism Development; p. 98: photo by M.P. Myers, courtesy Chamber of Commerce of Greater Cape May; pp. 108, 119: courtesy Delaware Tourism Office; pp. 149, 262: courtesy Washington, D.C. Convention and Visitors Association; p. 155: courtesy Peddler's Village; p. 184: photo by Milton Rutherford, courtesy Bucks County Historical Society; p. 195: courtesy Pennsylvania Dutch Visitors Bureau; p. 222: courtesy Gettysburg Convention and Visitors Bureau; p. 233: courtesy New York Convention and Visitors Bureau; p. 276: courtesy Virginia Tourism Corporation; p. 285: photo by Richard T. Nowitz, courtesy Virginia Tourism Corporation.

Cover photo by David Forbert/SuperStock
Cover design by Laura Augustine
Text design by Nancy Freeborn/Freeborn Design
Maps by MaryAnn Dube

Quick Escapes is a registered trademark of The Globe Pequot Press.

**Library of Congress Cataloging-in-Publication Data**

Odesser-Torpey, Marilyn.
      Quick escapes Philadelphia : 24 weekend getaways from the City of
Brotherly Love / by Marilyn Odesser-Torpey. — 1st ed.
         p. cm.
      Includes index.
      ISBN 0-7627-0444-6
      1. Philadelphia Region (Pa.) Guidebooks. 2. Middle Atlantic States Guidebooks.
I. Title.
F158.18.O34 1999
917.48'10443—dc21                                    99-15495
                                                      CIP

Manufactured in the United States of America
First Edition/First Printing

To my loves, Daniel, Dana, and Kristen
We made it home together!

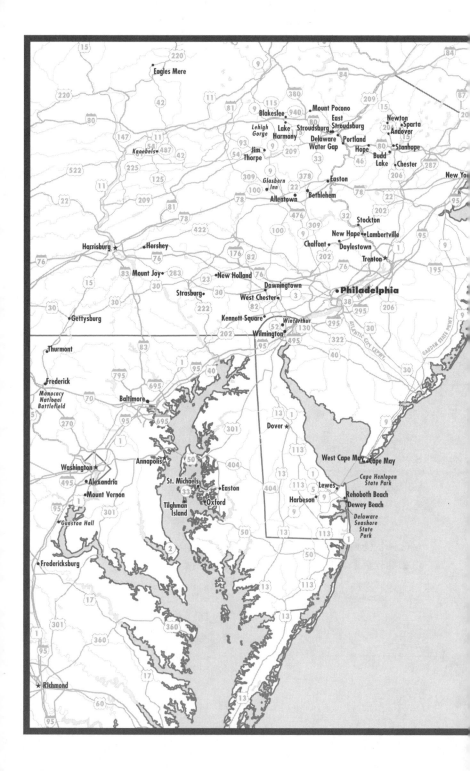

# CONTENTS

The information and rates listed in this guidebook were confirmed at press time. We recommend, however, that you call establishments before traveling to obtain current information.

# ACKNOWLEDGMENTS

As I journeyed up the mountains, down the shore, and between and beyond to research this book, I had a lot of company. There were, of course, my actual traveling companions, namely my beloved Dan and Kristen, and my good friends Mary Ellen Hatch, Michele Lerman, and Alonna Smith. Also crucial to my successful completion of this labor of love was my Dana, for helping to keep the home fires burning. Thanks, also, to my parents, Ben and Connie Odesser, for providing a home away from home for family members of the human and feathered varieties.

I would also like to express a sincere thank you to the many wonderful professionals I met along the way, especially Mindy Bianca, who has now become a treasured friend. Gratitude also to the many fellow diners, lodgers, travelers and locals in every town who so generously shared their favorite places, experiences and local lore with me.

To my wonderful editors, Laura Strom and Shelley Wolf, I know that working with first-time authors like me can be difficult. Your support and infinite patience made the experience of writing this first book so much easier (and a lot more fun) for this author.

And bottom-of-my-heart thanks to Elisabeth Rozin, my friend, role model and mentor. Your achievements are my inspiration.

# INTRODUCTION

Like most kids, I believed that the place where I lived was the center of the universe. It was kind of hard *not* to think that. After all, I lived in Philadelphia, and what place could have more history, more beauty, more fun things to do? Even our vacation destinations were close by—either "up the mountains" in winter or "down the shore" in summer.

"Up the mountains" generally meant the Poconos, where there were always countless fun ways to make your way down the glistening snow-covered slopes. "Down the shore" meant the beach, specifically any point from Ocean City to Cape May along South Jersey's Ocean Drive.

With age and experience came a broadening of my horizons. I learned that the pristine lakes and woodlands of the mountains make them as wonderful a place to visit in the summer as they are in winter. And I experienced the exhilaration of walking on a deserted windswept beach in the fall. But imagine my surprise when I realized that all mountains weren't part of the Poconos and all bodies of water weren't named Delaware, Schuylkill, or Atlantic!

Although I have lived here all my life, many of the sights, sounds, flavors, and feelings that make up the itineraries of this book were as much a revelation to me as I hope they are to you. I could always point out Philadelphia on a map, but it never really dawned on me how many exciting places and diverse experiences are easily within one to six hours driving time of the city. I hope this book will introduce you to some new ones . . . and, perhaps, put a few different twists on those you may have already discovered for yourself.

Whether your idea of a great time is going "up the mountains," "down the shore," or somewhere in between, whether you feel most comfortable in the lap of luxury or under Mother Nature's stars, and whether you prefer to be in the middle of nowhere or in the middle of everything, these quick escapes are for you. In fact, with so many escape options so close to home, you may well come to suspect, as I have, that Philadelphia really *is* the center of the universe.

# UP THE
# MOUNTAINS

# ESCAPES

*Raymondskill Falls.*

# The Lehigh Valley, Pennsylvania

## FORGED FROM STEEL, HEART OF GOLD

### 2 NIGHTS

*Thrills and Chills • Family Fun • Town and Country Cultural Diversity*

Once it was a place of green rolling hills, fertile fields, and sparkling waters ruled by Mother Nature and cared for by a tribe of Native Americans called the Leni Lenapes (also spelled Lenni Lenapes). Attracted by the shelter of the surrounding mountains and the promise in the rich soil, the Europeans came and settled in this virtual paradise. By the mid–1700s they had brought with them a diversity of cultures—Scotch-Irish, Moravian, English, and German. In the 1900s another wave of immigrants found their way to the valley, drawn by the hope of employment and a life of prosperity in its shining new cities, the largest of which were called Allentown, Bethlehem, and Easton.

Later in the century the steel industry went into a steep decline . . . and so did the fortunes of these cities and their inhabitants. But today the people are fighting back, determined to make their cities shine again. They still have a lot of work ahead of them, but a visit to the Lehigh Valley can yield some delightful surprises, as waterfronts are transformed into vibrant centers for the arts, shopping and dining; downtown areas are restored to their original charm; and the rich and varied cultural, religious, and historic heritages of its people are showcased.

Bounded on the north and northwest by the Kittatinny (Blue) Mountains, on the east by the Delaware River, and to the south by the Lehigh (South)

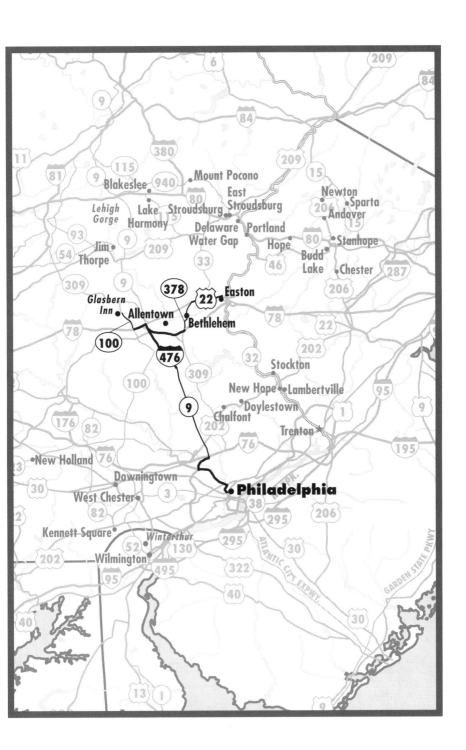

Mountains, the Lehigh Valley is still a beautiful area. Located only an hour or so north of Philadelphia, it is also an escape for all seasons . . . especially during Christmas when the valley becomes an old-fashioned winter wonderland of light, tradition, and song. And, after all, what more appropriate place to celebrate the season than in a little town called Bethlehem?

## DAY 1

## *Morning*

It's a 55-mile journey from Philadelphia to your first stop, Allentown. To get there, take the Pennsylvania Turnpike to Quakertown, exit onto Route 309 north and keep going until you see the exit for Cedar Crest Boulevard. Make a left onto Cedar Crest Boulevard and follow it past the light at the hospital. At the next light turn left onto Fish Hatchery Road for a don't-miss stop on the edge of town.

You will be experiencing a variety of different cultures during your visit to the Lehigh Valley. The **Lenni Lenape Historical Society and Museum of Indian Culture** (2825 Fish Hatchery Road, 610–797–2121) documents and celebrates the life and culture of the area's first inhabitants. Through exhibits, programs, historic trails, art, artifacts, and special events, it chronicles their history from the time they arrived in the valley through their early attempts to negotiate peacefully with the early European settlers. Open year-round; Wednesday–Sunday, noon–3:00 P.M. The museum's gift shop is also a wealth of Indian culture, offering books, music, and other native items. $3.00 for adults and children over twelve; $2.00 for children under twelve.

Next stop—the heart of Allentown's cultural and historic district. To get there, turn left out of the museum parking lot onto Fish Hatchery Road. At the stoplight turn left onto Twenty-fourth Street and continue until you get to Hamilton Boulevard. Park anywhere along Hamilton (at various points it is also called Hamilton Mall and Hamilton Street) and you'll be within walking distance of all the major downtown attractions.

If it's Thursday, Friday, or Saturday, it's market day in Allentown. So head to where Seventeenth Street intersects with Hamilton Boulevard and walk 3 blocks north to Chew Street and the **Allentown Fairgrounds Farmers Market** (610–432–8425). A tradition for more than four decades, the market features sixty-five merchants offering farm-fresh produce, baked goods (the Amish bakery's hot cinnamon buns are to die for), meats and cheeses, herbs and flowers. Open year-round; Thursday 9:00 A.M.–8:00 P.M., Friday 8:00 A.M.–8:00 P.M., Saturday 8:00 A.M.–6:00 P.M.

Then head back to Hamilton and walk over to the **Lehigh County Museum** (501 Hamilton Street; 610–435–4664 or 610–435–1704), a true gem housed in a circa 1814–17 courthouse. There's a lot of history covered in this museum, with exhibits that begin with the vertebra of a mastodon that roamed the area in 10,000–8,000 B.C. and end with displays of photos and memorabilia depicting agriculture, industry, and daily life in the valley up through the twentieth century. Open Monday–Friday 9:00 A.M.–4:00 P.M., Saturday 10:00 A.M.–4:00 P.M., Sunday, 1:00–4:00 P.M. Admission is free.

## *Afternoon*

**LUNCH: Federal Grill & Cigar Bar,** 536 Hamilton Street; (610) 776–7600. This spot across the street from the museum is a popular lunchtime hangout for lawyers and other official types from the nearby courthouse. But don't let the profusion of suits deter you; you'll be just as welcome in your jeans, shorts, and polo shirts. Housed in a one-hundred-year-old building, this dining establishment offers a moderately priced lunch menu featuring burgers, wraps, pizzas, and salads. For $6.25 you can "Do It Your Way" with a cup of homemade soup, half a sandwich, a small chopped salad, and beer-battered fries. Management credits the absence of cigar smoke in the air to their "state-of-the-art purification system."

Did you know that, during the Revolutionary War, the Liberty Bell "hid out" in Allentown? Fearful that it might come to harm at the hands of the British, the Philadelphia colonists smuggled our pride and joy here for safekeeping. Of course, the real McCoy has been back in Philadelphia for more than two centuries, but the **Liberty Bell Shrine Museum** (622 Hamilton Mall; 610–435–4232) still displays an exact replica. Open Monday–Saturday noon–4:00 P.M. (December through February, open Thursday, Friday and Saturday only). Donations.

The good news is it doesn't take a Rocky-like level of physical fitness to climb the outside steps to the **Allentown Art Museum** at Fifth and Court Streets (610–432–4333; Court runs perpendicular to Hamilton Street). The even better news is that at the top of these steps is a truly exciting museum. Among the permanent exhibitions are impressive collections of fourteenth- and seventeenth-century European paintings and sculptures, as well as works representing the last 200 years of American art. Open Tuesday–Saturday 11:00

A.M.–5:00 P.M.; Sunday noon–5:00 P.M. $4.00 for adults, $3.00 for seniors, $2.00 for students, free for children under twelve.

The Lehigh Valley is also home to two terrific amusement parks, one in Allentown and one in Easton, each with its own personality and following. If thrills, chills, and heart-stopping plummets are your idea of fun, you'll love **Dorney Park & Wildwater Kingdom** (3830 Dorney Park Road; 610–395–3724), where 200-foot-tall roller coasters, the world's longest elevated water slides, and giant wave pools await. All you have to do is head west on Hamilton Boulevard for about ten minutes and follow the signs. But don't think that the very young (or the older but not very brave) have been forgotten here. Among the one hundred rides and attractions at this 200-acre park are a circa 1921 Dentzel carousel, many kiddie rides, and a play area where you can visit with the Berenstain Bears of storybook fame. The park also offers live entertainment for the whole family. Both parks are open May–early September; Dorney Park alone remains open until mid-October. Prices are seasonal ranging from $22.00 to $28.00 for adults, $5.95 for children four and older, free for children three and under. Adult admission to Dorney Park alone is $16.50. Parking is $5.00.

## Evening

**LODGING: Glasbern Inn,** 2141 Pack House Road, Fogelsville; (610) 285–4723. The inn where you will be dining and lodging this evening is about 10 miles west of Allentown. From Dorney Park follow Route 22/78 west to the Fogelsville exit (exit 14B). Turn left at the first traffic light; go $^3/_{10}$ of a mile and make a right onto Church Street. Proceed $^6/_{10}$ of a mile and make a right onto Pack House Road; continue for about $^8/_{10}$ of a mile. The entrance to the inn will be on your right.

"It's just an old barn," manager Erik Sheetz explains, as you marvel at the soaring 28-foot cathedral ceiling, stacked slate and shale walls, and the ten two-story windows. ("Glasbern" is Middle English for glass barn.) But the only animals you'll find in this refurbished nineteenth-century German bank barn today are of the two-legged variety who come to stay in its twelve elegantly rustic guest rooms and feast on some of the Lehigh Valley's finest meals.

Outside there are lovely trails to stroll, romantic views to share, and a heated pool. Mountain bikes, a video library, and an on-site fitness center are also available. Room rates range from $120 to $155 weekdays, $145 to $200 weekends. *Note:* Management candidly acknowledges that some rooms tend to pick up sounds from the kitchen and/or upper floor, so if you're counting on total peace and quiet during your getaway, let them know when you make your reservation.

**DINNER:** Glasbern Inn. Rustic wooden posts and crossed beams and ladders that climb to the hayloft provide a dramatic contrast to the gleaming cherry tables and sideboards set with pewter, silver, and crystal in the Glasbern's candlelit dining room. It's the perfect place for enjoying expertly prepared American classics with a twist, such as the pan-seared red snapper over a scallop chowder with fresh truffles or roasted pheasant filled with wild mushrooms, foie gras, and risotto stuffing. Expensive. A special appetizer-to-dessert Glasbern Tasting Menu featuring some of the restaurant's specialties along with complementary wines is available for $55 (plus tax and gratuity).

## DAY 2

## *Morning*

**BREAKFAST:** Glasbern Inn. Bask in the morning sunlight in the same room in which you dined by candlelight the night before. The inn serves a bountiful eye-opener (included with the room) that begins with a buffet of oven-fresh muffins, fresh fruit, granola, and yogurt. Country-style entrees include fragrant fruited pancakes, waffles, and assorted egg dishes and accompaniments.

After breakfast it's on to Bethlehem. Take Route 22 going east for about 20 miles. Stay on Route 22 until you get to Route 512; take 512 going south until it turns into Center Street. Keep going south until Center intersects Broad Street, one of the main streets of Bethlehem. Turn right onto Broad and go two blocks down to Main Street. Park your car in the public lot at Broad and Main Streets (free evenings, Saturday, and Sunday) and forget about it for the day. This town is extremely walkable.

Bethlehem is a town of startling contrasts. In the course of a 2-block walk between Broad and Church Streets, you will pass back and forth through three centuries as rustic buildings of hand-hewn logs and limestone mingle with modern structures of steel, glass, and brick, and original Colonial and Victorian facades peacefully coexist next to twentieth-century chic. The majority of the town was built by members of the Moravian Church, who founded Bethlehem when they immigrated from Europe in 1741 to do missionary work among the Native Americans in the area.

To get a glimpse of early Moravian religious traditions, start at the **Moravian Museum of Bethlehem,** also known as **Gemein Haus** (Community House), located at 66 West Church Street (610–867–0173), right around the corner from Main Street. Built in 1741, it was home to the town's entire population while other buildings were being constructed, and it remained the center of worship and daily life. Today exhibits explain the ideals, arts, and culture of the early Moravians. The gift shop offers deliciously scented beeswax candles and other handmade items reflecting traditional early Moravian arts and crafts. Open February–December, Tuesday–Saturday 1:00–4:00 P.M. Admission is $5.00 for adults, $3.00 for students, children under six free. If you get there at the right time, you might even be able to tag along on one of the two-hour guided walking tours offered by the museum to groups of ten or more ($10.00 for adults, $8.00 for students).

Whether or not you join a tour, some of the key sites you should check out are:

- The **Central Moravian Church.** Constructed in 1806 when the total population of Bethlehem numbered only 580, this structure is designed to seat 1,500 because the Moravians planned to share their house of worship with the converted Indians and friendly colonists in the area.

- **God's Acre,** off Market Street between Heckewelder Place and New Street. All of the grave sites at this 1742–1912 Moravian cemetery are marked with identical flat stones to symbolize the Moravians' belief in equality in death as well as in life. One of these graves belongs to Tshoop, a member of the Mohican tribe who was immortalized as Uncas in James Fenimore Cooper's novel *Last of the Mohicans.*

- **Nain House,** at Heckewelder Place. This small 1758 log house is the only structure along the Delaware and Lehigh Heritage Corridor that was built by and lived in by Native Americans. Open by appointment; call the Moravian Museum. Admission is free.

After your walking tour, head for 427 North New Street, where you'll find 250 years of folk art, furnishings, paintings, and fine art at the **Kemerer Museum of Decorative Arts** (427 North New Street; 610–868–6868). The collections of Bohemian glass and regionally made tall case clocks are particularly dazzling. Open year-round Tuesday–Sunday noon–5:00 P.M.; daily during December. $3.00 for adults, $1.00 for children.

## *Afternoon*

**LUNCH: Bethlehem Brew Works,** 569 Main Street; (610) 882–1300. It's only a 1½ block walk from the Kemerer Museum to this fun spot that serves great food in a dramatic setting. The interior is all steel pipe, diamond plate, and copper tanks, attesting to Bethlehem's industrial heritage and the presence of a working brewery on the premises. The moderately priced menu includes salads, burgers, and sandwiches, along with some uniquely "spirited" offerings such as beer and cheese soup, porter beer chicken, diamond plate pork (medallions marinated in beer), and filet mignon with a stout-bourbon demiglaze. Kids' meals—of the nonspirited variety, of course—range from $2.95 to $4.95.

Even before steel came to town, Bethlehem was a thriving commercial center. In 1748 when the town had only 395 residents, thirty-eight industries were busily producing a variety of goods. Many of these industries were situated along the banks of Monocacy Creek in what is now called the **Colonial Industrial Quarter** (459 Old York Road; 610–691–0603). It's tucked off the road, but easy to get to; a little street called Ohio Road connects Main Street with the entrance. What you'll find are restored buildings that housed the **Tannery,** built in 1761; the **Waterworks,** the oldest pumped waterworks in America, built in 1762; and the **Luckenbach Mill,** here since 1869 (rebuilt from the ruins of its original 1743 wooden structure) and in operation well into the twentieth century. The three buildings now house interpretive exhibits and artifacts from those early industrial boom times. Open July and August, Saturday noon–5:00 P.M. Adults $5.00, children $2.00.

For the first part of the day you've been immersed in Bethlehem's early history. Now it's time to sample some of its more modern attractions . . . like shopping. The best place to do that is on the one-mile strip of Main Street that connects the north and south campuses of Moravian College, a location that has earned it the nickname "the Moravian Mile."

A new shining star in Bethlehem is **Main Street Commons,** two floors of mom-and-pop owned and operated shops at the corner of Broad and Main Streets. Some particularly interesting tenants include **Bone Appetit** (610–332–BONE), which offers all-natural, preservative-free, no salt or sugar-added treats for your best friend . . . the one named Spot or Fluffy. Since you deserve a treat, too, indulge in one of owner Barbara Garrison's super-premium concoctions at the **Heavenly Hedgehog Ice Cream Company** (610–332–1600). Barbara's signature flavor? A little something she calls "Forest Gump" (because "you never know what you're gonna get").

Wonder whatever happened to the part of town where the steel mills once dominated the landscape as well as the economy? Bethlehem's Southside is being revived, rejuvenated—actually reinvented—into a lively, energetic center for arts and culture. From downtown New Street to the heart of the Southside is a quick 1½-mile trip south and across the Fahy Bridge. At the **Banana Factory** (211 Plymouth Street; 610–332–1300), so named because it is housed in an old banana warehouse and distribution center, you can visit the studios of twenty-four emerging artists who work in a wide range of media. There's also a unique gift shop and an art gallery that exhibits works by artists from around the world. Open Monday–Thursday 8:30 A.M.–9:00 P.M., Friday until 7:00 P.M., and Saturday 9:00 A.M.–5:00 P.M. The Binney and Smith Art Gallery is open Monday–Friday 10:00 A.M.–7:00 P.M., Saturday until 5:00 P.M.

Talented local artists, artisans, musicians, authors, and illustrators are also the focal point at a Southside shop/gallery called **Legends, Traditions and Friends** (11 East Third Street; 610–865–4755).

**DINNER: Sun Inn,** 564 Main Street; (610) 874–9451. George Washington slept here . . . so did Martha, separated by three years and a set of stairs. John Adams called it "the best inn I ever saw." Since 1758 when the Moravians first constructed it as their first official *Gasthaus* for travelers, this building has been a place of gracious welcome and bountiful repasts. Today the first floor of the Sun Inn, furnished in eighteenth-century style with antiques and period reproductions, looks very much as it did back then. On the upper level are the dining rooms, including the particularly pretty Tile Room, named in honor of the composition of its centerpiece stove. The moderately priced menu, with selections such as Martha Washington Pecan Salmon and Marquis de Lafayette's Vegetable Napoleon, is a tribute to traditional and contemporary cuisine as well as to the illustrious clientele the inn has hosted over the years.

Rather than steel, higher education is probably the Lehigh Valley's most prized product today. Almost a dozen colleges and universities prosper here, bringing with them an indefatigable energy and a wealth of cultural activities. One example is the **Zoellner Arts Center** at Lehigh University (420 East Packer Street; 610–758–2787), which offers performances year-round in its three theaters, ranging from Broadway to Shakespeare, from country music to concertos and ballet to Irish dancing. While you're there, be sure to visit the center's galleries featuring exhibitions of painting, photography, sculpture, and other visual arts.

**LODGING:** Glasbern Inn.

*At the Banana Factory, you can visit the studios of emerging artists.*

## DAY 3

### Morning

**BREAKFAST:** Glasbern Inn.

Later today, you will be heading for the last of the trio of the Lehigh Valley's "big cities," Easton. But first a little side trip to Hellertown. Take Route 78 east to exit 21 (Hellertown/Bethlehem). Turn left at the bottom of the exit onto Route 412 south. Continue 1²/₁₀ miles to Penn Street; turn left. Go ½ mile. On your right-hand side will be **Lost River Caverns** (726 Durham Street, Hellertown; 610–838–8767). Formed sometime within the last 2,500 years and discovered in 1883, these natural limestone caverns are so beautiful that one, called the Crystal Chapel, was a popular ballroom in the late 1880s and is still used today as a wedding and christening chapel. During Prohibition, bootleggers also used the caverns for their illegal operations. On the walls crystal formations become strange and dazzling jewels, and minerals suddenly erupt in blazes of color under the illumination of an ultraviolet light. At the gift shop, rock, mineral, and crystal specimens, jewelry, and other related items range from twenty-seven cents to hundreds of dollars. Open year-round; Memorial Day–Labor Day 9:00 A.M.–6:00 P.M., remainder of year 9:00 A.M.–5:00 P.M. $7.50 for adults; $3.75 for children three to twelve.

To get to Easton, take Route 412 north to Route 378 north until you come to Route 22 east. Get off at the Fourth Street exit and follow signs for EASTON ATTRACTIONS. One of the most popular of these attractions is **Two Rivers Landing** and its focal point the **Crayola Factory** (30 Centre Square; 610–515–8000). The fun-filled tour includes a crayon-making demonstration (complete with free samples) and many opportunities to let the artist in you go wild. And remember, old crayon colors never die; they retire to the Crayon Hall of Fame. During the school year, the Crayola Factory is open Tuesday–Saturday 9:30 A.M.–5:00 P.M.; from Memorial Day–Labor Day it is open seven days a week; Monday–Saturday 9:00 A.M.–6:00 P.M., Sunday 11:00 A.M.–6:00 P.M. Adults and children over two, $7.00, seniors $6.50.

Your ticket also includes admission to the **National Canal Museum** (610–555–8000), located on the third floor of Two Rivers Landing, which takes you on a journey back to a time before railroads, highways, and airplanes through photographs, artifacts, and audio visual and interactive exhibits.

Now that you know what canal travel looked like, why not experience it firsthand on the *Josiah White II,* a real mule-drawn canal boat located right around the corner? Days and hours vary seasonally. The ticket ($5.00 adults, $3.00 children three to fifteen) also entitles you to visit the **Locktender's House Museum** in nearby **Hugh Moore Historical Park,** where you'll also find trails, picnic areas, and rental boats.

## *Afternoon*

**LUNCH: Pearly Baker's Ale House,** 11 Centre Square; (610) 253–9949. A huge crystal chandelier, brought here from Czechoslovakia in the 1940s, is the centerpiece of this razzle-dazzle pre-Prohibition-style restaurant/bar right across from Two Rivers Landing. One signature recipe on the moderately priced lunch menu is Brooklyn Brown Ale Onion Soup, regular or "boulder style" (baked with mozzarella and blue cheese). Some interesting entrees are grilled chicken and papaya quesadillas; mushroom ravioli; and flat breads (pizza toppings served on a hand-rolled whole-wheat crust). Children's selections are priced at $3.50.

# UP THE MOUNTAINS

Easton's **Bushkill Park** (2100 Bushkill Park Drive; 610-258-6941) is the second of the great Lehigh Valley amusement parks mentioned earlier. This one's for individuals and families who long for the good old days before bigger, faster, and scarier were the standard. Pay by the ride or purchase an unlimited ride pass to enjoy the seventeen classic old-fashioned delights, including a 1926 Allan Herschell carousel with Grand Wurlitzer band organ, and walk-through fun houses. Picnic grounds and free parking. Open weekends Memorial Day–June 15; Tuesday–Sunday June 17–Labor Day.

To return to Philadelphia, take Route 22 west until you get to Route 476. (northeast extension of Pennsylvania Turnpike). Drive south on 476 until you get to the Schuylkill Expressway. The trip home should take you a little more that an hour.

## THERE'S MORE

**Haines Mill Museum,** 3600 Dorney Park Road, Allentown; (610) 435–1074. Learn about farming and milling techniques at the turn of the century at this working grist mill built in 1760 and restored in 1909. Open May–September, Saturday and Sunday, 1:00–4:00 P.M. Admission.

**Allentown Symphony Hall,** 23 North Sixth Street, Allentown; (610) 432-6715. Home of the Allentown Symphony Orchestra and other performances for all ages from musical theater to professional concerts and lectures. Open year-round, Monday–Friday, 9:00 A.M.–4:30 P.M.

**Game Preserve,** 5150 Game Preserve Road, Schnecksville (6 miles north of Allentown); (610) 799–4171. More than 350 native and exotic animals and birds in a 1,200-acre setting of unspoiled beauty, hiking trails, and picnic areas. Kids will love playing detective in the environmentally themed feature "Where in the Zoo is Carmen Sandiego"™. The Game Preserve is open daily 10:00 A.M.–5:00 P.M. from late April to early November. Admission.

**Bethlehem Walking Tours,** Bethlehem Visitors Center, 52 West Broad Street, Bethlehem, PA; (610) 868–1513. Year-round one-hour tours ($6.00 for adults, $3.00 for children twelve and under) and holiday evening bus tours. Open seven days a week, 9:00 A.M.–5:00 p.m; until 9:00 P.M. from the day after Thanksgiving to January 1.

**Goundie House,** 501 Main Street, Bethlehem; (610) 691–5300. A Federal-style brick townhouse built in 1810 by a successful brewer and former mayor of Bethlehem. Peek into this 1810 brick townhouse and see a restored period kitchen, dining room, parlor, and bedroom. Free. Open year-round; Monday–Saturday 10:00 A.M.–5:00 P.M., and also Sunday from April–December, noon–4:00 P.M.

**Touchstone Theatre,** 321 East Fourth Street, Bethlehem; (610) 867–1689. An intimate theater in a restored 1875 firehouse where original and classic dramas are performed by a resident professional acting ensemble and distinguished guest artists. September–May, Wednesday, Thursday, Friday, 8:00 P.M.; Saturday, 4:00 P.M. and 8:00 P.M. Admission $9.00–$15.00 per person.

**Dutch Springs,** 4733 Hanoverville Road, Bethlehem; (610) 759–2270. Scuba diving in the Lehigh Valley? That's right, in a forty-seven-acre freshwater lake that has been especially designed for maximum sightseeing of submerged vehicles, aircraft, and plenty of fish. There are also facilities for picnicking, boating, swimming, and snorkeling. Open April–mid-December weekends and summer holidays, 8:00 A.M.–6:00 P.M.; Memorial Day–September 30, weekdays, 10:00 A.M.–6:00 P.M. No admission after 4:00 P.M. Only certified divers are permitted to scuba dive. Admission is $17.00 for divers, $10.00 for nondivers, $5.00 for children (nondivers).

**Godfrey Daniels,** 7 East Fourth Street, Bethlehem; (610) 867–2390. An intimate coffeehouse/listening club featuring folk, jazz, blues, Celtic, and Cajun music; poetry; and children's programs. Light menu featuring homemade vegetarian chili or soup ($3.50) and desserts. Performances are scheduled every Thursday–Sunday beginning at 8:00 P.M. Jams and special shows are often featured on Tuesday and Wednesday. Admission prices range from $9.50 to $17, depending on the performers.

**Discovery Center of Science & Technology,** 511 East Third Street, Bethlehem; (610) 865–5010. Science and technology come down to earth with interactive exhibits demonstrating how basic principles apply to our everyday lives. Open year-round, Tuesday–Saturday 9:30 A.M.–4:30 P.M., Sunday noon–4:30 P.M. Admission $3.00 per person.

**Passport to Color Fun,** Easton; (610) 555–8000. This program bundles admission to a number of Easton's major attractions into one economical ticket price.

**State Theatre, Center for the Arts,** 435 Northampton Street, Easton; (610) 252–3132 or (800) 999–STATE. Year-round live performances including comedians, headliners, drama, musicals, and children's shows.

## SPECIAL EVENTS

**March.** Bach Choir of Bethlehem, 423 Heckewelder Place; (610) 866–4382. Annual concert by America's oldest Bach Choir (its centennial birthday was celebrated in 1998). One hundred ten voices, the Bach Festival Orchestra, and distinguished soloists.

**Late July–August.** Philadelphia Eagles Training Camp at Lehigh University; (610) 463–2500.

**August.** Bethlehem Musikfest; (610) 322–1350. More than 650 free performances from Bach to bluegrass at an outdoor festival that also features ethnic foods, crafts, children's activities, and fireworks.

**Late August/early September.** The Great Allentown Fair, 302 North Seventeenth Street; (610) 433–7541. A weeklong extravaganza featuring agriculture, horticulture, domestic and fine arts, top-name musical performing artists, carnival rides and games, and "every food and gadget imaginable." Nominal admission.

**September.** Celtic Classic Highland Games & Festival, 437 Main Street, Bethlehem; (610) 868–9599. A celebration of the cultures of Ireland, Scotland, and Wales with Highland athletic, dance, and bagpipe competitions; Irish step dance; children's activities; food and wares from the Celtic isles; and continuous music. Free.

**November/mid-December.** Christkindlmarkt Bethlehem, Main and Hill Streets (under the Hill-to-Hill Bridge), Bethlehem; (610) 868–1513. A Yuletide family tradition modeled after European holiday markets. Features include juried crafts, holiday and specialty items, food, St. Nicholas, and entertainment. Three consecutive weekends (Thursday–Sunday) starting the Friday after Thanksgiving. Nominal admission.

**December.** Live Christmas Pageant, Bethlehem; (800) 360–8687 or (610) 868–1513. The Nativity story is reenacted in an outdoor setting by a large cast of costumed adults and children as well as live animals. Second weekend in December, one-hour program. Free.

### OTHER RECOMMENDED RESTAURANTS AND LODGINGS

## *Allentown*

King George Inn, Cedar Crest and Hamilton Boulevards; (610) 435–1723. A National Historic Site built in 1756, this pretty dining place serves veal, seafood, steaks, and pasta. Wine list offers more than one hundred selections. Seasonal outdoor dining. Moderate to expensive.

Yocco's "The Hot Dog King," 625 Liberty Street (610–433–1950) and 2128 Hamilton Street (610–821–8488). With or without chili sauce. Try the pierogies, too. Inexpensive.

## *Bethlehem*

Bethlehem Inn, 476 North New Street; (610) 867–4985. Conveniently located near many of the town's main attractions, this charming historic inn is renowned for its gourmet breakfasts. Room rates range from $75 to $105.

Cafe Havana, 313 South New Street; (610) 868–5733. The flavor of Cuba begins with the palm tree and fluorescent decor. Even more important, the food is authentic and homemade. Inexpensive.

Confetti Cafe, 462 Main Street; (610) 861–7484. This popular casual dining spot offers everything from cappuccino to full lunches and dinners. Sunday Brunch also serves up live acoustic jazz. Definitely don't skip the homemade ice cream, even if you can't handle the house specialty, a monstrous masterpiece served in a real kitchen sink! Inexpensive to moderate.

Sayre Mansion Inn, 250 Wyandotte Street; (610) 882–2100. Grace and luxury in an antiques-filled restored 1850s mansion. Room rates range from $80 to $150.

### *Easton*

Lafayette Inn, 525 West Monroe Street; (610) 253–4500. A fully restored 1895 brick mansion with Old World–style and modern-day amenities. Room rates range from $95 to $140.

## FOR MORE INFORMATION

Allentown Downtown Improvement Authority, 462 West Broad Street, Allentown, PA; (610) 776–7117.

Easton Visitor Trolley, Center Square in front of the Crayola Factory at Two Rivers Landing. A seasonal resource for brochures and other information.

Lehigh Valley Convention and Visitors Bureau, 2200 Avenue A, LVIP I, Bethlehem, PA; (800) 747–0561 or (610) 882–9200; www.lehighvalleypa.org.

# UP THE MOUNTAINS

# Jim Thorpe, Pennsylvania

## AMERICA'S LITTLE
## SWITZERLAND

### 1 NIGHT

*Fairy Tale Town • Mountain Majesty • Downhill Biking*
*Art-full Diversions*

At first glance, Jim Thorpe looks like a movie set, Mary Poppins' England come to life with rows of ornately trimmed Victorian homes and quaint little shops lining the winding, gently sloping streets. Brooding majestically from a high hilltop overlooking the town are two mansions that look as if they could have come straight from the pages of a gothic novel. And at the center of it all stands a bustling train station from which the clanging of the bell of an old-fashioned locomotive echoes cheerfully throughout the town.

Far from a fairy tale come to life, this is a town that has been known by a number of names and has had just as many personalities during its two-century-long history of fortune and misfortune. Called Coalville in the early nineteenth century, it was an important transportation center for the booming coal-mining industry. Later in the century, the arrival of the railroad made the town, which by then had been renamed Mauch Chunk (Lenape for Bear Mountain), a popular tourist destination often referred to as "America's Switzerland" because of its glorious mountain surroundings.

Mauch Chunk's glory days abruptly ended with the collapse of the coal-mining industry and the onset of the Great Depression in the 1920s, followed by years of hard economic times. In 1954, the town got a new name, Jim Thorpe, along with a new spirit and new hope. Jim Thorpe was a Native

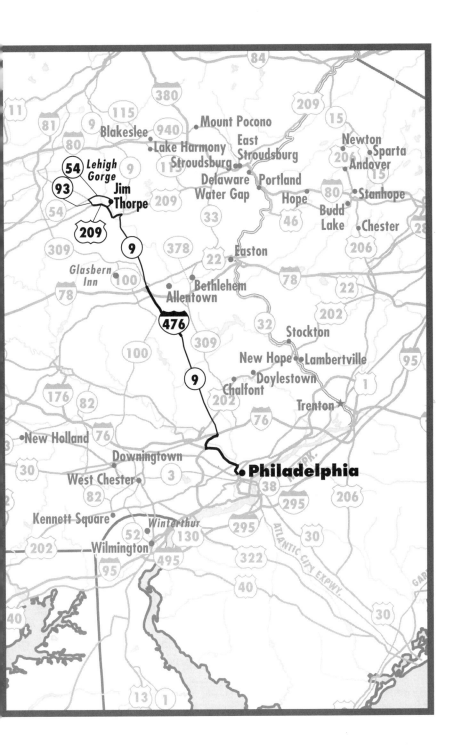

American athlete who had won glory and two gold medals at the 1912 Olympics in Stockholm, Sweden, only to be stripped of them later because he had earned a little bit of money playing semipro baseball in his younger years. Although the Olympic Committee eventually restored the medals after Thorpe's death, his widow thought the man once regarded as "the greatest athlete in the world" deserved more. She proposed that the struggling little town in the Pennsylvania mountains build a monument to Jim Thorpe, take his name, and make his memory the focus of a concerted effort to restore his name—and the town—to their former glory.

## DAY 1

## *Morning*

Jim Thorpe lies about 90 miles north of Philadelphia, about a 1½-hour drive. Your day is going to be quite full, so be sure to get an early start. To get there, take the Schulkyll Expressway (I–76) west for 15 miles; get on the Blue Route (Route 476) west for 4 miles. Get on the Northeast Extension (I–476) of the Pennsylvania Turnpike going north for 55 miles; get off at exit 34 and follow Route 209 south 7 miles through Lehighton to Jim Thorpe.

As you enter town on Route 209 you can't miss the centrally located and architecturally distinctive **Jersey Central Railroad Station** (open weekdays June–October 9:00 A.M.–4:30 P.M., until 4:00 P.M. November–May; summer weekends 10:00 A.M.–5:00 P.M., other weekends 9:30 A.M.–4:30 P.M.). Constructed in 1888 as the hub of the town's passenger train activity, it now houses the **Tourist Welcome Center** (888–JIM–THORPE) and a museum filled with artifacts from the town's heyday as an industrial and tourist railroading center. The station still functions as the home base of **Yesterday's Train Today** (570–325–4606), an old-fashioned locomotive with vintage coaches that offers forty-minute ($9.00 per adult) to 2¾-hour ($14 per adult) excursions through this scenic mountain region.

The decidedly ecclesiastical architecture and high ornate ceilings of the **Mauch Chunk Museum & Cultural Center** (41 West Broadway; 570–325–9190) are reminders of its origins as a church in 1843. Today it is home to a comprehensive collection of artifacts and photos that trace the history of the area from its geological formation to present times and describe the enormous impact the discovery of coal and its subsequent mining and production had on this and other nearby mountain towns. Pay particular attention to the working model of the once world-renowned Switchback Gravity Railway. This extraordinary collaborative effort of man and nature will play a key role in your activities later on in the day. The museum is open Tuesday–Sunday, 10:00 A.M.–4:00 P.M. Admission is $3.00.

**LUNCH: Sunrise Diner,** 3 Hazard Square; (570) 325–4093. Normally, it might be a bit early to think about lunch. But you're going to be a long way from town when those midday hunger pangs start to make themselves known. So before you head for the hills, take a short walk down to the diner and grab something hearty to go . . . perhaps a triple-decker club or other big, freshly made sandwich. Inexpensive. Breakfast, lunch, and dinner daily; Friday and Saturday, twenty-four hours.

## *Afternoon*

Head past the railroad station and turn right onto the bridge on North Street (Route 903). About 2 miles down the road, just at the edge of town on your left-hand side, you'll see the **Jim Thorpe Mausoleum,** a twenty-ton granite monument to the athlete. Continue on Route 903 about 5 more miles and you'll come to the **Pocono Whitewater Adventure Center** (570–325–8430), where you'll begin your afternoon's explorations on the back of a mountain bike.

Jim Thorpe has been rated as one of the top three mountain-biking destinations in the United States by *Cycling* magazine. One popular ride is along a downhill 9-mile trail that was once the site of the **Switchback Gravity Railroad**. The first railroad in Pennsylvania, and the second in the United States, the Switchback was originally built in 1827 to transport coal down the mountain from nearby mines to Mauch Chunk for shipment to Philadelphia. In addition to being a railroad industry pioneer, it was unique in that it made its downhill runs powered solely by gravity. In the 1870s, after the major railroad lines had begun servicing the mines, the Switchback continued to make its 65-mile-per-hour downhill runs, this time carrying thrill-seeking visitors who came from far and wide just to take this hair-raising plunge. In fact, it became one of the top tourist attractions in the United States, second only to Niagara Falls. One of the passengers loved the railway so much he made it the prototype for a new kind of amusement park ride—the roller coaster.

Although the Switchback ceased operation in 1933 and the tracks are long gone, the route still provides a breathtaking ride for bikers who take the descent down the mountain, past a lake and along a creek through a forest dense with hemlock and rhododendron. For your efforts, you will be rewarded with awe-inspiring scenery as you ride and some of the most beautiful backdrops you'll find anywhere for enjoying your picnic lunch. Pocono Whitewater Adventure Center offers bike rentals and shuttle service to the Lehigh Gorge and Switchback Railway Trails ($25 full day rental, $15 half day, $35 shuttle with rental, and $10 Switchback shuttle). Maps, parking, and child seats are free with rental. Open seven days year-round.

If, upon your return to downtown Jim Thorpe, you find yourself in need of a little relaxation and refreshment, go right over to **Java Rock** (89 Broadway; 570–325–8891). where owner Terry Rock will greet you with a comfy chair, cup of specialty coffee or tea, and a piece of delectably homey cake or fresh fruit pie.

For another glimpse into Jim Thorpe's history, take a late afternoon stroll up and down the town's historic district right across from the Jersey Central Railroad Station. Once known as **Millionaires Row,** the ornately designed Victorian era townhouses that line both sides of Broadway were home to families made wealthy by the coal, lumber, and transportation industries. In reality, few of those who resided in these royal rowhouses were actually millionaires, but their working class neighbors viewed them as if they were. Today many of these lovingly maintained houses are living second lives as enticing—and sometimes curious—little shops and art galleries.

At **Maria Monteleone Design** (97 Broadway; 570–325–3540), the art, which highlights the best of local and national talent, is of the wearable variety. Open Saturday and Sunday, noon–5:00 P.M.; weekdays by appointment. And for some dramatic handcrafted jewelry to go with your unique new wardrobe, **Chatelaine** is just a few doors away at 81 Broadway (570–325–2224).

If you happen to be in the market for a new crystal ball, there's the **Emporium of Curious Goods** (15 Broadway; 570–325–4038), which is presided over by Barrett Ravenhurst, Ph.D., and a Red Lored Amazon parrot named Chester. And if you think twenty-four-hour automatic money access machines were a great invention, stop by **Four Seasons Sporting Goods** (29 Broadway; 570–325–4364) and see how far modern technology has really come. Right outside the door is a twenty-four-hour bait vending machine that dispenses six different kinds of worms for those day- or night-fishing emergencies.

*A visit to Jim Thorpe is like a journey back to yesterday.*

## Evening

**DINNER: Sequoyah House,** 68 Broadway at Victoria Ann's Bed and Breakfast; (570) 325–8824. To top off an athletic day of biking and walking, there's no more appropriate place to take your evening meal than Sequoyah House. Calling itself "a natural emporium of gourmet world cuisine," this distinctive dining spot serves innovative all-organic vegan, vegetarian, and nonvegetarian dishes in an atmosphere of casual elegance. Prices are moderate. Byob.

If you're visiting during the months of December, March, or May, be sure to catch one of the four seasonal performances by the **Bach and Handel Chorale** (570–325–9440), an exquisite collection of local voices. The concerts are held at various locations throughout the town. A donation ranging from $10.00 to $15.00 for adults and $5.00 to $7.50 for students is requested.

**LODGING: Harry Packer Mansion,** Packer Hill; (570) 325–8566. This eighteen-room Victorian creation of the most elaborate sort has watched over the town from high atop its perch on Packer Hill since 1874. The home was a wedding gift from Harry's father, the illustrious and exceedingly wealthy Asa Packer, and mother. Its distinctive design and otherworldly quality have long fascinated visitors—including the designers of the Haunted Mansion attraction at Walt Disney World, who used the house as their model. Completely restored, the mansion retains many of its original features and appointments, including the four-hundred-pound front doors with cut-glass windows, hand-painted ceilings, carved mantles, and even the detailed English Minton fireplace accent tiles depicting Shakespearean scenes. This place is definitely worth seeing, even if you're not staying overnight. Tours of the first floor are available for a moderate fee for nonguests. Room rates range from $75 to $150 for the mansion; $95 to $125 for the carriage house. The Harry Packer Mansion also hosts monthly Murder Mystery Weekends with package prices ranging from $350 to $495.

## DAY 2

## *Morning*

**BREAKFAST: Harry Packer Mansion Bed & Breakfast.** A full breakfast is included in the room rate. Innkeeper Pat Handwerk is justifiably proud of the feasts she lays out each morning for guests, including such house specialties as French toast stuffed with strawberries and cream cheese in a strawberry glaze, croissants l'orange, and a savory crustless quiche.

Before you descend Packer Hill, stop by the mansion next door. You can't sleep at the **Asa Packer Mansion** (570–325–3229), but you can take a fascinating tour of this nineteenth-century home owned by one of the town's only true millionaires and the man responsible for the building of the Lehigh Railroad and Lehigh University in Bethlehem. The inside of the mansion is much the same as it was in 1878 when Packer and his wife moved in on their golden wedding anniversary. Among the many treasures on display is a crystal chandelier, a copy of which was used in the movie *Gone With the Wind*. Tours are offered weekends in April, May, and November; daily June–October, 11:00 A.M.–4:15 P.M. Admission is $5.00 for adults, $3.00 for children under twelve.

At the bottom of Packer Hill and a few blocks straight up on Broadway is the **Old Jail Museum** (128 West Broadway, 570–325–5259), formerly the old

Mauch Chunk Jail. It was here that, in the late 1800s, seven Irish immigrant coal miners were hanged for being members of the Molly Maguires, an organization formed to fight the dangerous and deplorable working and living conditions imposed on the immigrants by the mine owners. Legend has it that before the hanging, one of the men placed his hand on the wall of his cell and declared that if he was innocent, the print would stay on the wall forever. It's still there. Tours are offered Memorial Day–October, every day except Wednesday, noon–4:30 P.M. $4.00 for adults, $3.50 for seniors and students, and $2.50 for children six to twelve.

When Hollywood decided to tell the story of the Molly Maguires in a 1969 film, they came to Jim Thorpe for historical authenticity. One of the sites they used was the courtroom at the **Carbon County Courthouse** (570–325–3637). Check out the impressive interior features such as the oak paneling and spectator pews, the wooden spindle "peacock fans" above the judge's bench, and the gorgeous stained glass, including a skylight depicting Justice in the center of the courtroom—all created by local craftsmen. Open for tours weekdays 8:30 A.M.–4:30 P.M. Free.

Around the corner from Broadway and running parallel to it is Race Street, a charming part of town best known for its group of sixteen houses called **Stone Row.** Said to have been copied from Elfreth's Alley in Philadelphia, these houses are basically identical in design, yet each is individualized by some distinctive decorative feature. Once the homes of railroad engineers and foremen, some of these buildings remain private residences while others provide studio and shop space for local artisans and merchants.

## *Afternoon*

**LUNCH: Black Bread Cafe,** 45–47 Race Street; (570) 325–8957. This terrific lunch and dinner spot on the ground floor of a 150-year-old Stone Row townhouse has a moderately priced menu that spotlights the cuisines of Spain, Cuba, Jamaica, the Middle East, and northern Italy, as well as original inspirations from owners Barbara and David Yamrich. Even the burgers reflect the restaurant's international influence with Mexican (corn salsa and sharp cheese), Greek (feta cheese, black olives, and peppers) and Bavarian (sauerkraut, Thousand Island dressing, and Swiss cheese) selections—all priced at $6.50. Fresh game is also a specialty. Moderate to expensive.

Before you leave town, treat your inner child to a visit to the **Old Mauch Chunk H.O. Scale Model Train Display,** right across the street from the railroad station on the second floor of the Hooven Mercantile Company Building (41 West Susquehanna; 570–325–2248). Aspiring engineers of all ages will marvel at the extensive collection of working trains and automobiles, which is open to the public weekends from April to mid-June and daily from June 15 to Labor Day (Sunday, Monday, Tuesday, Thursday, and Friday, noon–5:00 P.M.; Wednesday and Saturday, 10:00 A.M.–5:00 P.M.). Admission is $3.00 for adults, $2.00 for seniors, $1.00 for children five and older.

On the lower level of the Hooven Building are some interesting stores, including the **Virginia Smith Shops** (570–325–2248; open daily 10:00 A.M.–5:00 P.M.). Be sure to ask about the unique collectibles and jewelry made by local artisans out of coal mined from the nearby mountains. They are really quite beautiful and make highly appropriate souvenirs of your trip to Jim Thorpe.

To return to Philadelphia, simply retrace the route you took to get here. The trip home should take about 1½ hours.

## THERE'S MORE

**Lehigh Gorge State Park,** Jim Thorpe. A 25-mile, gentle downhill, packed-dirt bike trail between 800–1,000-foot-high mountains. One of the highlights is a stop at Glen Onoko Falls. Pocono Whitewater Adventure Center (570–325–8430) offers bike rentals; guided mountain, wetland, and waterfall hikes; and whitewater rafting trips through the Gorge from March to November.

**Mauch Chunk Opera House,** Opera House Square, Jim Thorpe; (570) 325–4439. Throughout the year this rustic 1882 entertainment center hosts concerts, children's theater, workshops, art and fashion shows, and sidewalk festivals.

**No. 9 Mine 'Wash Shanty' Anthracite Coal Mining Museum,** Dock Street, Lansford; (570) 645–7074. This recreation of the lives, work, and times of the miners when coal was king is only 10 miles south of Jim Thorpe on Route 209. Opened in 1855, it was the world's oldest operating deep anthracite mine when it closed in 1972. Open Wednesday–Sunday, 8:00 A.M.–4:00 P.M. Adults $3.00, children twelve and under $2.00.

**Camping.** Jim Thorpe Camping Resort, Lentz Trail, Jim Thorpe; (570) 325–2644. Features include level wooded sites, 60-foot swimming pool and 15-foot wading pool, playground, camping cabins, free hot showers, laundry facilities, grocery and camping supply store, games and planned activities. Fees for two people are $20 per site, $35 per day for camping cabins. Water, electrical, and sewer hookups; air conditioning or electric heaters; and cable TV hookups are available at additional cost.

### SPECIAL EVENTS

**October.** Fall Foliage Festival, (888) JIM–THORPE. Local crafters, music, ethnic foods, train rides, tours of museums, historic mansions, and other sites.

**December.** Old Time Christmas; (888) JIM–THORPE. Weekends in December leading up to Christmas. Horse-drawn trolley rides with Santa, concerts, Victorian carolers, talking snowman.

### OTHER RECOMMENDED RESTAURANTS AND LODGINGS

## *Jim Thorpe*

Emerald Restaurant & Molly Maguire's Pub, 24 Broadway at the Inn at Jim Thorpe; (570) 325–8995. During its days as a bustling coal transportation center, Mauch Chunk attracted many immigrants from Ireland. So it should be no surprise to find a bona fide Irish pub serving shepherd's pie, bubble and squeak, and Dublin fish and chips right in the center of town. Prices range from inexpensive to moderate for lunch, moderate to expensive for dinner. A $5.95 children's dinner menu is available.

Inn at Jim Thorpe, 24 Broadway; (800) 329–2599. Located right in the heart of the town's historic district, this restored hotel has been charming guests including General Ulysses S. Grant, President William Taft, Buffalo Bill, Thomas Edison, and John D. Rockefeller for over a century. Rates range from $65 to $95 for a standard room to $159 to $250 for a suite. Continental breakfast buffet is included.

J. T.'s Steak & Ale House, 5 Hazard Square at the Hotel Switzerland; (570) 325–4563. The J.T. stands for—who else?—Jim Thorpe. And the hearty fare is, indeed, suited to the most athletic of appetites. A specialty of the house is the twenty-four-ounce prime rib steak ($11.95). Moderate.

# UP THE MOUNTAINS

A Suite on Broadway, 97 Broadway (above the Mary Monteleone Design Gallery); (570) 325–3540. Artist and shop owner Monteleone and her husband Darryl have created this "B&B alternative," actually one extremely private suite for one couple complete with king-sized bedroom, stained glass, antiques, sitting room, European kitchen, balcony, private bath, and homemade treats. $125 per night.

Victoria Ann's Bed and Breakfast, 68 Broadway; (570) 325–8107. A true nineteenth-century getaway with period furnishings, welcoming atmosphere, and a lovely Victorian garden. Rates range from $50 to $95 for a standard room to $125 to $150 for a suite. Rates include a full breakfast.

## FOR MORE INFORMATION

Carbon County Tourist Promotion Agency; (888) 546–8467 or (570) 325-3673.

# The Western Poconos, Pennsylvania

## BLAKESLEE AND LAKE HARMONY

### 2 NIGHTS

*Downhill Skiing • Sporty Days • Romantic Nights*
*Spectacular Views*

In a dictionary of purely Philadelphia terminology, this is the area that would define "up the Poconos" best. Between the generosity of Mother Nature and man's own contribution, the snow-making machine, these mountains are ready to give you the ultimate experience no matter what time of winter the skiing (or other winter sport) bug bites.

Actually, the Poconos are wonderful for a getaway any time of year. In summer, there are shimmering lakes for swimming, boating, waterskiing, and fishing; championship golf courses; breathtaking mountains for hiking, biking, and horseback riding; even NASCAR racing. With its slopes covered in the sparkling snow of winter, the lush greens of summer, or the flaming foliage of fall, it's hard to believe that the hustle and hassles of home are only 1¾ hours away.

This itinerary describes a winter escape to the western Poconos. For a summer-oriented Pocono getaway, see the itinerary for Escape Four, Delaware Water Gap.

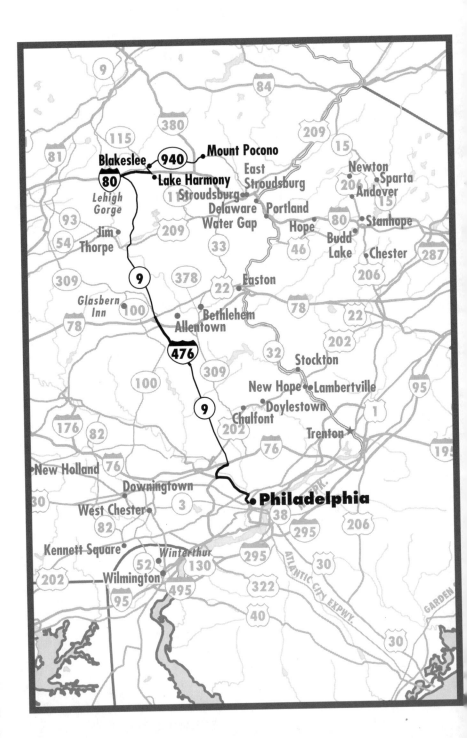

# UP THE MOUNTAINS

## DAY 1

## *Evening*

Leave right after work so you can enjoy a nice dinner and some evening entertainment in the mountains. To get to this area of the Poconos, take the Schuylkill Expressway (I–76) to the Northeast Extension of the Pennsylvania Turnpike (I–476)—about 74 miles. Get off at I–80 and continue west about 5 miles to White Haven; get off at exit 40 and you will see the sign for your dinner destination on your right-hand side.

**DINNER: Power House Eatery,** I–80, exit 40, White Haven; (570) 443–4480. In this converted turn-of-the-century coal-to-electricity power plant, you'll dine amid original construction and hardware, surrounded by valves, boilers, and fire doors. Surprisingly, all of this makes for a pretty dramatic setting for a contemporary menu featuring some very innovative dishes such as shrimp and crab française and pork a la Powerhouse stuffed with crabmeat and topped with dill sauce. Moderate to expensive.

If you want to sample a little bit of the area nightlife, two of the mountain's hot spots are within the resort complex at **Split Rock Lodge** (Lake Drive; 800–255–7625) on beautiful Lake Harmony. From the Power House Eatery, take I–80 east until you come to Route 940, then continue east on Route 940 about 10 miles. Every evening at 9:30 (except Sunday) you can enjoy live music, followed, on Saturday evenings, by comedy at 11:30 P.M. at the **Galleria Night Club.** The **Rock Bar** features open mike night on Wednesday; DJ/dance music on Thursday; live bands on Friday and Saturday; and billiards, darts, and electronic trivia every day. Both clubs open at 9:30 P.M.

Time for a good night's rest before your day on the slopes tomorrow. From Split Rock Lodge take Route 940 east until you come to Route 115 in Blakeslee.

**LODGING: Blue Berry Mountain Inn,** Thomas Road, just off Route 115, Blakeslee; (570) 646–7144. Although it is located off the beaten path (in this case Route 115) on a dirt road that winds through a beautiful wooded area, don't expect your typical rustic mountain hideaway. When owner Grace Hydrusko decorated her home in 1994, she was inspired by the sunshiny colors of Bermuda . . . which means you can't miss the salmon-colored stucco structure with its white wide-board shutters, unique architecture, and graceful verandas. Just as you think you have Blue Berry Mountain pegged as a totally modern inn, Grace surprises you again with a warm and cozy interior filled with books, antiques, and country charm. Another surprise . . . the inn doesn't have one massive stone heart- and soul-warming fireplace such as you'd expect in the heart of ski country—it has *two*! The five guest rooms and one suite are spacious and individually decorated. Other amenities include a complimentary full country breakfast, indoor swimming pool and year-round outdoor spa. Weekend rates are $90 for a room, $115 for the suite. A 10 percent discount is offered for midweek stays.

## DAY 2

### *Morning*

**BREAKFAST:** Blue Berry Mountain Inn. Every day, Grace offers juices, a huge fresh fruit salad, a bread basket teaming with a variety of breads and home-baked muffins, and an egg or other entree served with breakfast meats. Saturday mornings she really goes all out with semolina French toast, pancakes or waffles, and perhaps some oven-fresh strudel or apricot-cheese pastries. And Sunday brunch is a buffet featuring Grace's famous crustless, creamless quiche; crepes (or blintzes) with hot strawberry sauce; oven-roasted red potatoes; lemon-poppyseed cornbread; and a homey dessert. Lots of guests also make special requests for her old-fashioned oatmeal. Ask in advance and she'll be happy to whip some up for you.

Whether or not a single snowflake has fallen from the sky today, you can be assured of a great time on the slopes at **Big Boulder** and **Jack Frost Mountain,** two major ski areas with one ticket price. To get to Big Boulder, take Route 115 south to Route 903 south; turn right and follow the signs.

For novices, families, and anyone who prefers an easygoing downhill run, **Big Boulder** (800–468–2442 or 570–722–0100) is the place to go. Opened in 1946, it was the first commercial ski area in Pennsylvania and the first to perfect snowmaking. The terrain here is beginner-friendly with vertical drops of 475 feet for runs that are thrilling without being heart-stopping. Adults who have never put on a pair of skis before (and the more experienced skiers around them) will appreciate the resort's **Snowsport Learning Center,** which offers traditional group lessons. For more individualized instruction, there are also a Discovery Program ($50 each includes lift/lesson/rental for ages sixteen and older) and individual private coaching sessions ($45 per hour, $110 for half day—three hours).

If you prefer a more challenging run, the Free Domain area at **Jack Frost Mountain** (Route 940 east just a few minutes away from Big Boulder, 570–421–7231) has all the trees, glades, bumps, and cliffs your adventurous heart desires—as well as vertical drops of 600 feet.

For a single ticket price, you can move back and forth between the ski areas at will. For adults, a day/night (open to close) ticket is $36 midweek, $42 weekends and holidays; night prices (4:00 P.M. to close) are $20 midweek, $25 weekends and holidays; and multiday/night $36 per day anytime. Together these two neighboring resorts also offer other popular winter sports, including cross-country skiing, snowboarding, snowmobiling, and tubing (more about that this afternoon). Baby-sitting is available at both locations.

## *Afternoon*

**LUNCH:** The **cafeteria** at Big Boulder or Jack Frost Mountain Lodges. The decor isn't fancy, and neither is the food; but it's good, plentiful, inexpensive, and, best of all, nearby. Try to plan an early (11:00 A.M. or so) or late (after 2:00 P.M.) lunch to miss the noontime rush. Then relax over your choice of mealtime options ranging from pizza, nachos, burgers, and hot dogs to soups, chili, topped baked potatoes, or other homemade hot entrees.

Add $10 to your Big Boulder/Jack Frost Mountain lift fee and you can trade in your skis for a tube and spend the afternoon gliding down hills as much as twelve stories high and more than 1,000 feet long. (Full-day tickets for tubing alone are also available for $20 for adults, $15 for youths fifteen and under.) As with skiing, Big Boulder tends to be mild, while Jack Frost tends to be wild. After the sun goes down, you can continue tubing (or skiing) "under the lights" at Big Boulder until 10:00 P.M.

**DINNER: Villa Virella,** Route 115, Blakeslee; (570) 646–3265. "Casual, but nice" attire and a reservation are required at this family-operated restaurant, but you will be rewarded for your efforts with an eight-course Italian feast so exquisite the locals consider this their favorite special-occasion spot. To get there from the Blue Berry Mountain Inn, turn right onto 115 south and follow it for twelve miles; Villa Virella, marked by a little oval sign, will be on your left. The entire meal—from Bagna Caoda (a warm dipping sauce for vegetables and bread sticks) to Cappuccino—is traditional northern Italian with an emphasis on homemade freshness and family recipes. How fresh is the food? Well, the Virella family requests that you choose your entree when you call for reservations to ensure that they order everything in just the right amounts. It's

*Horseback riding in the Poconos.*

hard to believe this elegant old building was once a roadside service station! Fixed price dinner costs $45 plus tax and gratuity.

**LODGING:** Blue Berry Mountain Inn. After dinner, cozy up to one of the inn's two fireplaces. If you like (and if you have room), your host Grace will pop some corn or fix you a nice cup of cocoa or a hot buttered rum (BYOB). You can also play some pool in the game room or settle in with a good book from the inn's library.

# UP THE MOUNTAINS

## DAY 3

## *Morning*

**BREAKFAST:** Blue Berry Mountain Inn.

Before you set out on your day's adventures, take some time to stroll the inn's 440 acres of nature-decorated walking trails. There's a private lake for admiring, fishing (no license required, but bring your own equipment), or boating in season. Or take a refreshing dip in the indoor pool.

We'll get to the athletic stuff later. For now stay in a leisurely mode for a trip to the **Morgan Gallery of the Arts** (800–621–1654 or 570–646–5333), located on Route 940 about 1 mile east of the inn. In this 1,500-square-foot gallery, owner and self-proclaimed "chief cook and bottle washer" James Morgan exhibits and sells original paintings, sculptures, and other works by regional artists.

If you think horseback riding isn't a winter sport, tell that to the people at **Deer Path Riding Stable** (Route 940, White Haven; 570–443–7047). Only about 12 miles south of the inn on Route 940, Deer Path is open year-round offering guided one- and two-hour guided trail rides through beautiful woods, farms, and state game land teeming with deer, wild turkeys, and other wildlife. The easy walk and jog pace is nonthreatening to beginners and, at the same time, it allows seasoned riders to really have a chance to drink in the dazzling scenery. For total novices, Deer Path also offers a combination instruction/trail ride package. A one-hour guided trail ride costs $22 for adults, $20 for children ages nine to twelve. Two-hour rides are $38. Ask about monthly specials. Trail rides are scheduled seven days a week, every hour from 10:00 A.M. to 4:00 P.M. in winter (subject to weather conditions) and from 9:30 A.M. to 5:30 P.M. in summer.

## *Afternoon*

**LUNCH: Piggy's of Lake Harmony,** 1 Lake Shore Drive; (570) 722–8493. A Pocono tradition famous for its generous portions, inexpensive prices, and fun atmosphere. The specialty of the house is a signature version of French toast called Piggy's Batter Toast. The lunch menu might make you feel nostalgic for home with its Philly cheesesteaks, hoagies, and other locally adored delicacies.

From the restaurant, it's about a fifteen-minute drive to **Hickory Run State Park** (570–443–0400). Take 940 east to Route 80 west, get off at the Hickory Run exit and follow the signs to the park. All year round this 15,500-acre park offers a veritable smorgasbord of recreational facilities, activities, and options. Bring your own gear, and in winter you can choose from cross-country skiing (16 miles of designated trail), ice-skating, sledding, or tobogganing. If hiking is more your sport, there is a 37-mile trail system in the park. Make sure you pick one ending at Hawk Falls, a natural 25-foot waterfall, or at Boulder Field, where the dramatic 400-by-1,800-foot landscape with its absence of vegetation and boulders as much as 26 feet long has remained relatively unchanged for the past 20,000 years. There's also a large, guarded (Memorial Day–Labor Day) sandy beach for swimming, a family campground (open April–December); picnicking, hunting, and fishing.

**DINNER: Britannia Country Inn,** Swiftwater; (570) 839–7243. Take Route 940 east to the junction of Route 611. Turn right onto Route 611 south and follow it through the town of Mt. Pocono. The road will become a divided highway. Turn left at the second traffic light (there is a gas station on the left and the Swiftwater Inn on the right). Go approximately ²/₁₀ of a mile and the road makes a "Y," bear to the left. The inn is 1½ miles on the right. Owners Joan and Steven Matthews have truly brought a taste of British style, hospitality, and, of course, dining to the Poconos with this charming restaurant. The menu is fun and hearty, and emphasizes such traditional British favorites as roast beef and Yorkshire "pud," "ye olde" steak and kidney pie, pork sausage and potatoes (aka bangers and mash), and Lancashire hindle wakes, a chicken dish created by Oliver Cromwell. Look for other dishes the menu says were relished by such historical luminaries as Sir Frances Drake and the Duke of Wellington.

To return to Philadelphia, start at the intersection of Routes 611 and 314 in Swiftwater. Take Route 314 west for about 3 miles until you reach Route 940; go south for 1 mile on 940 to I–380. Go east for 3 miles to get to entrance ramp of I–80. Take I–80 west for 17 miles to Pocono Interchange of Northeast Extension of Pennsylvania Turnpike (I–476). Go east on I–476 for 74 miles until you come to Schuylkill Expressway; go east for 15 miles. The trip home should take you about two hours.

## UP THE MOUNTAINS

### THERE'S MORE

**Alvins Snowmobile Rental,** Long Pond; (570) 646–0705. Head east on Route 940 to Long Pond Road on your right, just before Route 380. Turn onto Long Pond Road and drive 4 more miles to Alvins. If there's enough white stuff on the ground, you can go for an hour-long, sixty-acre spin. $50 for single; $75 for double. Call ahead to check conditions.

**Whitewater Challengers,** White Haven; (800) 443–8554 or (570) 443–9532. Take Route 940 west to Route 80 west. Get off at exit 40 and make a left onto 940 west and continue approximately 2 miles. Challengers will be on the left. Rafting, biking, kayaking, overnight camping, and outdoor adventure weekend packages. Breakfast buffets ($5.00), box lunches ($5.00), and dinner buffets ($7.95) are available.

**A. A. Outfitters,** Blakeslee Corners; (570) 643–8000. Guided fishing tours and private instruction available year-round, seven days a week. $150 per person for a full day ($125 per person for two people) and $85 for half-day rates include equipment rental.

**Peterson Ski & Cycle,** Route 115, Blakeslee; (570) 646–9223. This convenient shop will rent you all the equipment and accessories you'll need for mountain biking, skiing, and snowboarding. Open year-round.

**Memorytown,** Grange Road (between Routes 611 and 940), Mt. Pocono; (570) 839–1680. Open year-round, seven days a week. In operation for more than half a decade, this fun-filled attraction is a complex of museums, eating places, old-time country shops, and a lake for fishing and boating.

**Moyer Aviation,** Route 611, Mount Pocono; (570) 839–7161. If you think the mountains are magnificent from the ground, you should see them from the air! Ten-minute mountain tours ($15 per passenger) and twenty-five-minute Delaware Water Gap tours ($25 per passenger) are among the options offered seven days a week, year-round (including weekends and holidays). Flights are scheduled from 8:00 A.M. to sunset.

## SPECIAL EVENTS

**April.** Annual Great Brews from Around the World International Beer Festival, Split Rock Resort; (800) 255–7625. A day filled with international music, food, beer-related crafts, and more than twenty of the world's best brews.

**May.** Poconos Greatest Irish Festival, Jack Frost Ski Area, (800) 468–2442. A Memorial Day Weekend (Saturday and Sunday) extravaganza featuring three stages of Irish performers, specialty vendors, and lots of food.

**June.** Pocono NASCAR Winston Cup Series Race, Pocono International Raceway, Long Pond; (800) RACEWAY or (570) 646–2300.

**June.** Annual Great Tastes of Pennsylvania Wine & Food Festival, Split Rock Resort; (800) 255–7625. Two days, usually the last weekend in June, of more than one hundred of Pennsylvania's finest wines from twenty of the state's premier wineries, three stages of live entertainment, wine and food-related seminars, grape stomping, crafts, food, and children's entertainment. Saturday and Sunday, 11:00 A.M.–6:00 P.M.

**July.** Pocono NASCAR Winston Cup Series Race, Pocono International Raceway, Long Pond; (800) RACEWAY or (570) 646–2300.

**August.** Annual Poconos Blues Festival, Big Boulder Ski Area; (800) 468–2442. Enjoy a weekend (usually the first Saturday and Sunday of August) of performances by and workshops with more than a dozen blues artists.

**August.** Poconos Annual Gathering on the Mountain, Big Boulder Ski Area; (800) 468–2442. This national festival pays tribute to the legendary artists and spirit of the psychedelic San Francisco music scene of the late sixties. Regain your oneness with the Universe as you groove to the cosmic tunes of name performers and shop the "bizarre bazaar."

**September.** Grand Emerald Fling, Jack Frost Ski Area; (800) 468–2442. This Labor Day weekend tradition dedicated to the Emerald Isle features dozens of Irish performers on three stages, specialty vendors, and food.

**September.** Annual Native American Festival and Powwow, Memorytown, Grange Road, Mt. Pocono; (570) 839–8821. A wonderful three-day event featuring authentic Native American dancing, story telling, music, food, and crafts.

**November.** Great Brews of America Classic Beer Festival, Split Rock Lodge; (800) 255–7625. More than 200 beers from classic and microbreweries across the country will be served up along with food; live entertainment; and beer-related crafts and seminars (including one specifically for home brewers) during this two-day festival traditionally held the weekend before Thanksgiving.

## OTHER RECOMMENDED RESTAURANTS AND LODGINGS

### Blakeslee Area

Edelweiss International Restaurant, Pocono Lake, Route 940 between Mt. Pocono and Blakeslee; (570) 646–3938. This charming German restaurant, which serves, among its traditional and contemporary fare, a variety of schnitzels, sauerbraten, and spaetzle, is as much at home in the Pennsylvania Poconos as it would be in the Alps. Don't miss the old country desserts, especially Austrian apple strudel—served warm. Moderate to expensive.

Woody's Country House, Route 115, south of Route 903 (next to Pocono International Raceway) and 4 miles from Blakeslee Corners; (570) 646–9932. Chilis, soups, sandwiches, and the like to chase away the winter chill are available from 11:30 A.M.–4:00 P.M. Moderately priced dinner fare includes pastas, fresh seafood, charbroiled steaks, and baby back ribs.

### Lake Harmony

Close Quarters Bar/Restaurant, Lake Drive, ½ mile north of Big Boulder Ski Area; (717) 722–8127. Italian-style veal, chicken, beef, seafood, and, of course, pasta in a lakeside setting. Pizza and sandwich platters available for takeout only on Saturday evenings. Inexpensive to moderate.

The Resort at Split Rock, five miles east of exits 42 and 43 off I-80; (800) 255–7625 or (570) 722–9100. This 500-acre, four-season resort offers a number of options from the traditional rustic ski lodge to a contemporary posh hotel. Rates, which vary by season and time of week, can range from $160 to $190.

## *Swiftwater*

Britannia Country Inn, (570) 839–7243. Transplanted Brits (as they like to refer to themselves) Joan and Steven Matthews have transformed a historic old inn into one with English countryside personality. The decor in each of the rooms ($50 per person) and suites ($60) is pure Laura Ashley. You can also rent a private cottage ($70 per person) or a room in a cottage ($60). Add $10 to include a full English-style dinner in the inn's restaurant/main dining room.

### FOR MORE INFORMATION

Pocono Mountains Vacation Bureau, Inc.; (800) 762–6667 or (570) 424–6050; www.poconos.org.

Snow conditions; (800) 475–SNOW (800–475–7669).

# UP THE MOUNTAINS

# Delaware Water Gap, Pennsylvania

## PLY ME A RIVER

### 2 NIGHTS

*River and Mountain Sports • Breathtaking Overlooks*
*Fun Restaurants • All That Jazz*

It doesn't take much imagination to picture this magnificent area as it was when the ancestors of the Leni Lanape tribe first discovered it sometime between 12,000 and 10,000 B.C., a place of lush woodlands teeming with wildlife, miles of crystal clear waters, and awe-inspiring waterfalls. That's because it still looks very much like that today.

Inspired by the more than one-mile-wide S-shaped cleft the river had carved into the mountain ridge they knew as Kittatinny ("endless hills") millions of years before, the Native Americans called the area Pohoqualin, or "termination of two mountains with a stream passing through them." Over time that name evolved into "Pocono" and came to represent an entire mountain range. However, back then, "Pohoqualin" referred specifically to one area in the eastern part of the mountains, an area we now call Delaware Water Gap.

When people talk about Delaware Water Gap, they are usually referring to the 70,000-acre national recreation area in Pennsylvania and New Jersey. And it truly is an idyllic spot for nature lovers of all kinds with its more than sixty hiking trails; 40 miles of Delaware River; wide variety of birds, fish, and other wildlife; and virtually unlimited opportunities to enjoy the great outdoors in whatever way you choose. Although each of the seasons has it own distinctive charm, beauty, and activities in the Poconos, spring and summer are really the

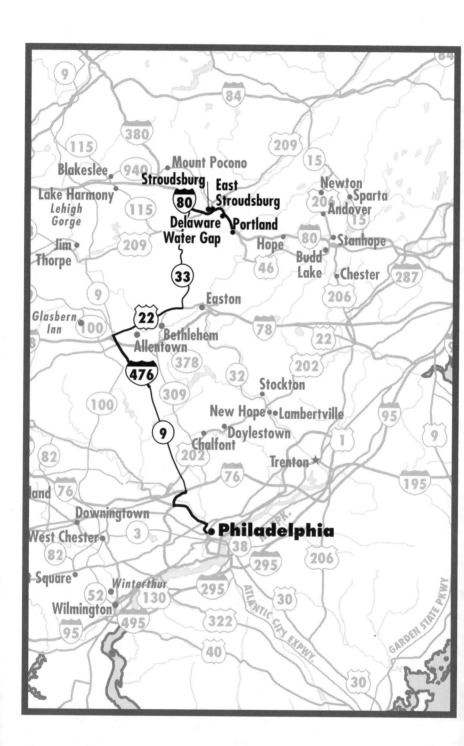

best times to fully enjoy this area of the mountains. August is peak tourist time here and the area can get pretty crowded so you may want to plan your escape for earlier in the season or even the first few weeks of September.

These are also the best times to explore the *other* Delaware Water Gap, a small nearby town, along with neighboring Stroudsburg, East Stroudsburg, Bushkill, and Portland at your leisure. Their histories and personalities are as varied as the river that flows through the mountains.

## DAY 1

## *Morning*

Start out early in the morning so you can do some basic sightseeing and grab some lunch in Delaware Water Gap, the town, before you make your way to Delaware Water Gap, the national recreation area. From Philadelphia, take the Schuylkill Expressway (I–76) to the Northeast Extension of the Pennsylvania Turnpike (I–476); go north to Route 22 east. Take 22 east to Route 33 north then to Route 80 east. Get off at exit 53 for Delaware Water Gap and travel Route 611 south, which will take you into the center of town.

As you enter town on Route 611, you'll see the **Water Gap Trolley Depot** (570–476–9766) on your right. Make that your first stop and take the forty-five-minute scenic tour. Of course, you could easily drive the route along 611 yourself, but the history and local lore offered up by your trolley driver/guide make the excursion much more interesting. For example, you might just drive on by and miss **Cold Air Cave**, aka "Mother Nature's Refrigerator," tucked into the mountainside along the road, or the breathtaking Resort, Arrowhead Island, and the Point of the Gap overlooks.

Along the route you can also see the remains of the grandest of the nineteenth and early twentieth century grand hotels that catered to well-to-do families from Philadelphia and New York who would summer here. Then there's historic 1752 Shawnee Presbyterian Church, the oldest church in the Poconos, with tombstones from the adjacent cemetery incorporated into its back wall. There's also a natural formation that looks like the profile of an Indian head in the mountain rocks and the place on Main Street where the Appalachian Trail cuts right through the center of town on its 25-mile stretch through the mountains. And if you're of a "certain age," you will probably get a kick out of seeing the home of Captain Kangaroo's longtime sidekick Mr. Greenjeans. Trolley tours are available seven days a week, 10:00 A.M.–4:00

P.M. rain or shine until the weather turns very cold and/or the tourists disappear. Call for current prices.

Right across Main Street from the Trolley Depot is the **Antoine Dutot School and Museum** (570–421–5809). In the 1920s, this was the site of a school that was a model for others of its time. Today it is the town's main cultural center and houses an extensive collection of Native American and other historical artifacts, audio and visual exhibits on education in the twenties, and changing displays of works by local artists. Open every Saturday and Sunday from Memorial Day Weekend–October. Call for hours and admission prices.

## Afternoon

**LUNCH: Trails End Cafe,** 14 Main Street; (570) 421–1928. Don't worry, formal dress is not required at this circa 1920 former bus station turned cozy little bistro even though the doorman—a bigger-than-life wooden raccoon—is wearing coattails. Inside, the sunny country cabin interior bids you warm welcome with its antiques, pressed-tin ceiling, and colorful array of dried-flower wreaths and swags. The breads are baked on the premises (or "imported" from one of Philadelphia's top artisan bread bakeries on the weekends), and there are more than a few surprises (pierogies Poblano and Thai pie) on the menu. Even such old-fashioned favorite desserts as fruit crisps, bread pudding, and carrot cake are jazzed up with complementary sauces, ice cream, and other delicious additions. Inexpensive to moderate.

Although the restaurant you just dined in is called Trails End, it's actually the beginning of the trail you'll be taking for your afternoon in the sun. Head north on 611 until it intersects Route 402. Follow 402 north about 18 miles to **Pocono Backwater Outfitters** (570–775–7237) at Pecks Pond. When you see the large wooden fisherman on the right-hand side of the road, you'll know you're there.

There are many places where you can rent canoes, kayaks, tubes, and other watercraft, but Pocono Backwater Outfitters offers a different kind of vehicle . . . and a unique kind of river experience. Upon arrival, you'll be issued a twenty-one-pound "float," which you will carry on your back as you follow your guide on a hike that will take you off the beaten path and onto backwater streams, ponds, and waterways that cannot be accessed by boat. At that time you will don a wet suit and frog fins, place your float in the water, and instantly become one with nature as you glide silently along using only your own kicking power and a small paddle to propel yourself. Because you are creating almost no disturbance or noise, you can enjoy the exquisite beauty of your surroundings and observe the wildlife around you under the most natural of circumstances. A three-hour outback nature trip with guide and all equipment costs $49 per person and can be tailored specifically for individuals who want to fish, bird-watch, or take photographs. Eight-hour trips are also available at a cost of $90 (includes a hot or cold lunch). Outings may be scheduled during fall, spring, and summer (as long as the water level is high enough for floating).

## *Evening*

**DINNER: Everybody's Cafe,** Main and Ninth Streets, Stroudsburg; (570) 424–0896. Coming from Delaware Water Gap, head south on 611 for about 3 miles until you come to Main Street. The restaurant is right across the street in a converted home. This is one of those places that has wonderful architectural or decorative surprises such as ornate doorways with leaded glass, graceful arches, and back-to-back fireplaces just about everywhere you look. The prices are surprisingly modest on the very ambitious, multipage menu. Even more surprising are the huge portions. In light of both these factors perhaps the biggest surprise of all is that the food is excellent, prepared and seasoned with obvious care to preserve and enhance its fresh flavors. Everybody's is well known for its innovative vegetarian offerings. But as the name suggests, this restaurant isn't just for vegetarians. There are a number of American and internationally inspired meat, seafood, and fowl selections along with infinite pasta combinations. Don't skip dessert—especially the hot fudge pudding cake served warm with ice cream; it's satisfyingly gooey without being overly sweet.

**LODGING: Stroudsmoor Country Inn,** Stroudsmoor Road; (570) 421–6431. Take Route 611 south until you come to Route 191 south; turn right and follow 191 to the top of the mountain where you'll make the first right onto Stroudsmoor Road (the entire trip, including the mountain-climbing expedition, should take five minutes or less). Glowing lanterns line the path leading to the inn, nestled on its 200-acre mountain overlooking the city and surrounded by nature. Gleaming dark woods, colorful flower arrangements, and a big central fireplace greet you at the front door. Owned and operated by the Pirone family, the inn's pretty guest rooms are furnished in turn-of-the-century style, using as many original pieces and designs as possible. Most guests opt for the B&B plan, which includes a bountiful breakfast each morning. Among the many on-site amenities are the natatorium with its indoor 40-foot swimming pool and 10-foot whirlpool spa; the outdoor pool; fitness center; bikes; and scenic trails. The Marketplace, right on the property, sells everything from furniture and antiques to clothing (vintage and new), pottery, fine art, and jewelry. B&B rates start at $94 per couple; suites begin at $120 and luxury suites at $195.

## DAY 2

## *Morning*

**BREAKFAST:** Stroudsmoor Country Inn. When staff and guests speak of family matriarch and executive chef Bernadette Pirone's culinary skills—and especially her baking—you can hear the reverence in their voices. The display of some of Bernadette's baked goods (including giant cookies and raisin bread topped with a thick layer of confectioner's sugar icing) in the lobby of the inn hints at her prowess. But breakfast is the real clincher. Aside from a multitude of warm, aromatic muffins, she also whips up some mean pancakes, eggs, just about anything you could possibly be craving. Sunday morning's meal is an extravagant buffet (it's included in your room tab; otherwise, it's $16.90 to the general public).

Dress comfortably and pack plenty of suntan lotion. You're going to be spending a good part of the day outdoors exploring the trails, waterfalls, and other natural attractions of the Delaware Water Gap National Recreation Area. Before you head there, however, pick up a single- or triple-decker sandwich-to-go at the **Watergap Diner,** a block off Main Street (Route 611) at 55 Broad Street (570–476–0132). To make your sweet tooth happy, make a quick stop at the **Village Farmer and Bakery** (on Main Street, Route 611, across from the Water Gap Trolley Depot; 570–476–9440), an old-fashioned farm stand that sells oven-fresh cookies (three for $1.00), brownies, and other home-baked goods. The Cooper family, which has been operating at this location for twenty years, also makes thirty varieties of fruit pies (apple is their specialty), crumb cake, apple dumplings, and pot pies.

On your way to the park are two interesting museums situated directly opposite one another on Route 209, but in two different towns. On the left-hand side of the road, off 209 at McCole Road in East Stroudsburg, is the **Mary Stolz Doll & Toy Museum** (570–588–7566). Owner Bill Stolz and his wife Jan lovingly preserve and display more than 125 dolls from around

*The Shawnee Mountain Annual Rodeo.*

the world collected by Bill's grandmother Mary. The collection includes dolls from the 1800s through today, many of which are in original condition, others that were repaired and clothed in authentic period attire handmade by Mary. Also on display are exquisitely detailed miniature rooms. The museum's gift store features—what else?—dolls of all description as well as houses for them to live in, teddy bears, and tin and mechanical toys. Open seven days 11:00 A.M.–5:00 P.M. Admission is $2.50.

On the left-hand side of the road in Bushkill is the **Pocono Indian Museum** (570–588–9338), dedicated to portraying the history of the Delaware (Leni Lenape) tribes from prehistoric times (somewhere in the area of 10,500 B.C.) to their first contact with the Europeans prior to the American Revolution. Using the cassette player and thirty-minute tape issued to you with your admission, you can take a narrated self-guided tour through six rooms of artifacts—most of which were discovered within a 20-mile radius of this site—and exhibits showing how these Native Americans lived, worked, and fought for their lives and their land. Highlights include re-creations of a Paleolithic cave and a bark longhouse The gift shop has an extensive collection of Indian jewelry, crafts, clothing, and other items. Open seven days a week. Call for hours. $4.00 for adults, $3.00 for seniors, $2.00 for children, and free for children under six.

Whether you're an experienced hiker at the top of your form or someone who simply appreciates fabulous scenery, the **Delaware Water Gap National Recreation Area** (570–588–2541) has a trail for you. At **Dingmans Falls Trail** (1 mile west of Route 209 at Dingman's Ferry) a ½-mile walk along the forest floor through a hemlock canopied grove will bring you face-to-face with Silver Thread Falls, with its graceful 80-foot drop, and Dingmans Falls, with its two-tiered, 130-foot drop. The 1⁸⁄₁₀-mile forested loop at nearby **George W. Child Recreation Site** takes you to three additional waterfalls along Dingmans Creek. Wooden stairs and boardwalks make it easy for you to safely get a close look. About 12 miles north is **Raymondskill Falls,** a seven-tiered 175-foot beauty that drops in seven stages.

## *Afternoon*

**LUNCH: George W. Child Recreation Site.** A wonderful spot to enjoy your picnic lunch is in the hemlock-shaded glen along Dingmans Creek.

Before you leave the park area, get in your car and take the Dingmans Ferry access road to Route 209; then follow 209 north to the toll bridge to **New Jersey.** A few hundred yards after you cross the bridge, take the right-hand turn and follow the signs for about 2½ miles to **Peters Valley Crafts Center** (19 Kuhn Road, Layton, New Jersey; 973–948–5200). Located in a green peaceful valley, this center is actually a community of working/teaching studios for resident artists ranging from blacksmiths to photographers to woodworkers. In the summer, the artists open their studios to the public for classes or pop-in visits (Saturday and Sunday, 2:00–5:00 P.M.). On-site galleries display and sell current works by the artists-in-residence as well as by craftspeople from around the country. Gallery hours are 11:00 A.M.–6:00 P.M., Friday–Monday in June and Thursday–Tuesday July–early September. Fall hours are Friday–Sunday noon–6:00 P.M.

## *Evening*

**DINNER: Deer Head Inn,** 5 Main Street, Route 611, Delaware Water Gap; (570) 424–2000. During the town's annual Jazz Fest weekend in September, this modest little gathering spot is known as "jazz central" because it's such a popular hangout for the performers and their fans. Actually, that nickname applies all year long–and has for the past forty years. The moderately priced dinner menu is an eclectic mix where the chicken is likely to have a Moroccan or other exotic accent, salmon might come adorned with a cilantro and lime-spiked sauce, and New York strip steak is, well, New York strip steak. For an extra $5.00–$10.00 (depending on the performers) you can stay for the music. Usually the Deer Head Inn is very easygoing and relaxed . . . except during Jazz Fest . . . then it's insane (so make reservations and don't be late)!

**LODGING:** Stroudsmoor Country Inn.

## DAY 3

## *Morning*

**BREAKFAST:** Stroudsmoor Country Inn.

From Stroudsburg take Route 80 west; get off at exit 46A onto Route 209. Turn right at Shafer's School House Road, then left on Route 209. Follow the signs to **Quiet Valley Living Historical Farm** (1000 Turkey Hill Road, Stroudsburg; 570–992–6161) about 1½ miles down the road. In the mid-1700s, this sprawling sixty-acre farm was the home of German immigrant Johann Peter Zepper and his family. Today, the original house, barn, smokehouse, and tool sheds have been restored, and you can still visit a period-clad farm family, much like the Zeppers, as they go about their spinning, weaving, meat smoking, gardening, fruit and vegetable drying, and cooking. Open mid-June–Labor Day; Tuesday–Saturday 10:00 A.M.–5:30 P.M., Sunday 1:00–5:30 P.M. Admission for adults $7.00, $4.00 for children three to twelve.

## *Afternoon*

Returning to Stroudsburg, don't miss the multitude of antiquing opportunities starting with the town's two sister co-ops, one housed in a one-hundred-year-old former machine shop and the other, only blocks away, housed in an equally historic former vinegar distillery. Together the **Olde Engine Works** (62 North Third Street; 570–421–4340) and the **Olde Vinegar Works** (70 Storm Street; 570–421–4441) total 140 dealers and 35,000 square feet. If books are your passion, head for 740 Main Street where at **Carroll & Carroll Booksellers** (570–420–1516) owners George and Lisa Carroll specialize in history, philosophy, and fiction—including science fiction—offering thousands of new, used, rare, and out-of-print volumes. For new and old toy soldiers from every era and every part of the world go to **Stockade Miniatures** at 4 North Sixth Street (570–424–8507).

It's a 7-mile drive south along spectacularly scenic Route 611 to get from Stroudsburg to the tiny town of Portland.

**LUNCH: Eva Luna's Cafe and Restaurant,** 425 Delaware Avenue, aka Route 611; (570) 897–6005. This local favorite filled with personality is one of Portland's star attractions. With its big checkerboard, nonfussy furnishings, and fun things to look at scattered throughout, this absolutely wonderful little dining spot seems more like an old-time country store than it does a restaurant. Owner/chef Daniel Hicks named it after his grandmother (yes, there really was an Eva Luna) and, in her honor, serves real home cooking— American and Mexican style—for breakfast, lunch, and dinner along with what Dan humbly calls "the best pies this side of the Mississippi" made from fruits in season. Prices are extremely reasonable–from ninety-nine cents to $4.50 for breakfast (served all day); $1.25–$5.95 for lunch; and nothing over $10.00 for dinner.

Right across from the restaurant is a footbridge that connects Pennsylvania with Columbia, New Jersey. Walk across to the sleepy town of Columbia and take a leisurely stroll along the river, visit a Civil War cemetery, and admire the restored Victorian era homes.

**Portland** is such a little town that the guy who runs the old-fashioned barbershop is also the tax collector and borough secretary. So it may come as somewhat of a surprise to find such a heavy concentration of interesting little shops and co-ops along its main street (Delaware Avenue). While you won't find a lot of glitz and tourist trappings, what you will find is at least one of anything and everything you could possibly want in the way of antiques and collectibles—vintage clothing, Revolutionary War and other military memorabilia, railroad-related items, household goods, whatever. The mix of shops is certainly an eclectic one, but that just makes it all the more fun to poke around. By the way, if you want to tour the 1800s jailhouse just down the street from "antiques row," stop in at **Knott Necessarily Antiques** (570–897–7140) at 501 Delaware Avenue—owner Nancy Knotts has the key.

From Portland, it's a little more than a two-hour drive back to Philadelphia, heading north on Route 611.

## THERE'S MORE

**Pecks Pond Rentals,** same building as Pocono Backwater Outfitters, Route 402, approximately 18 miles north of Route 611; (570) 775–7237. Take out a canoe or other small craft for a day of fishing for native bass and trout on one of eight nearby Pocono lakes. They'll take you out in the morning, provide you with a guide, equipment, and supplies, and pick you up at the end of the day. Also available are mountain bikes and paddle/pedal combinations including a half day (five hours) of biking and half day (five hours) of canoeing for $25. In winter, you can enjoy their outdoor ice-skating rink (including skate rentals) and snowmobile tours.

**Pennsylvania Fishing Museum,** Pecks Pond; (570) 775–7237. Equipment displays and other exhibits follow the history of fishing from the late 1700s to the 1950s. Particularly interesting is the display on ice fishing. Open 9:00 A.M.–6:00 P.M. most times of the year—call for winter hours. $4.00 admission for adults; $2.00 for children six to twelve. There's also a gift shop featuring fishing-related antiques and gifts, handmade wood carvings, tables, and home decor items.

**Pennsylvania Craft Gallery,** corner of Route 209 and Bushkill Falls Road, Bushkill; (570) 588–9156. This 1746 former house-general store-post office-bar is now the home of the Pennsylvania Guild of Craftsmen, one of the largest craft guilds in the United States, and showcases the traditional and contemporary works of juried members who work in a variety of media from wheat to bronze. Free admission. Call for seasonal hours.

**Stroud House,** 900 Main Street, Stroudsburg; (570) 421–7703. During the French and Indian War, this was the site of Fort Hamilton, one of a chain of frontier forts extending across Main Street. In 1795, it became the home of Daniel Stroud, the man who planned the town that bears his name, and whose artifacts and personal belongings are on display here today. Open year-round Tuesday–Friday 10:00 A.M.–4:00 P.M.; call for Sunday hours. Admission is $2.00 for adults, $1.00 for students.

**Shawnee Mountain,** Shawnee-on-Delaware; (570) 421–7231. Skiing, snowboarding, snow tubing on twenty-three slopes and trails, with special instruction for kids as young as three and four years of age, teens, and adults. Late November–late March. Call for hours and rates. There's also a water park that's open Memorial Day–Labor Day 10:00 A.M.–5:00 P.M.

**Camping.** Delaware Water Gap KOA Campgrounds, Hollow Road, East Stroudsburg; (800) KOA–0375 or (570) 223–8000. Open April 1–October 1. Tent sites ($25), RV campsites ($28 with water and electric hookups), and "kamping kabins" ($45) convenient to all local activities and attractions. Special off-season rates are also available.

## SPECIAL EVENTS

**September.** Annual Jazz Fest, Delaware Water Gap; (570) 421–5791. Held annually the weekend after Labor Day, this three-day outdoor event attracts thousands of jazz fans from all over for music, arts and crafts, and all kinds of food.

**September.** Annual Shawnee Mountain Rodeo, Shawnee Mountain Ski Area, exit 52 off I–80, Shawnee-on-Delaware; (570) 421–7231. A real old-fashioned rodeo featuring bull riding, calf roping, saddle and bareback bronc riding. This two-day event also offers music and, of course, a real country barbecue.

**September.** Annual Scottish and Irish Festival. Shawnee Mountain Ski Area, exit 52 off I–80, Shawnee-on-Delaware; (570) 421–7231. A weekend of nonstop music and dancing including bagpipe bands and parade, working sheepdogs, Highland athletics demonstration, pony rides, traditional dancing, gift shops, and lots of food.

**October.** Annual Lumberjack Festival, Shawnee Mountain Ski Area, exit 52 off I–80, Shawnee-on-Delaware; (570) 421–7231. Witness amazing feats of strength and skill by world champion lumberjacks competing in three days of forest sport events. Also craft exhibits and demonstrations, "Racing Stinkers" (aka skunks), a petting zoo, country line-dancing, jug band and other musical entertainment, food vendors, and a "Paul Bunyan Lumberjack Feast."

### OTHER RECOMMENDED RESTAURANTS AND LODGINGS

## *Delaware Water Gap*

Shepard House, 108 Shepard Avenue; (570) 424–9779. Antique furnishings, a wraparound front porch, and country/Victorian charm make this bed-and-breakfast, located just 1 block from the Appalachian Trail, a delightful place to stay. Rates range from $60 to $110.

## *Shawnee-on-Delaware*

Mimi's Streamside Cafe, River Road (Route 611) next to the Shawnee Inn; (570) 424–6455. If you're in the mood for some real native Pocono Mountain brook trout, this moderately priced little restaurant tucked into the mountain is the place to come. Charbroiled steaks are another specialty.

Shawnee Inn, 1 River Road, exit 52 off I–80; (800) SHAWNEE or (570) 424–4000. This historic one-hundred-room inn, situated 2½ miles from Shawnee Mountain, features a large indoor pool and Jacuzzi, the area's only full-size indoor ice rink, four dining spots, and a large fireplace in the lobby.

## *East Stroudsburg*

Dansbury Depot, 50 Crystal Street, exit 51 off I–80; (570) 476–0500. This circa 1864 former railroad station is now a charming restaurant serving moderately priced seafood, chicken, and steak.

### FOR MORE INFORMATION

Pocono Mountains Vacation Bureau, 1004 Main Street, Stroudsburg, PA; (570) 421–5791; www.poconos.org.

Snow report: (800) 721–7321.

Delaware River Water Gap National Recreation Area, (570) 588–2541.

Town of Portland, (570) 897–5606.

# The New Jersey Skylands of Sussex County

## SO NEAR, YET SO FOREIGN

**1 NIGHT**

*Rainbow Caverns • Crystal Lakes • Anglers' Paradise
Cowboys and Outlaws*

A number of my friends are regular weekend escapees. They think nothing of throwing a few necessities into the trunk of the car and heading down the most scenic road they can find in search of idyllic adventures. So needless to say, I was rather surprised when virtually all of them greeted my announcement of an impending trip to the New Jersey Skylands with a resounding "Never heard of it."

It was their turn to be surprised when I told them that the Skylands begins only about an hour away from Philadelphia, right on the other side of New Hope in Lambertville, New Jersey. However, the place where I have set my itinerary about an hour farther north in a county called Sussex is the same driving distance from Philadelphia as Cape May—only in the opposite direction.

In total, the Skylands is composed of five counties—Morris, Somerset, Hunterdon, Warren, and Sussex—situated in the northwest part of the state. At its edges are two national parks, 60,000 acres of state parkland, and a diverse geographical makeup of lakes, rivers, hills, and farmlands dotted with small-towny residential areas that invite you to slow down your pace and stay awhile. Sussex County alone contains one state forest and six state parks, accounting for one-third of its total land mass, and the Kittatinny Mountains stretch north and south along its western boundary.

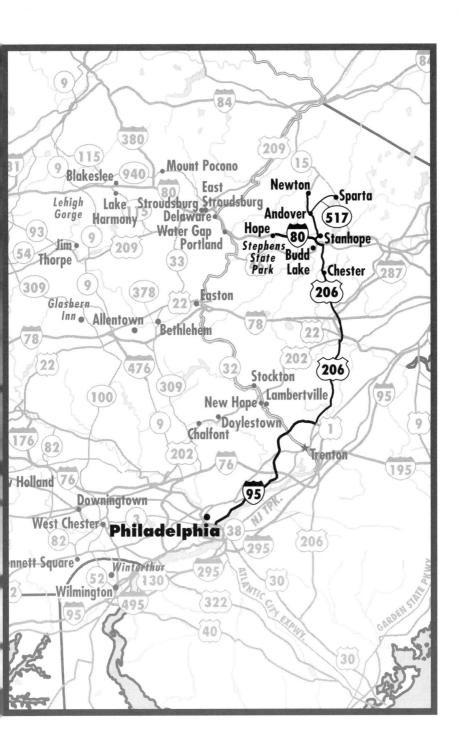

Peak time in the Skylands is summer; that's when all the natural and fantasy attractions are in top form. But keep in mind that this area also affords a spectacular view of the fall foliage, which is particularly brilliant because of the many, many different kinds of trees that thrive here. There's also skiing—both cross-country and downhill—nearby.

## DAY 1

### *Morning*

To get your bearings, find your way to the Sussex County town of Stanhope and the Whistling Swan Inn, where you will be spending the night. I found that, by using the inn as my focal point, the area was a lot easier to navigate. To get there, take I–95 north to the Lawrenceville, New Jersey, exit (7B); then go north on Route 206 to Somerville. Get onto I–287 north for 5 miles to exit 22B, which will take you back onto Route 206 north. Follow 206 through the towns of Chester and Flanders. As it goes under I–80, stay to the right and go one-third of the way through the traffic circle, following the signs for Route 183 to Netcong. Travel ½ mile north on Route 183 to the Hess gas station; turn left onto Main Street directly across from the station, and go to 110 Main Street, where you'll find the inn. Look for the big swan mailbox on your left. The trip should take between 2–2½ hours.

Probably the most prominent man-made attraction in this part of the Skylands is **Waterloo Village** (524 Waterloo Road, 973–347–4700), only a few minutes drive from the inn. Turn left out of the Whistling Swan drive and go to the end of Main Street; then turn left again. At the second traffic light, make a left onto Route 206, then another left at the bottom of the hill. Or, if you happen to be on Route 80, follow it west to Exit 25 (2½ miles).

Yes, this re-creation of an actual 200-year-old village that thrived on this site along the Musconetcong River and Morris Canal is named for the Belgian town in which Wellington defeated Napoleon, but that is its only connection to Belgium or to that momentous event. Once a prosperous mill town and key supplier of armaments to George Washington's Continental Army, today's Waterloo Village features more than twenty-eight mills, shops, and houses restored from its Colonial and Victorian heydays and populated with costumed "locals" demonstrating the practical and aesthetic arts of those eras. There's also a very well-researched, interpretive re-creation of a circa 1625 Leni Lenape village.

Authentic bone-rattling, horse-drawn wagon rides around the site are available Saturday, Sunday, and holidays, $4.00 for adults, $3.00 for seniors and children. Waterloo Village is open Wednesday–Sunday, mid-April–mid-October, 10:00 A.M.–5:00 P.M. Admission is $9.00 for adults, $8.00 for seniors, and $7.00 for children six to fifteen.

## *Afternoon*

**LUNCH: The Pavilion,** Waterloo Village. At this charmingly rustic cafeteria-style restaurant in Waterloo Village, you can pick up an inexpensive bowl of homemade soup or chili, a salad, or a sandwich to eat inside or, better yet, outside at one of the picnic tables.

For a refreshing afternoon, head over to **Tomahawk Lake** (973–398–7777) in nearby Sparta. From Waterloo, get back onto Route 206 and head south to Route 80. Take 80 east to exit 34 and Route 15. Take 15 north to the Woodport–Lake Forest exit (you'll go over Route 15). Then make a second right onto Route 181 and follow Sawmill Road/Tomahawk Trail to the entrance. For forty-seven years, this privately-owned twenty-five-acre lake has offered visitors crystal-clear, mountain-fed waters for swimming and boating, and the largest (500 feet wide) white sand beach in Sussex County for sunning and sand castle-building. For an additional cost, you can also visit the adjacent water park with its six water slides, including one that plummets downhill more than 500 feet and another that shoots out 100 feet over the lake. There is also a Kiddie Water World for children four and under. Combination admission to the lake and water park is $8.00 weekdays, $12.00 weekends for adults, $5.00 all the time for children eight and under, $3.00 for all after 3:00 P.M. on weekdays. Tickets can also be purchased separately. Bumper-paddle-, and rowboat rentals are available at extra cost. Open weekends end of May through mid-June, daily from June 15–early September. Hours vary by season, but are generally somewhere between 8:30 and 9:30 A.M. to between 5:30 and 7:00 P.M.

## *Evening*

**DINNER: Black Forest Inn,** 249 Route 206, Stanhope; (973) 347–3344. A good many of the house specialties on the German continental menu center around veal in just about every form from schnitzelette to noisette and every part from kidney to saddle. Whatever you choose, pair it with the homemade spaetzle or potato dumpling. The desserts are authentic, too, especially the flaky apple strudel, Schwarzwälder kirschtorte, and black cherries in red wine over silky vanilla ice cream. Entrees range from $14.75 to $23.50 per person for chateaubriand or roasted rack of lamb for two.

After dinner, head for **Stanford House** (45 Main Street; 973–347–0458), less than two blocks from the Whistling Swan Inn. This unassuming 200+-year-old former stagecoach stop/hotel is now one of the nation's top blues clubs. According to co-owner Maureen Myers, legends such as Muddy Waters and John Lee Hooker have been coming here to perform and jam for the past twenty-five years. Stop by any Saturday or Sunday around 10:00 P.M. and you might see one of these big-name performers or some other local, regional, or national blues or zydeco artists. On various other days of the week there might be a special rock, acoustic, or folk performance. Because you never quite know who will be performing here on any given evening, Maureen and her husband Ed offer a money-back guarantee—if, by the end of the third song, you decide you don't want to stay for the performance, they'll give you your money back, no questions asked. Average cover charge is $5.00–$7.00. It can be higher for artists who must be transported in from other parts of the country.

**LODGING: Whistling Swan Inn,** 110 Main Street, Stanhope; (973) 347–6369). It may sound like a cliché, but as soon as you set foot in the door you feel as if you're home. It could be the 1905 house with its majestic 10-foot ceilings, working fireplace, and carved tiger oak woodwork restored to its original turn-of-the-century splendor. It could also be the ten cozy guest rooms, each individually furnished with antiques and heirlooms from periods and places ranging from 1920s art deco–era America to the soothingly harmonious Orient. (There's even a big bathroom with his and hers claw foot tubs, bubbles, and big fluffy robes for romantic evenings.) But most of all, it has to be owners Paula Williams and Joe Mulay, a truly hospitable couple who provide gracious service, great conversation, and a constantly full cookie jar. Rates range from $95 to $150.

## DAY 2

## *Morning*

**BREAKFAST:** Whistling Swan Inn. It's hard to forget Paula's strawberry soup and rich oatmeal pancakes topped with warm spiced apples or black cherry syrup and almonds. The camaraderie among your hosts and fellow guests is also quite memorable.

To learn more about the county's history as an important mining center and at the same time view some truly dazzling natural phenomena, take a ride about 12 miles north on Route 206 to Route 517, continue north until you come to the town of Ogdensburg. Cross the railroad tracks and pass the Green Thumb Nursery on your right. On your left you will see **Sterling Hill Mine & Museum** (30 Plant Road, 973–209–7212). New Jersey's only underground mine tour takes you on a two-hour guided walk through ¼ mile of tunnels and chambers of what was once one of the most renowned mines in the world. Displays of equipment, artifacts, and rare minerals plus lifelike tableaux of men at work serve as reminders of the days from the 1800s to the mid-1900s when the mine was a source of prosperity and peril for so many towns in this part of the country.

Even the generation raised on special effects can't help but be awe-struck by the dramatic display of fluorescent minerals that make the walls of the chamber called the Rainbow Room glow red, green, and yellow when bathed in shortwave ultraviolet light. The mine has yielded a world-record of eighty different species of fluorescing minerals, some of which can be purchased at the aboveground gift shop (along with the shortwave ultraviolet light you'll need to see the various colors). Mine tours are offered seven days a week, June through August at 11:00 A.M., 1:00 P.M., and 3:00 P.M. Call for off-peak season hours. Admission is $9.00 for adults, $8.00 for seniors, $6.00 for children.

Take Route 206 south, past Stanhope to the neighboring town of **Chester,** a turn-of-the-century former stagecoach stop with tree-lined streets and lanes, hidden courtyards, lovely restored buildings, and several blocks of boutique shops offering original and one-of-a-kind items. Grab a parking space on Main Street (Route 24) and head for **Alstede Farms** (Routes 206 and 24; 908–879–7189), a real working farm where you can pick your own strawberries, raspberries, pumpkins, and flowers in season and purchase just-picked fruits, vegetables, and herbs all year round. Family fun includes hayrides

*The pristine rivers and lakes of The Skylands.*

(in season) and lots of farmyard animals. Stock up on the fruit pies and other baked goods as well as farm-made honey, preserves, and relishes.

## *Afternoon*

**LUNCH: Publick House Restaurant,** 111 Main Street, Chester; (908) 879–6878. In 1810, when Route 24 (Main Street) was the Washington Turnpike, this building was a well-known stagecoach stop. For a delicious seafood double-whammy, start off with the rich, creamy lobster bisque laced with brandy and chablis, then move on to shrimp, lobster, and sea scallops served Wellington style or prawns stuffed with crab meat. Moderate to expensive. Like the public houses of old, this one also features ten antiques-appointed guest rooms for overnight accommodations.

At **Chester Crafts and Collectibles** (28 Main Street; 908–879–2900), you'll find the works of more than seventy of the region's top artisans in a gallerylike setting. Exquisite jewelry handcrafted by more than 350 artisans is the featured attraction at **Ciao Bella!**, 41B Main Street (908–879–5153). Check out the kaleidoscopes and "teleidoscopes" at the **Stained Glass Boutique,** 76 East Main Street (908–879–7351). And be sure to say hello to Cosmo the cockatiel and all the other resident pets who welcome you to the fifteen rooms of fine vintage furniture at **Aunt Pittypat's Parlour,** 57 Main Street (908–879–4253).

To go with the fresh produce you picked and/or bought at Alstede Farms, try your luck at **Go Fish!,** a private fishing reserve located at the Wharf at Drake Lake (33–08 Newton–Sparta Road, 973–579–6633) in Newton. To get there from Route 206 north, bear right onto Woodside Avenue (Route 621), then turn right onto Sparta Road (Route 616) and follow to Drake Lake, which will be on your left. No license is needed to catch the native and stocked fish at this nine-and-one-half-acre natural lake. Trout season is from March through mid-June, then again from September through November. In summer, the striped bass, channel catfish, pickerel, crappie, and sunfish are more active. All fish are $4.99 per pound. You can fish from the pier or rent a boat (from $8.00 per hour to $40.00 for a full day). Fishing rod rentals are also available for $6.00 and there is an on-site bait and tackle shop. Admission is $8.00 per adult, $6.00 per child (under fourteen). Open March 15–December 15, Monday–Friday 8:00 A.M.–6:00 P.M., Saturday and Sunday 8:00 A.M.–7:00 P.M.

## *Evening*

**DINNER: Barone's,** 77 Route 206, Byram Township; (973) 347–1812. A local favorite, this charming restaurant offers an extensive menu of Italian specialties including chicken- and prosciutto-stuffed dumplings, veal prepared nine different ways, and elegant treatments of filet mignon. Prices range from $9.95 to $19.95. The circa 1807 Lockwood Tavern downstairs features pub fare and microbrews in a rustic setting.

To return to Philadelphia, take Route 206 south and reverse your steps from Day 1. The trip home should take between 2–2½ hours.

### THERE'S MORE

**Allamuchy Mountain and Stephens State Parks;** (908) 852–3790. A total of 9,200 acres of park lands bisected by Route 80. Located 3 miles north of Hackettstown between Willow Grove/Waterloo Road (Route 604) on the east, Route 517 on the west, and Cranberry Lake (Route 206) on the north, Allamuchy Park lies mainly on the uplands and features an expansive natural area with 15 miles of trails and a variety of natural habitats. Stephens State Park, situated in the valley below along the Musconetcong River, offers a forty-site campground and world-class trout fishing at the Saxton Falls dam. Both areas have an abundance of birds and other wildlife and are beautiful spots for hiking, horseback riding, and cross-country skiing.

**Franklin Mineral Museum and Mine Replica,** Route 517 (3 miles north of the Sterling Hill Mine); (201) 827–3481. In addition to viewing thousands of local and international specimens of minerals, crystals, fossils, and gemstones, you can do some mineral mining of your own (no tools required) in the Buckwheat Dump, a mine waste pile from the 1870s. Combined admission to the museum and "mining rights" at the dump are $7.00 for adults, $3.00 for students. Open April–November Monday–Saturday 10:00 A.M.–4:00 P.M., Sunday 12:30–4:30 P.M. Also open March, weekends only.

**Fairy Tale Forest,** 140 Oak Ridge Road, Oak Ridge; (973) 679–5656. Follow the winding paths through this forty-year-old enchanted forest to more than twenty handcrafted, life-size decorated cottages and scenes from fairy-tale classics. Kids will feel as if they have stepped into their favorite stories; adults will be enthralled by the artistry. Open every day June 15–Labor Day from 11:00 A.M.–6:00 P.M.; weekends April–mid-June and after Labor Day to the third week in October. Admission is $6.00 for adults, $5.00 for children (under two free).

**Land of Make Believe,** Route 80, exit 12, Hope; (908) 459–5100. At this fun attraction that was first built in 1954, every member of the family can indulge in his/her favorite fantasies at the Haunted House, Old McDonald's Farm, Candy Cane Forest, Pirate's Cove, and the Middle Earth Theatre. Open daily 10:00 A.M.–6:00 P.M. in summer. Admission is $14.50 for children two to eighteen, $11.50 for adults, $10.00 for seniors.

**Lakota Wolf Preserve,** 85 Mount Pleasant Road (at Camp Taylor), Columbia; (908) 496–4333. For centuries wild wolves ran free in these and other mountains across the United States. However, for the last one hundred years, they could be seen only in Alaska and Minnesota. This recently opened 350-acre preserve high up on a ridge in the Kittatinny Mountains has brought them back—the tundras, timbers, and arctics, adults and pups—to live in peace and safety. Not a zoo, this is a sanctuary where they can roam and interact freely and where we can observe them in all their natural splendor. Admission is $15 for adults, $10 for children.

**Skylands Park,** Augusta (just north of Newton); (888) NJ–CARDS. This 4,500-seat stadium is the home of the New Jersey Cardinals, the farm team of the St. Louis Cardinals. Tickets for home games are $3.00–$8.00. Call for schedule.

**Pax Americus Castle Theatre,** 23 Lake Shore Drive, Budd Lake; (973) 691–2100. An Equity theater presenting a mix of performances from September–May including comedies, dramas, and classic plays by the Centenary Stage Company; stand-up comedy; ballet; concerts and children's theater.

**Mountain Creek,** 200 Route 94, Vernon; (973) 827–2000. Day and night skiing, snowboarding, snowshoeing, snowblading, tubing, and hiking. Winter season goes from early December to mid-March. Open 9:00 A.M.–10:00 P.M. daily. Eight-hour lift tickets are $44 for adults, $33 for juniors (ages seven to twelve) and seniors (sixty-five and over); four-hour tickets are $40 and $30. Other ticketing options are available.

**Wild West City,** Route 206 north (follow the signs), Netcong; (973) 347–2355. You're transported back to the nineteenth-century American West—Dodge City, to be exact—complete with wooden sidewalks, saloons, gold prospecting, live action gunfights, Texas Rangers on horseback, and outlaws the likes of Jesse James or the Sundance Kid. Open daily late June–Labor Day 10:30 A.M.–6:00 P.M.; weekends only in May, September, and October. Admission is $6.75 for adults, $6.25 for children (two to twelve), $5.25 for seniors.

**Camping.** Panther Lake Camping Resort, 6 Panther Lake Road, Andover; (800) 543–2056 or (973) 347–4400. Trailer and cabin rentals on a private lake with sandy beaches, boat rentals, Olympic size swimming pool, tennis, and minigolf. Call for rates.

## SPECIAL EVENTS

**July/August.** Sussex County Farm and Horse Show, Sussex County Fairgrounds, Plains Road (1 mile north of the intersection of Routes 15, 206, and 565), Augusta; (973) 948–5500. New Jersey's largest livestock and horse show offers ten days of tractor and oxen pulls, demolition derby, carnival rides and games, educational exhibits, and live entertainment in a country fair setting.

**August.** American Indian Powwow and Western Festival, Vasa Park, Wolfe Road, Budd Lake; (973) 627–2595. Three days of Native dance and foods, crafters, artisans, traders, Western shows, storytelling, exhibits, and pony- and hayrides.

**September.** Scandinavian Fest, Waterloo Village, Stanhope; for information call (732) 542–8150. Held on the Sunday of Labor Day weekend, this event celebrates and demonstrates the culture, traditions, customs, and contemporary life of Sweden, Denmark, Norway, Iceland, Finland, and Estonia through foods, craft demonstrations, and visual and performing arts.

## OTHER RECOMMENDED RESTAURANTS AND LODGINGS

### *Netcong*

El Coyote, Route 46; (973) 347–8313. Inexpensive-to-moderately priced Tex-Mex specialties.

### *Chester*

Country Road Cafe, 137 East Main Street; (908) 879–5128. This is a good, inexpensive breakfast (great stuffed French toast and fruit-topped pancakes) and lunch (chili is the specialty) spot with a great location right in the heart of the village's shopping area.

## *Stanhope*

Chef Bill's Gourmet Deli and Catering, 44 Main Street; (973) 426–9101. Inexpensive breakfasts and picnic fare including an "international series" of subs with names like the Italian Stallion, Brazilian Bombshell, and Red October (Red October . . . sub . . . get it?).

## *Andover*

Andover Diner, 193 Main Street/Route 206; (973) 786–6641. This chrome-and-red piece of nostalgia has been recently renovated, but the waitresses still good-naturedly smart-mouth one another and vie for the title of "sore feet queen." The portions are gigantic so don't be ashamed to ask for a doggie bag for the remains of your sandwich, salad, or platter. Inexpensive.

Andover Inn, 136 Main Street; (973) 786–5640. Renowned for its twenty-two-ounce rib-eye steak for $11.95.

## *Hope*

Inn at Millrace Pond, Route 519; (908) 459–4884. This 1769 Moravian grist-mill still retains it original Colonial charm from its elegant exterior to its antiques-appointed guest rooms. Rates range from $110 to $160 on weekends; $100 Sunday–Thursday. On-premise tennis courts and continental breakfast are included. The inn also has a splendid gourmet restaurant for dinner.

### FOR MORE INFORMATION

Sussex County Chamber of Commerce; (973) 579–1811.

Skylands Visitor Information; (800) 4–SKYLAND; www.njskylands.com.

Camping Information; (800) GO–CAMP–1 or (973) 948–4941.

# UP THE MOUNTAINS

# Eagles Mere, Pennsylvania

## WILD IN THE MOUNTAINS

### 2 NIGHTS

*Norman Rockwell Revisited*
*Up Close and Personal With Nature • Simple Pleasures*

When the people of Eagles Mere tell the story of *The Three Bears,* their version has a local twist. As they tell it, once upon a time (not very long ago) a momma bear and her two cubs who lived in the nearby woods decided to come into the village to have a romp in the playground. Unlike Goldilocks, however, the residents didn't run away in terror, they simply alerted the forest rangers and kept an eye on the frolicking family until the authorities came to gently escort them home.

This story tells a lot about Eagles Mere, an easygoing small town in the Endless Mountains where human and wild residents peacefully coexist. Located in virtually unspoiled Sullivan County, an area that remains 94 percent forest land and is the least populated county in the state, Eagles Mere is the ultimate escape from anything resembling hustle or bustle, deadlines or traffic jams—which is amazing when you realize that the nearest traffic light is 16 miles from town.

The Native Americans named this area perched atop a 2,126-foot-high mountain "Lake of the Eagles." In the 1880s crowds of vacationers, mostly from Philadelphia's Main Line, came for the beautiful scenery and stayed in the town's grand hotels and cottages. The old hotels are gone, but the cottages remain, and many Main Liners (along with others who have been let in on this well-kept secret) continue to make the 123-mile, 3 to 3½-hour pilgrimage northwest to this Shangri-la every summer. In peak season, the popula-

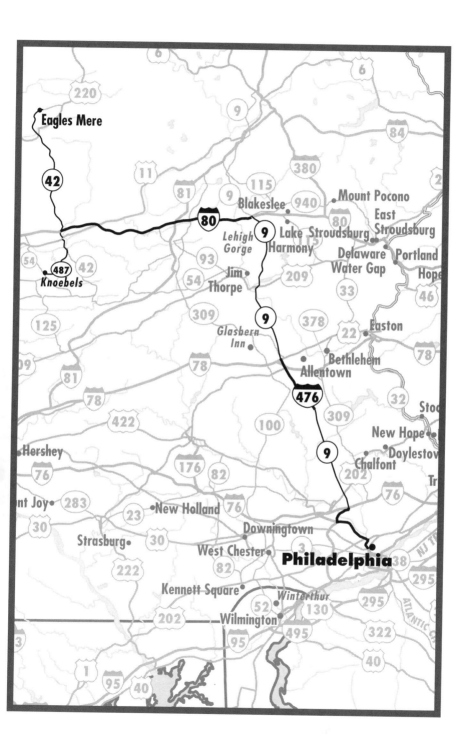

tion of Eagles Mere swells from its usual 125 to 1,200, but even then it retains its small-town character as visitors become assimilated into its daily life and activities.

## DAY 1

## *Morning*

Leave as early in the morning as possible to allow yourself maximum time to decompress from your usual routine and get into the Eagles Mere mode of laid-back living. To get there, take the Schuylkill Expressway (I–76) to the Northeast Extension of the Pennsylvania Turnpike (I–476). Get off 476 at I–80 west, and take I–80 to Route 42 north (exit 34 Buckhorn); follow 42 north for about 34 miles on country roads through small villages and cornfields, and past a smattering of rustic farms, farm markets, and country stores. Route 42 north will take you directly into the village of Eagles Mere.

Even if it's too early to check in, make your first stop the **Eagles Mere Inn** at Mary Street (800–426–3273 or 570–525–3273). It's the second right and 1 block downhill from the big free-standing clock in the center of town. Owners Peter and Susan Glaubitz are happy to share their wealth of information about the area along with some great maps and recommendations with their guests. In the summertime, the best way to get to know Eagles Mere is to walk to the **Village Green** you passed earlier. Remember the big clock? Well, it's one of the area's most famous man-made landmarks; a two-ton, almost 19-foot-tall cast-iron timepiece made in the early 1900s by the Seth Thomas Company.

Adjacent to the green are the **Eagles Mere Village Shoppes** (570–525–3503), a charming collection of mom and pops that sell everything from antiques and handmade pottery to clothing and fine handcrafted jewelry. Most of the shops are open daily from Memorial Day–Labor Day, and weekends year-round.

As part of your get-acquainted tour, visit the **DeWire Center** (at the corner of Laporte and Allegheny Avenues; 570–525–3232), the town's combination firehouse and community, cultural, and arts center. During July and August, the Eagles Mere Friends of the Arts hold art shows and musical concerts here. Across the street from the center is a circa 1920s church that houses the **Eagles Mere Museum.** Here you'll find exhibits of artifacts that tell the story of Eagles Mere from the time it was a glassworks town to its turn-of-

## UP THE MOUNTAINS

the-century glory days as a resort with five grand hotels. The museum is open every Wednesday–Sunday, July until after Labor Day. At other times of the year, you may call one of the board members listed on the outside wall to come and let you in. Donations are welcome.

## *Afternoon*

**LUNCH: Sweet Shoppe,** Route 42; (570) 525–3525. Located right in the heart of Eagles Mere's shopping area, the Sweet Shoppe is more than a restaurant and ice cream parlor. It's the social hub of the town and a fun place to grab a sandwich or other inexpensive light meal. Be sure to leave room for one of their killer sundaes. Even the nonhuman inhabitants of the area seem to think this is a great place to eat. Come at just the right time and you might just see a deer or two nibbling the grass right outside.

Head back in the direction of the inn. Along the way you'll come to a steep hill leading to a lake encircled by a green and blooming forest. This is a private lake, but as a guest of the Eagles Mere Inn you are invited to enjoy it and all of its facilities. For example, right at the bottom of the hill is **Edgemere Dock,** where you can borrow a canoe or small sailboat for a tour around the lake. Or, if you'd rather let someone else do the work, hop aboard the motor launch whimsically named the *Hardly Able.*

For swimming and fishing, there's a small, old-fashioned beach with a big wooden raft a few yards out. Adjacent to the beach is a rustic little playground—complete with rubber tire swings—for the kids, and a refreshment stand with picnic tables.

If you want to feel your city stress just melt away, take a relaxing walk on the narrow, 2-mile-long **Laurel Path** around the lake. You'll be instantly soothed by the earthy smells of the forest floor, the embracing canopy of giant hemlock trees, the songs of the birds, and the riotous colors of the mountain laurel and rhododendrons. Tucked here and there among the trees and shrubs are turn-of-the-century and modern houses, cottages (some with as many as sixteen rooms), and log cabins.

As you walk back up the hill, try to envision it covered from top to bottom with 12–14-inch-thick ice blocks that have been harvested from the frozen lake. You can almost hear the shrieks of excited laughter as adults and children alike pile onto toboggans for the 45-mile-per-hour plummet down this 1,400-foot-long ice-paved hill. Open only during appropriate natural conditions; call (610) 525–3368 for information and prices.

# UP THE MOUNTAINS

**DINNER:** Eagles Mere Inn. One of the many compelling reasons to stay at Eagles Mere Inn is the inclusion of a full gourmet dinner (as well as a bountiful country breakfast) with your room tariff. At dinnertime the inn's cozy L-shaped dining room is elegant and romantic, with white lace cloths and Victorian gas lamps at each table. In keeping with this genteel atmosphere, appropriate dress (nice shirt, sport jacket, tie optional) is required. The menu for the nightly five-course feast changes regularly and may feature any combination of a wide range of signature dishes, including Roquefort soup, West Indian rum stew, apple-smoked game hen, and duck Huli Huli. Susan Glaubitz's desserts are also superb, especially the pecan pie made from her grandmother's recipe and the chocolate cream puffs with raspberry sauce that are a favorite of a number of the inn's regular guests.

Outside is a spacious covered porch where you can savor a before- or after-dinner drink and the still night air while lounging in a comfy rocking chair.

**LODGING:** Eagles Mere Inn. When you enter the front door to this 1887 inn, Molly the Lhasa apso lazily wags her tail in typical warm yet understated Eagles Mere fashion. You could easily while away hours sitting under the lazily spinning ceiling fan or, in winter, in front of the blazing fireplace in the cozy living room, flipping through the pages of the inn's photo albums or getting lost in a book from the small library. Guest rooms and suites are split between the original Main Inn and the Garden House, built one hundred years later and 30 feet away. Each room is individually decorated with antiques and reproductions. Rates vary by day and date and begin off-season at $139 weekdays, $150 weekends; on-season $150 all the time.

## DAY 2

## *Morning*

**BREAKFAST:** Eagles Mere Inn. In the morning the inn's dining room takes on a warm and sunny personality and the menu is pure country, with eggs any style, bacon or sausage, warm muffins and breads, and French toast served with local maple syrup or raspberry brandy sauce.

With thousands of acres of pristine and protected forest land to be explored in and around Eagles Mere, it may be hard to decide where to begin. But if you get an early start, you can experience a number of the area's highlights.

## UP THE MOUNTAINS

Make your first stop **J.R.'s** (570–525–3050), a gas station/minimart about 2 miles south of the Eagles Mere Inn, where you can gas up the car and pick up a picnic lunch of big, fresh subs, deli sandwiches, and snacks all in one stop. Really, the sandwiches are great, just as the year-round residents of Eagles Mere promised they would be.

Take Route 42 south to Route 238 south. This will lead you to Route 118 east which you will follow to Route 487 north to **Ricketts Glen State Park** (570–477–5675), a 13,050-acre expanse of woodland paradise that is widely regarded as one of the most scenic areas in Pennsylvania. One of the park's main attractions is the **Glens Natural Area** with its giant pine, hemlock, and oak trees, many 100 feet tall and almost 5 feet in diameter. A large number of these trees are more than 500, and some as much as 900, years old. Take a hike along all or part of the 7-mile trail along crystal clear streams and past many of the park's twenty-two named waterfalls, which range in height from the 11-foot Cayuga to the 94-foot Ganoga. The trail tends to be rather strenuous, but the scenery is unbelievable. If you're not up for something quite so athletic, the Evergreen Trail offers an excellent view of the final series of falls along an easier ½-mile path.

## *Afternoon*

**LUNCH:** Enjoy your brown bag lunch at one of the picnic pavilions that border sparkling Lake Jean in the Glens Natural Area.

After lunch you can take a refreshing dip in the lake, relax in the sun on the 600-foot guarded beach (open Memorial Day weekend–Labor Day weekend) or rent a rowboat or canoe ($5.50 for ½ hour, $7.00 per hour) from the concession that operates during the summer season. In winter Lake Jean is a prime spot for skating or ice fishing.

## *Evening*

**DINNER:** Eagles Mere Inn

The best place to watch the sunset is from **High Knob Overlook** in nearby **Worlds End State Park** (570–924–3287), located only about fifteen minutes from the inn. You can get there by taking Route 42 south for approximately 1½ miles to Double Run Road. Turn right onto Double Run Road and continue for approximately 2½ miles until it intersects with Dry Run Road. The intersection is marked by a large wooden recreation map sign for nearby Wyoming State Forest. Turn left onto Dry Run Road and stay on the blacktop road for approximately 3 miles to High Knob Vista. No matter what time of day you come, this is probably the most dramatic view around, overlooking mountaintops in seven counties and making it instantly clear why this area is called the Endless Mountains. For the ultimate scenic experience, come in June with the mountain laurel in full bloom or in September when the fall foliage is flaming with color. Speaking of Nature's fall art exhibit, neighboring **Canyon Vista** affords the best view of the season's changing colors.

Head back to the Eagles Mere Inn for a nightcap at The Pub, a full bar located on the inn's lower level. With its stone fireplace, sink-in sofas, TVs, games and puzzles it feels like a family room in a friendly home (which it is). Pop in the twenty-five-minute Eagles Mere video for some interesting insights into the town's past. And be sure to check out the murals of local scenes painted on the room's walls. The Pub is open all the time for guests of the inn and on Friday and Saturday evenings from 5:00 to 10:00 P.M. it also becomes a lively gathering spot for the locals.

**LODGING:** Eagles Mere Inn.

## DAY 3

*Morning*

**BREAKFAST:** Eagles Mere Inn.

As a guest of the inn, you are entitled to visit **Eagles Mere Country Club** (about $\frac{6}{10}$ mile away on Country Club Drive; 570–525–3475) where you can enjoy eighteen holes of championship golf. Greens fees (including the cart) from June 15 through Labor Day are about $75 per round; $50 per round the rest of the year. Special package rates are available for guests who stay at the inn for multiple days.

**LUNCH:** Eagles Mere Country Club. Relax over a delicious soup, salad, sandwich, or entree from the moderately priced menu while you savor the spectacular mountain view.

If you want to take a piece or two of Eagles Mere home with you, take Route 42 south to Route 220 and go south on 220 for about 2½ miles. On the left-hand side of the road you'll see **Katie's Country Store** (570–482–2911), where you can buy locally made maple syrup, jams, honeys and chocolates, penny candy, upscale clothing for women and children, and all kinds of gifts. And if you've been looking for some good "rat cheese" (ched-

*Small-town pleasures abound in Eagles Mere.*

dar by its more refined name), here's where to come. Even in summer, Katie's all-year-round Christmas shop is a fun place to visit.

Continue south on 220 about 7 miles until you reach Sonestown; then follow the signs that will lead you to **Nature's Way Herbary & Nursery** (570–946–5707). If you want to attract more butterflies and hummingbirds to your home garden, owners Donna and Donald Iarkowski will help you select just the right field-grown herbs, perennials, evergreens, and plants to do the job. The couple also designs and handcrafts a wide variety of herbal and floral gift items. Make sure you take the time to take a stroll through the colorful and fragrant gardens.

Start your return trip to Philadelphia by taking Route 220 south to Route 42 south. On the left-hand side of the road before you get to Route 118 is **Swisher's Country Store** (570–482–2162), a genuine small-town 1879 general store where you can buy just about anything from a fishing or hunting license to fresh fruit in season to a pickle crock. Open seven days a week from Memorial Day to Christmas; Friday, Saturday, and Sunday only the rest of the year.

From Swisher's, follow Route 42 south until you reach I–80. Take I–80 east to the Northeast Extension of the Pennsylvania Turnpike (I–476) and head south on 476 to the Schuylkill Expressway heading east to Philadelphia. The return trip should take about 3½ hours.

## THERE'S MORE

**Children's activities.** Throughout the summer the Eagles Mere Athletic Association (570–525–3515) plans a daily schedule of activities that include softball, hikes, swimming, and arts and crafts for children of all ages. The activities are free of charge (the association operates on donations) and offer a great way for mom and dad to get some grown-up time while the kids have a blast. The Eagles Mere Conservancy (507–525–3725) also schedules nature hikes and activities three times a week.

**Ice-skating.** From the Eagles Mere Inn turn right onto Route 42, go down to the bottom of the hill, turn left, and go over the bridge to the Outlet Pond (or Lily Pond as it is also called), which will be on your right. No charge. Bring your own skates.

**Covered bridges.** Within easy driving distance of Eagles Mere are three distinctive covered bridges, all built between 1850 and 1880. Innkeepers Peter and Susan Glaubitz offer a complimentary booklet to guests called *Covered Bridges of Sullivan County* that includes a comprehensive driving tour of the areas leading to these bridges.

**Camping.** Pioneer Campground, Route 220, about 8 miles north of Eagles Mere; (570) 946–9971. Cabin rentals, water and electrical hookups, boat rentals, fishing, hunting, swimming pool. Open April 1–October 31. Basic cabin rental fee is $35– $40 per night.

**Fishing.** Local lakes and streams teem with native and stocked fish. Excellent trout fishing. Warm water game fish and panfish may be found in Lake Jean.

**Hunting.** There are more than 83,000 acres of state game lands to the west and north of Ricketts Glen State Park, plus approximately 9,000 acres inside the park that are open for hunting in season.

## UP THE MOUNTAINS

**Historic Walking Tours;** (507) 525–3632. Barbara and Bush James offer walking tours of the area as well as daylong hikes that leave from Outlet Pond to various points of beauty and interest every Thursday at 9:30 A.M.

**Brace's Stables Inc.,** near Ricketts Glen State Park; (570) 925–5253. For a truly exhilarating experience, take a 4-mile-long horseback ride on a tree-shaded trail in the forest ($20 per person) or a 6-mile-long ride to a water-fall ($25 per person). Pony rides ($3.00) are also available for children under ten years old.

**Eagles Mere Mountain Bikes;** (570) 575–3368.

**Knoebels,** Route 487, 13 miles south of I–80, Elysburg; (800) ITS–4FUN. With more than forty rides, live entertainment, a 750,000-gallon swimming pool, and four water slides, this is the state's largest free admission (pay as you play) amusement park. Open late April–September, hours vary.

### SPECIAL EVENTS

**January.** Annual Sullivan County Winter Sleigh Rally, Montanvale Farm, Route 87, Forksville; (570) 946–4160. Horse-drawn bobsled rides and antique sleigh competitions, rides, food. Admission.

**January.** Endless Mountains Sled Dog Races, Camp Brule, Forksville; (570) 924–3458. U.S. and Canadian teams compete in sprint races and a 50-mile event for cash prizes over two days. Hot food and beverages are available.

**June.** Eastern Delaware Nation's Annual Pow-Wow. Sullivan County Fairgrounds, Route 154, Forksville; (570) 924–9082. This annual gathering of Native Americans from all over the United States and Canada features traditional crafts, storytelling, dancing, drumming, princess contest, food, and children's programs.

**July.** Sullivan County Rodeo, Sullivan County Fairgrounds, Route 154, Forksville; (570) 924–9082. All kinds of traditional rodeo activities, including bareback and saddle bronc riding, steer wrestling, calf roping, and bull riding.

**August.** Eagles Mere Water Carnival, (570) 525–3503. Celebrated annually on the third Saturday in August, this is a big community day when local and summer residents collaborate to create the most imaginative and elaborate water-worthy float based on a given theme. A highlight is the unveiling of the creative craft and the crowning of the Water Carnival Queen.

**September.** Sullivan County Fair, Fairgrounds, Route 154, Forksville; (570) 924–2843. A real old-fashioned agricultural fair with dairy and livestock shows, truck and tractor pulls, demolition derby, and outside stage shows.

**October.** Annual Sullivan County Flaming Foliage Festival and Woodsmen's Competition, Sullivan County Fairgrounds, Route 154, Forksville; (570) 946–4160. Two days of woodsman activity demonstrations and competitions; juried crafts, art and photography; quilt show and sale; free horse-drawn wagon rides; children's activities; apple butter and apple cider making; horseshoe pitching; entertainment and lots of food.

### OTHER RECOMMENDED RESTAURANTS AND LODGINGS

## Eagles Mere

Shady Lane Bed and Breakfast Inn, Allegheny Avenue; (570) 525–3394. A pretty Victorian inn with an inspiring view. Afternoon tea or wine and full home-cooked breakfast every morning. Even a hammock for swaying the day away under the trees. Room rates begin at $85.

The Barn, World's End Road, just outside of Eagles Mere (take Route 42 north about 35 miles to World's End Road, turn right and continue ¼ mile to restaurant); (570) 525–3092. Inexpensive dinner menu specializes in American and Italian favorites including spaghetti and meatballs, lasagna, and roast beef.

## Sonestown

Sonestown Country Inn. Route 220; (570) 482–3000. Dining and overnight accommodations at an old-fashioned country inn. Inexpensive to moderate.

### FOR MORE INFORMATION

Endless Mountains Visitors Bureau, (800) 769–8999 or (570) 836–5431.

Endless Mountains Heritage Region, (888) 868–8800.

# UP THE MOUNTAINS

# Frederick, Maryland

## EYE OF THE STORM

### 2 NIGHTS

*Angels in the Streets* • *Presidential Retreat* • *Unsung Heroes*
*Poetic Heroines*

You won't find the name of this Maryland town written in fire and brimstone in any history book. Nor will you see it on a list of America's most famous battlefields. But through the centuries Frederick has played an important role in many of the major events that have helped to shape our nation.

What is it about Frederick that has so often put it in a position of such prominence? One simple explanation is its location. During the French and Indian War, this was the edge of the wild and perilous Western frontier, making it the perfect strategic planning post for then-Colonel George Washington and British General Edward Braddock. During the Civil War it was sandwiched between the Union right above the Mason-Dixon Line and the Confederacy across the Potomac, making it a busy crossroads of troop movement and a crucial center of medical care for soldiers from both sides wounded in the nearby battle of Antietem. Today its position halfway between Baltimore and Washington continues to make it a favorite R&R spot for business and leisure travelers.

But Frederick is more than just a town to breeze through on your way to somewhere else. It has a wealth of historical and recreational attractions, absolutely incredible art, fabulous shopping, fine and fun dining, and world-class lodging to share with those who choose to make it the focal point of a quick escape.

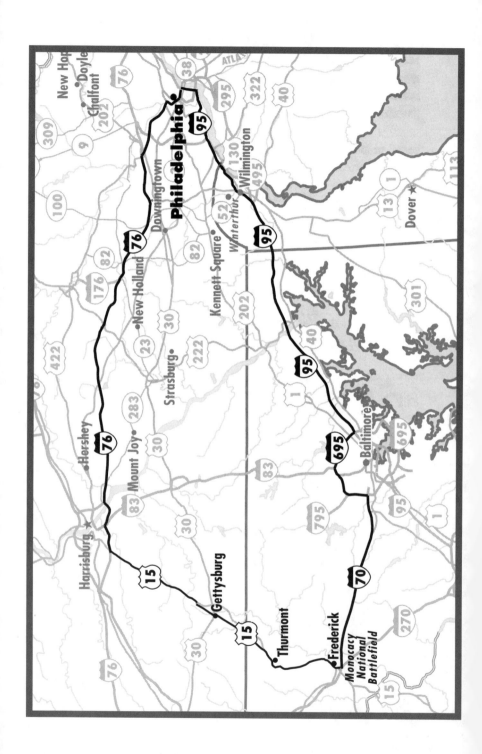

# UP THE MOUNTAINS

## DAY 1

## *Morning*

As the crow flies, Frederick, Maryland, is about 128 miles southwest of Philadelphia. But unless you have wings too, give yourself at least three hours to get there. Take I–95 south past Baltimore until you come to exit 49 for the Baltimore Beltway (I–695) west toward Towson. Take the Beltway to Exit 16 (I–70 west toward Frederick) and stay on 70 for approximately 35 miles. Take exit 54 to Market Street/Buckeystown. At the end of the ramp, turn left onto South Market Street and follow the signs for the **Visitor Center,** 19 East Church Street; (301) 663–8687.

Before you embark on the ninety-minute historic district walking tour offered by the center, get yourself a primo caffeine jolt. You can choose from fifty kinds—all roasted on the premises—and freshly baked pastry at **Frederick Coffee Company & Cafe,** 100 East Street at Everedy Square and Shab Row (301–698–0039). While you're there, order a lunch-to-go to pick up after your tour. The chicken salad is famous, and most of the rest of the inexpensive menu is innovative vegetarian.

During your walking tour, the stories your guide shares will be as interesting as the sites. There are stories of Civil War–era families torn apart by divided loyalties. And stories of how the population came together to create makeshift hospitals in their homes, churches, and other public buildings to care for soldiers from both sides wounded on the battlefield at Antietem. Along the route, you will also see beautifully preserved eighteenth- and nineteenth-century homes and churches, the homes and/or workplaces of such famous Fredericktonians as Francis Scott Key and Barbara Fritchie (more about her later); and the Tory Gaol, a log jail that housed British prisoners in 1776. Walking tours are offered April–December at 1:30 P.M. on Saturday, Sunday, and most major Monday holidays. Cost is $4.50 for adults, $3.50 for seniors, and free for children under twelve.

The city of Frederick's skyline is famous for the graceful **clustered spires** that rise above its many churches. You can get a breathtaking view of six of these spires (including the tallest at St. John the Evangelist Roman Catholic Church) from the top of the parking deck adjacent to the Visitor Center. It's the best view in town.

Grab your picnic lunch and head southeast on Route 355 south/Urbana Pike to **Monocacy National Battlefield** (Visitor Center is at 4801 Urbana

Pike, 301–662–3515), the site of a strategically important, yet little known Civil War encounter often referred to as "the battle that saved Washington." It was here that Union troops held off the Confederates who planned to invade Washington, D.C., even though the Southerners outnumbered them by more than three to one. This two-day engagement gave the Union troops time to fortify against and eventually repel the Confederate advance. You can take a ½-mile walking tour of the beautiful farmland and orchards that look much the same as they did on the day of the battle and view artifacts, monuments, and an electronic map presentation that offers a detailed account of the action. Open daily Memorial Day–Labor Day 8:00 A.M.–4:30 P.M., Wednesday–Sunday only from September–June.

## *Afternoon*

**LUNCH:** Have your picnic at one of the designated spots along the now-peaceful river at **Monocacy National Battlefield Park.**

Back in Frederick's historic district, there are several sites from this morning's tour that you might want to explore in more detail. The first, and most extensive, is the **National Museum of Civil War Medicine** (301–695–1864), the only museum in the world dedicated to the practice and development of medicine during the war. The museum's usual site at 48 East Patrick Street is temporarily closed to allow for major restoration and is scheduled to reopen sometime in spring of 2000. In the meantime, the exhibits will be on display at 100 Adventist Drive (near the Harry Grove Stadium and Mt. Olivet Cemetery).

Authentically detailed exhibits and videos trace the medical care soldiers from both sides received from their initial examination at recruitment stations to the dismal breeding grounds for disease that served as camps to the primitive field facilities and, finally, "fixed bed" hospitals. Particularly fascinating are the exhibits explaining how such important breakthroughs as triage, plastic surgery, and prosthetics had their origins during this dire period in medical history.

Open Monday–Saturday 10:00 A.M.–5:00 P.M., Sunday 11:00 A.M.–5:00 P.M. from mid-March through mid-September; closing at 4:00 P.M. every day the rest of the year. Hour-long guided tours of the museum cost $3.50 per person. There is also a museum store filled with medical-related Civil War books and other items.

"Shoot if you must this old gray head, but spare your country's flag" go the words of John Greenleaf Whittier's poem. It was inspired by the legendary bravery of a ninety-year-old woman named Barbara Fritchie who waved her American flag in the face of advancing Confederate troops. Although her original home was ruined by a flood, the **Barbara Fritchie Museum** (154 West Patrick Street; 301–698–0630), built on the site in 1926, is an exact replica featuring much of the salvaged woodwork and hardware as well as Fritchie's clothes, furnishings, and other personal effects. Open April–September, Monday, Thursday, and Saturday 10:00 A.M.–4:00 P.M., Sunday 1:00–4:00 P.M.; October–November Saturday and Sunday only. $2.00 donation.

If you would like to visit the final resting places of Barbara Fritchie, Francis Scott Key, and many other of Frederick's most prominent citizens, walk the couple of blocks to **Mt. Olivet Cemetery,** 515 South Market Street (301–662–1164). On the western edge of the cemetery, you can also see the graves of more than 800 Union and Confederate soldiers who died at the battles of Antietem and Monocacy River. Open year-round.

Frederick County is apple country, and since 1938 the name McCutcheon's has been synonymous with fine apple products, not just locally, but nationwide. You can get your apples in any form you like them—right off the tree or crafted into butter, cider, or syrup—at **McCutcheon's Factory Store,** 13 South Wisner Street (301-662-3261). Located at just west of Market Street off of South Street, this very popular shop also carries local preserves and jellies, honeys, mustards and relishes, hot sauces, and other condiments.

Sue Shatto's **Victorian Millinery** (401 Fairview Avenue; 301–694–8950), specializing in authentically styled and reproduced ladies' Civil War era headwear, is open by appointment only. So check out her offerings on her Web site at www.victorianmillinery.com to choose your style, then make an appointment for a fitting during your visit. Sue also offers clothing (from underpinnings to ball gowns), shoes, and all kinds of other great stuff from the Civil War and other eras.

## Evening

**DINNER: The Province,** 129 North Market Street; (301) 663–1441. The indoor dining room's cheerful gardenlike setting and view of the real seasonal flower and herb garden outside set the scene for a romantic or just plain relaxing meal. The menu is officially characterized as American bistro, but it also contains more than a few interesting international accents and elegant fillips such as the made-on-the premises pâté du jour and the flambé finish on the veal Amontillado. Entree prices range from $16 to $20. The Province is also well-known for its fabulous desserts, but don't worry if you don't have room for a slice of that luscious-looking cake, pie, or torte after dinner. You can get some to go at the restaurant's takeout location close by at 12 East Patrick Street.

**Lodging: Hill House Bed and Breakfast,** 12 West Third Street; (301) 682–4111. Innkeepers Damian and Taylor Branson have turned their circa 1870 Victorian townhouse into a cozy downtown getaway. Wonderful furnishings collected from antiques hunts and international travels, heirloom family treasures, and original works of art created by Damian and other Maryland artists give each of the four guest rooms its own distinct personality. The third floor Steeple Suite ($175 per night) offers a spectacular view of the spires of Frederick. The Mexican Room ($125 per night) is a grand and colorful affair filled with acquisitions from the Bransons' frequent forays South of the Border. Even the bathrooms are works of art. Room rates start at $105. A full breakfast is included.

## DAY 2

## *Morning*

**BREAKFAST:** Hill House Bed and Breakfast. This is no ordinary breakfast; this is a Maryland breakfast, says Damian, as she sets out baskets of homemade biscuits and dishes of French toast, country ham, bacon, sausage, home fries, some of the best grits I ever tasted, and such in-season delicacies as fried apples or green tomatoes. Long live Maryland breakfasts!

For more of Maryland's best seafood, meats, fresh produce, and homemade baked goods, make your first stop of the day the **Frederick County Fairgrounds Market** on East Patrick Street (301–663–5895). This colorful farmer's market is open year-round on Saturday from 8:00 A.M. to 2:00 P.M.

If thousands of people were asked to suggest a symbol that best represents the spirit of community, what would they choose? The answers (actually more than one hundred of them), ranging from the whimsical to the profound, are now part of an amazing piece of art and cultural and sociological revelation known as **Community Bridge** on Carroll Street, 1 block east of South Market. This trompe l'oeil masterpiece, actually a 2,500-square-foot mural, created by local artist William Cochran over a five-year period appears to be an old-fashioned stone bridge covered with carvings of icons and symbols. Other "fool the eye" triumphs on the mural include an intricately sculpted statue in a niche, a bronze gate, and a marble fountain. For information call Shared Vision at (301) 698–2647.

You can see three more of Cochran's trompe l'oeil creations adorning—and seeming to leap out from—the walls of buildings along Market Street. Part of a series he calls "Angels in the Architecture," they are *The Edge of Gravity* (at Citizen's Way), *Earthbound* (at Church Street), and *Egress* (at Second Street).

To see one of the most intriguing features of Community Bridge exactly the way the artist intended, you must view it from a certain window inside the adjacent **Delaplaine Visual Arts Center,** 40 South Carroll Street; (301) 696–0656. Housed in a restored old mill, the center also offers exhibitions of local, national, and regional fine arts, crafts, and photography all year round. Open Thursday–Saturday 10:00 A.M.–5:30 P.M., Sunday 1:00–4:00 P.M. Admission is free.

## *Afternoon*

**LUNCH: Pretzel & Pizza Creations,** 210 North Market Street; (301) 694–9299. If all of this art has awakened the Picasso, Degas, or Cochran in you, why not use that inspiration to create a masterpiece of a lunch or snack? Owner Natalie Nastovici provides close to twenty sweet and savory toppings which translate to an almost infinite variety of mix and match possibilities (including somebody's idea of a yummy meal, sauerkraut pizza). The specialty of the house is the pretzel dog, a hot dog coated with homemade honey mustard, topped with different cheeses, rolled in pretzel dough, and baked. If you're daring, ask for the deluxe model, stuffed with onion and sauerkraut. Inexpensive.

From May to July, one of the most popular destinations in the Frederick area (actually in Buckeystown about 8 miles south of Frederick on Route 85) is **Lilypons Water Garden,** 6800 Lilypons Road; (800) 999–5459 or (301) 874–5133. During the summer blooming season this sixty-acre aquatic nursery's outdoor displays of water lily–filled ponds, pools, and lush wetlands are breathtaking in color and dimension. Birders also delight in visits by the wide variety of species that are attracted to this natural setting. If you're into aquatic gardening at home, you'll find lots of tips, ideas, plants, statuary, and fountains to create your own paradise. Open year-round Monday–Friday 8:00 A.M.–8:00 P.M., Saturday 9:00 A.M.–8:00 P.M., Sunday until 6:00 P.M.

Return to Frederick and take East Patrick Street out toward the highway (I–70). But instead of taking 70, follow the signs for Route 144 east; keep a sharp eye out for these signs and be sure you turn left when they tell you to do so. Follow 144 until it becomes Main Street in the 200-plus-year-old village of **New Market** (301–864–5651) aka "the Antiques Capital of Maryland." Main Street's antique mile with its restored eighteenth-century buildings and small-town-of-long-ago feeling is in perfect harmony with the art to armoires, books to beer steins, teddy bears to textiles array of antiques and vintage and collectible items on display in its thirty individual shops. A number of these shops are open during the week, but for the full effect—and the widest selection—try to visit on a weekend.

## Evening

**DINNER: Mealey's Restaurant,** 8 Main Street; (301) 865–5488. I'll long remember the salmon and crab Wellington from this spot in the heart of New Market. Housed in an eighteenth-century log building enclosed in a larger nineteenth-century brick former hotel, Mealey's is renowned for steak and seafood and offers a generous taste of both with such house specialties as prime rib of beef and hickory shrimp, and filet mignon and broiled crab cake. Desserts are well worth the calories, especially the homemade peanut butter and key lime pies. Or you could innocently order a Girl Scout Cookie coffee and pretend that you didn't know it was laced with white menthe and dark cacao. Entrees range from $11.95 for pasta to $26.95 for a "seafood feast."

**LODGING:** Hill House Bed and Breakfast.

## DAY 3

## Morning

**BREAKFAST:** Hill House Bed and Breakfast.

You're going home to Philadelphia today, but you won't be reversing your original route. Instead get on to Route 15 in Frederick and follow it about 10 miles north. From Route 15, take Route 77 west for 3 miles and follow the signs to **Catoctin Mountain Park** (Visitor Center; 301–663–9388) in the town of Thurmont.

Aside from its beauty, scenic mountain overviews, and virtually unlimited recreational opportunities, the park is probably best known as the site of the presidential retreat known as Camp David. Although the chief executive's get-away is closed to the public, you can still share the presidential vacation experience by hiking, snowshoeing, or cross-country skiing some of its more than 45 miles of trails, admiring the wildflowers and visiting the remains of farms once inhabited by early European settlers. You can also go rock climbing if you obtain a free permit from the Visitor Center.

One particularly interesting site in the park is the **Blue Blazes Whiskey Still,** originally built by western Maryland farmers during the Whiskey Rebellion of the 1790s and later enlarged for use by Prohibition-era bootleggers.

Right across Route 77 is **Cunningham Falls State Park** (Visitor Center; 301–271–7574) where you'll find a 78-foot waterfall, more hiking trails, and forty-three-acre **Hunting Creek Lake,** where you can swim, fish, or canoe. Only fifty-some years ago, this beautiful park was a devastated area, depleted by years of logging, mountain farming, and the wanton harvesting of resources to fuel a major iron furnace from Revolutionary War times up until 1903. The remains of the **Catoctin Furnace** still stand, but the land, 10,000 acres of which were purchased by the federal government in 1935, has come a long way toward returning to its natural state.

The parks are open daily year-round from sunrise to sunset. Peak visitor time is in October when the foliage is in its most magnificent finery.

## *Afternoon*

**LUNCH: Cozy Restaurant,** 103 Frederick Road, Route 806, Thurmont; (301) 271–4301. Normally I would suggest getting a picnic lunch and enjoying it amid the trees and wildflowers of one of the parks. But just about everyone who visits the Catoctins or Camp David—from high-ranking government officials to foreign dignitaries to members of the news media—makes at least one special pilgrimage to this 70-some-year-old spot, as the jam-packed celebrity memorabilia cases will attest. "The Cozy" is also famous in its own right for its outstanding, yet outrageously inexpensive, daily lunch and dinner buffets. Call for weekday and weekend hours.

To return home to Philadelphia from Thurmont, Maryland, it should take about three hours. Follow Route 15 north 16 miles into Gettysburg, Pennsylvania; then take Route 30 east for 2 miles and get back on Route 15 north for another 29 miles until you reach the Pennsylvania Turnpike (I–76). Take the turnpike east 92 miles until you come to the Schuylkill Expressway (I–76); then take the expressway east for 22 miles into Philadelphia.

## THERE'S MORE

**Rose Hill Manor Park,** 1611 North Market Street, Frederick. This former retirement estate of Thomas Johnson, Maryland's first elected governor, is the site of two separate attractions that are accessible for a single ticket price of $3.00 for adults, $1.00 for children:

- Children's Museum; (301) 694–1648. Designed to teach elementary school-age children and their families about life in the late eighteenth and early nineteenth centuries, this tour of a 200-year-old Georgian manor house and its outbuildings offers many interactive exhibits and activities to make the learning fun. Open daily April–October Monday–Saturday 10:00 A.M.–4:00 P.M., Sunday 1:00–4:00 P.M. Also open weekends in November.

- Farm Museum. Upon request, you can take a self-guided tour of these exhibits depicting nineteenth- and twentieth-century agricultural tools and techniques.

**Weinberg Center,** 20 West Patrick Street, Frederick; (301) 694–8585. The setting is a restored 1926 movie palace complete with plush velvet rocking chair seats, massive crystal chandeliers, satin brocade walls, marble columns, and an old Wurlitzer organ. The fare is everything from silent and classic films to music and dance to community theater. Evening and matinee performances October–May.

**Schifferstadt,** 1110 Rosemont Avenue, Frederick; (301) 663–3885. This pre-Revolutionary War farmhouse, the oldest standing structure in Frederick, is considered one of the finest examples of German Colonial architecture in America. Open May–mid-December Tuesday–Saturday 10:00 A.M.–4:00 P.M., Sunday noon–4:00 P.M. $2.00 donation.

**Frederick Carriage Company,** departure points at 124 Market Street, Baker Park, or Everedy Square, Frederick; (301) 694–RIDE (7433). Scenic and romantic horse-drawn carriage rides through Frederick's historic district. Price for a ½-hour carriage ride for up to six adults is $35; $60 for one hour.

**Catoctin Wildlife Preserve & Zoo,** 13019 Catoctin Furnace Road, Thurmont; (301) 271–3180 or (301) 271–4922. This twenty-six-acre woodland setting is home to more than 300 animals including many rare and endangered species. Open April–October, seven days a week, 9:00 A.M.–6:00 P.M. Admission for adults (thirteen and over) $8.95, seniors (sixty and over) $7.00, children (two to twelve) $5.75, under two free.

**Camping.** Catoctin Mountain Park in Thurmont has two public campgrounds:

- Owens Creek Campground; (301) 663–9330. Twelve dollars per night per site for five people, available on a first-come-first-served basis. Open April 15–third week in November.

- Camp Misty Mount; (301) 271–3140. Individual cabin rentals begin at $40 per night. Open mid-April to end of October.

**National Shrine of St. Elizabeth Ann Seton,** 333 South Seton Avenue, Emmitsburg (north of Thurmont on Route 15); (301) 447–6606 (Monday–Friday), (301) 447–3121 (Saturday and Sunday). Home and shrine of the first American saint to be canonized by the Catholic Church. Open daily, 10:00 A.M.–5:00 P.M., except two weeks in January and Mondays in December.

## SPECIAL EVENTS

**May.** Frederick Art & Craft Festival, Frederick Fairgrounds; (717) 369–4810. This annual three-day festival featuring more than 300 of America's top artisans is considered one of the top juried shows in the country.

**June/July/August.** Summer Concert Series, Baker Park Bandshell, Second Street and Carroll Parkway; (301) 663–8687. Outdoor musical performances every Sunday evening at 7:00. Free.

**End July/Early August.** Country Peddler Show, Frederick Fairgrounds, 797 East Patrick Street; (301) 663–0559. A two-day gathering of folk artists and their one-of-a-kind crafts from around the nation.

**September.** The Great Frederick Fair, Frederick Fairgrounds, 797 East Patrick Street; (301) 663–5895. This eight-day event is one of the oldest agricultural fairs in the country. Features include animal exhibitions, food, carnival rides and games, harness racing, and national headliner musical entertainment.

**October.** In the Street, downtown area; (301) 663–8687. Nine downtown blocks are closed to traffic to accommodate vendors, events, and celebrants at Frederick's most vibrant festival. Lots of food from local restaurants, crafts, live entertainment, and children's activities.

### OTHER RECOMMENDED RESTAURANTS AND LODGINGS

## *Frederick*

Brewer's Alley, 124 North Market Street; (301) 631–0089. If you've never tried Louisiana alligator, you can get a side of sausage or an entree of medallions. Other Big Easy fare includes a foot-long muffuletta, smoked sausage po'-boy, gumbo du jour, and boudin (Cajun pork and rice sausage). Inexpensive to moderate.

Tyler Spite House, 112 West Church Street; (301) 831–4455. A faithfully restored pre-Civil War home with a unique history in the heart of downtown Frederick. Rooms range from $150 to $250 double occupancy on weekends; $120 to $175 weekdays.

Morningside Inn, 7477 McKaig Road; (800) 786–7403 or (301) 898–3920. Set on 300 acres of fields and forest, this renovated early 1900s Amish-style barn has cozy country-style furnishings and on-site activities that range from an exercise room to playing fetch with Sydney, the resident golden retriever. Rates, which include a full breakfast, range from $95 to $105 Sunday–Thursday, $115–$125 Friday, and $125–$135 Saturday.

## *New Market*

New Market General Store and Cafe Maryland, 26 West Main Street, Old National Pike (Route 144); (301) 865-6313. This combination turn-of-the-century general store/casual breakfast and lunch spot offers an opportunity to enjoy inexpensive fare and shop for antiques at the same time! What bliss!

## *Buckeystown*

Inn at Buckeystown, 3521 Buckeystown Pike; (301) 874-5755. This elegant inn, housed in a nineteenth-century former mansion and church, offers five guest rooms and two cottages furnished with period pieces and filled with amenities. You can choose from the traditional bed-and-breakfast plan ($140–$240 per night) or a plan that includes breakfast and a gourmet dinner ($200–$300).

## *Thurmont*

Cozy Country Inn, ½ mile off Route 15 on Route 806; (301) 271–4301. The Cozy offers executive rooms, suites, and cottages ranging from $46 to $130 per night (depending on type of accommodation and time of year), all individually decorated to commemorate the presidents, foreign leaders, and news organizations who have visited the inn or nearby Camp David. Deluxe continental breakfast is included on weekdays.

## FOR MORE INFORMATION

Maryland Office of Tourism Development; (410) 767–6298; www.mdisfun.org.

# DOWN THE
## SHORE

## ESCAPES

*Crabs are a specialty all along Maryland's Eastern Shore.*

# DOWN THE SHORE

# Cape May, New Jersey

## BEYOND THE GINGERBREAD

### 1 NIGHT

*Brilliant Monarchs • Water Safaris • Whales*
*Diamond-Studded Beaches*

Cape May ... the name undoubtedly sets visions of cozy gingerbread cottages and Victorian painted ladies dancing in your head. And they are well worth seeing, these survivors of history, reminders of an era so prim and proper that men and women were assigned separate hours to bathe in the sea.

But it was the wild side of this beautiful peninsula bounded by the Atlantic Ocean to the east and the Delaware Bay to the west that attracted the first seasonal visitors here almost four centuries ago. In the 1600s, the Leni Lenape tribe used it as their summer home, returning year after year to feast on the bounty offered by its waters, lands, and skies. Later in the century the abundance of whales off the coast brought the Dutch as well as William Penn's Quakers and migrating colonists from New York and New England, including a few original Mayflower families from Plymouth, Massachusetts. Even birds have long recognized this southernmost tip of New Jersey as a hospitable feeding and resting place along their annual migration routes.

Today that wild side of Cape May, the oldest and still one of the most popular of the nation's seashore resorts, remains a major draw for visitors, not just in summer, but throughout the year. Like the Indians, they still come to fish the ocean and bay. Like the English colonists, they continue to hunt the whales—only now with cameras instead of harpoons. And nature lovers from all over the world follow the hundreds of thousands of birds and over one

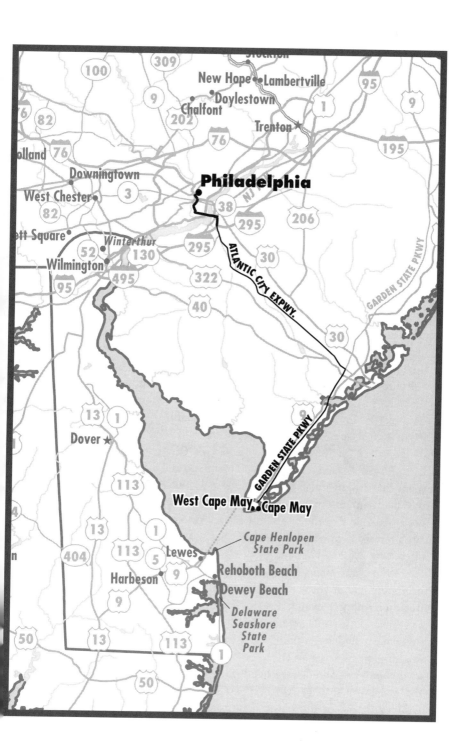

hundred species of butterflies as they converge here each year on their way to warmer climates.

As with most seaside resorts, summer is peak time for tourists. That's when the population swells from its year-round figure of about 5,000 to about 80,000 on any given weekend. If you must come in summer, try to make it during the week rather than on the weekend. Better yet, come in the fall when there are fewer visitors (unless you count the thousands of migrating raptors and other birds) with whom you will have to share the beaches, trails, cruises, wonderful restaurants, intriguing shops, and awe-inspiring sunrises over the ocean and sunsets over the bay.

## DAY 1

## *Morning*

The wildlife gets up early in Cape May, so try to hit the road right after break-fast. To get there, take the Walt Whitman Bridge to New Jersey Route 42 south. Take 42 south to the Atlantic City Expressway east until you come to the Garden State Parkway. Take the Parkway south to Route 109 and follow 109 into Cape May. The total distance from Philadelphia is 97 miles, which translates to two days by stagecoach (the way vacationers came in the 1800s) or about 2½ hours (depending on seasonal traffic) by car.

In 1976 Cape May became one of the only entire cities in America to be designated a National Historic Landmark. Along its lovely tree-lined, gas lamp-lit streets stand more than 600 preserved and restored buildings—among them the famous gingerbread houses and painted ladies—representing all of the Victorian era's most popular architectural styles. One of the best ways to get an overview of these beauties and learn some interesting tidbits about the city's history is to take one of the variety of regularly scheduled trolley tours offered by the Mid-Atlantic Center for the Arts. You can purchase tickets at the Washington Street Mall Information Booth, where all the center's tours begin and end. If you have the time, take one of the ninety-minute **Combination Trolley/Physick Estate Tours** ($11.00 adults, $5.50 children three to twelve). This guided excursion takes you through Cape May's historic district and includes a tour of the **Emlen Physick House & Estate** (1048 Washington Street), the city's only Victorian home museum. Open daily in spring, summer, and fall; weekends in winter. Also included with your tour of the estate is a stop to see the current exhibition at the **Carriage House Gallery,** home of the oldest county art league in America. For additional information about arts center–sponsored tours and the Emlen Physick House & Estate, call (609) 884–5404.

If a visit to the shore means stocking up on your favorite fudge and salt-water taffies, you're in luck because **Morrow's Nut House** (609–884–3300) and **Fralingers** (609–884–5695), both of which have been making their famous confections for more than a century, sit right across Washington Street (below Jackson) from one another.

## Afternoon

**LUNCH:** Pick up a lunch-to-go at **Van Scoy's Bistro, Bakery and Gourmet Carry-out,** Carpenters' Square Mall, 312 Carpenters' Lane; (609) 898–9898. Freshly made sandwiches range from $5.95 to $8.75. The signature model has artichoke hearts, sprouts, sun-dried tomato, cucumbers, cheddar, lettuce, and olive oil on six-grain bread. (Dinner here emphasizes fresh seafood and a global perspective. And daily in summer from 3:30 to 5:00 P.M. is "cappy hour," cappuccinos and dessert for two for $9.95.)

**Cape May Point State Park,** off Sunset Boulevard at the southern tip of New Jersey, about 2 miles west of the city of Cape May (609–884–2159), is a beautiful spot to relax over your picnic lunch. Near the entrance to the park there's a still-working 157-foot-tall 1895 lighthouse (609–884–5404)—one of the nation's oldest in continual operation—that you can climb day or evening for a panoramic view. Admission for climbing the tower is $3.50 for adults (one child free per adult) and $1.00 for additional children. Right off-shore you can spot a World War II bunker, once 900 feet inland, now slowly eroding away in the sea.

In the skies and on the beach, you can watch the year-round residents and migratory visitors that come for rest and food to the nearby National Audubon Society's **Cape May Bird Observatory**. In mid-September thousands of monarch butterflies add their brilliant colors to the view as they wing their way to Mexico. The park is open daily from dawn to dusk from April to mid-October and weekends from mid-February to March and mid-October to January 1. Closed January to mid-February.

## Evening

**DINNER: Louisa's,** 104 Jackson Street; (609) 884–5882. At this tiny family-owned dining spot (across from Washington Street Mall) the hand-painted door, walls, and tables are only a preview of the real artistry, which comes from the kitchen. Fresh fish gilded with tomatilla and red pepper salsa or papaya mustard sauce. Chicken breast made sassy with Jamaican jerk seasoning. Savory vegetable cakes made from the season's harvest. For dessert, there are oven-fresh fruit cobblers and irresistible bread puddings. The blackboard menu changes daily. Prices are moderate to expensive. Louisa's is a quirky kind of place with hours that change according to the whim of the owners. It's also extremely popular so call early for a reservation.

After dinner, walk back to the parking lot of the Washington Street Mall to see if you're in the right place at the right time to catch one of the free open-air concerts at the **Victorian Bandshell** (Wednesday and Saturday at 8:00 P.M. July–Labor Day). Or you could take a moonlight stroll on Cape May's answer to the boardwalk, an oceanside path stretching from Madison Street to just beyond Broadway called the **Promenade**. If you're looking for a noisy, razzle-dazzle, circus midway, you'll have to go to Wildwood. Although Cape May's version does have a smattering of arcades, cafes, fudge, and T-shirt shops, it is a relatively peaceful place, perfect for some romantic star- and surf gazing.

**LODGING: Albert Stevens Inn,** 127 Myrtle Avenue, West Cape May; (800) 890–CATS or (609) 884–4717. West Cape May is only a ten-minute walk from the beach and the Washington Street Mall, but, for some reason, it is considered by many tourists to be off the beaten path. But the Albert Stevens Inn has become a destination all by itself, especially for feline fanciers from all over the world who come to have afternoon tea in its famous "cat's garden." But more about that later. The house, a fine specimen of a Victorian painted lady, is furnished with period pieces and distinctive bed and wall treatments. Adding warmth and whimsy to the accommodations is owners Curt and Diane Diviney-Rangen's collection of kitty memorabilia, with frolicking fur balls decorating everything from the walls to the bedsheets.

But the Rangens aren't just your ordinary cat lovers. Deeply concerned about the number of feral cats that were roaming the streets of Cape May after being abandoned by vacationing families, they turned their garden into a refuge for these strays and provide them with food, shelter, and medical care (which includes neutering). Of course, the house is primarily human territory; the kitties have their own playing and living accommodations (although one or two have learned to con guests into opening the front door for them). Rates range from $85 to $165 per night double occupancy, depending on the room and the season. A full breakfast and beach tags are included.

## DAY 2

## *Morning*

**BREAKFAST:** Albert Stevens Inn. Curt's Norwegian ancestry is a delightful influence on the meals—especially the daily three-course breakfasts—that come from his and Diane's kitchen. Airy apple fritters with a lingonberry-based sauce and a Norwegian-style vegetable quiche are among their breakfast specialties.

Head for the beach or, for a truly unique perspective on the Cape May seascape, head north on Ocean Drive over the Cape May inlet bridge into Wildwood Crest and travel about ¼ mile until you see Two Mile Landing Restaurant and Marina on your left. This is the home base of **Atlantic Parasail** (609–522–1869), where you will begin your one-hour adventure 300 feet ($38) or, for the truly courageous, 500 feet ($48) over the ocean. There is no age limit and you don't even have to get wet if you don't want to. Open Memorial Day–end of September. During peak season boats depart hourly from 8:00 A.M.–sunset; call for off-peak hours.

## *Afternoon*

**LUNCH: Zoe's Beachfront Eatery,** Beach and Stockton Place, Cape May; (609) 884–1233. Here you can get another view of Cape May over lunch on the white picket-fenced, flower-box, and planter-adorned patio. Lunch favorites include big-chunk fruit salads, a truly delicious signature veggie hoagie, and fresh-roasted turkey sandwiches. Prices are inexpensive; inside seating is available.

One of West Cape May's best-kept secrets is its abundance of wonderful antiques shops, a number of which are within blocks of the Albert Stevens Inn and are open year-round. On 405 West Perry Street you'll find **Rocking Horse Antique Center** (609–898–0737), an eighty dealer co-op that can provide a morning's entertainment by itself. **Tabby House Antiques** at 479 West Perry (609–898–0908) features eighteenth- and nineteenth-century American antiques in room settings. Broadway is home to **Finestkind** (139 Broadway, 609–898–1622), a five-shop co-op featuring works of regional fine and folk artists, antique and vintage American pottery and dinnerware, Victorian and Edwardian vintage and reproduction fashions, and home furnishings.

By now it's late afternoon, time to follow the sun and Sunset Boulevard to the southernmost tip of the peninsula and the state. This lovely spot is called

*Welcome to Louisa's in Cape May.*

**Sunset Beach**—for good reason. Out in the water you can see the weathered hull of the *Atlantus,* a World War I–era concrete ship that went aground here more than fifty years ago and has been slowly sinking deeper into the sands with each passing year. And while you won't find a lot of seashells on this beach, you will find Indian arrowheads and a wealth of Cape May diamonds, pure quartz crystals of various shapes, sizes, and colors believed by the early Native Americans to possess supernatural powers and bring good luck. While that might be merely wishful thinking, these "diamonds" are still treasured for their beauty; when polished and cut into facets, they closely resemble the real thing. Even if you don't have much luck on the beach, you don't have to go away empty-handed. The adjacent **Sunset Beach Gift Shops** (609-884–7079) carries a large selection of sterling and gold-filled Cape May diamond jewelry ranging in price from just over $20 to more than $100. You can also purchase small uncut polished stones for 94 cents.

# Evening

**DINNER: Peaches at Sunset,** 1 Sunset Boulevard, West Cape May; (609) 898–0100. The sunsets here are so spectacular, it's no wonder the beach is named in their honor. Quite frankly, with its unparalleled view of the sunset, a beachfront restaurant here could probably get away with serving a pretty ordinary menu. But it isn't likely that anyone would call coffee roasted filet mignon with shiitake mushroom sauce, Mexican-style corn and black bean lasagna or pistachio-crusted salmon with five star spice and beurre blanc ordinary. For starters be sure to order the signature roasted garlic served on slices of grilled sourdough bread with imported mascarpone cheese. Prices range from moderate to expensive.

To return to Philadelphia, retrace your route from Day 1. The return trip should take about 2 to 2½ hours.

## THERE'S MORE

**Cape May Stage,** Welcome Center, Lafayette and Bank Streets; (609) 884–1341. The town's resident Actors Equity theater company performs contemporary and regional historical plays from spring through December. Also on the schedule are a children's theater series and poetry readings. Tickets are $18 for adults, $15 for seniors and students.

**Hauntings of Cape May Tour,** across from Hotel Macomber, 727 Beach Avenue; (609) 463–8984. Tickets are available and tours meet at the Promenade across from the hotel. Your guide will regale you with tales of buried pirate treasure and other scary stuff on this ninety-minute ghost tour along Jackson and Washington Streets. Available May–November, 7:00 P.M. and 9:00 P.M.; call for specific days. Tickets are $9.00 for adults, $5.00 for children ten and under.

**Shields' Bike Rentals,** 11 Gurney Street; (609) 898–1818. Hourly and daily rentals for the family plus tandems and beach cruisers. Call for hours and rates.

**The Colonial House,** 635½ Washington Street, behind City Hall; (609) 884–9100. Built before the Revolutionary War, this museum hosts changing exhibits of art and artifacts from Cape May's (or as it was called then

Cape Island) Colonial past. Open daily June 15–September 15, 10:00 A.M.–2:00 P.M. $1.00 donation. Call about off-season special exhibits.

**Cape May National Golf Club,** Route 9, exit 4A Garden State Parkway; (609) 884–1563. A uniquely beautiful and environmentally sensitive course set amid wetlands, ponds, flower beds, and a private nature preserve and sanctuary. Open year-round. Prices, including cart, range from $25 to $30 in winter and from $68 to $74 in summer.

**Cape May–Lewes Ferry,** Route 9 south to Ferry Road, terminal is between Bay Shore Road and Beach Drive; 800–64–FERRY or 609–886–1725. Take a relaxing 17-mile (seventy minutes one-way) ride across the Delaware Bay aboard the newly renovated MV *Twin Peaks* or MV, *Cape May,* state-of-the-art vessels, each with expansive passenger decks, cushy lounges, and a fine restaurant. Fare: $18–$20 for passenger car and driver (other passengers are additional); $4.50–$6.50 for foot passengers six and over. Operates 365 days a year.

**Nature Center of Cape May,** 1600 Delaware Avenue; (609) 898–8848. Take a Harbor Safari, a fascinating ninety-minute exploration of this fertile habitat led by a marine biologist, to you get up close and personal with the native fish, other vertebrates, and plants. Offered April–November; call for days, hours, and prices.

**Camping.** Cape Island Campground, 709 Route 9, directly across from Cold Spring Village, Cape May; (800) 437–7443 or (609) 884–5777. Spacious campsites with accommodations for everything from tents to RVs set on 175 acres of forests and fields. Amenities include two large swimming pools, tennis courts, all hookups, modern bathhouses, and convenience store. Call for rates.

## SPECIAL EVENTS

**April.** Spring Festival; (800) 275–4278 or (609) 884–5404. Ten days of seasonal celebration including the new Spring Victorian Weekend (a three-day version of October's Victorian Week) and Tulip and Garden Weekend with secret garden tours, concerts, trolley rides, and golf and tennis tournaments.

**May.** Cape May Music Festival; (800) 275–4278 or (609) 884–5404. Convention Hall and other venues. This six-week, twenty-concert series features the forty-piece Cape May Festival Orchestra and classical and classic music from the Renaissance to the jazz era, and from Bach to the Beatles.

**October.** Victorian Week; (800) 275–4278 or (609) 884–5404. Throughout the city. A ten-day extravaganza of historic city and house tours, Victorian fashion shows, vaudeville, brass bands, craft and antiques shows, lectures, and workshops.

**October.** Lima Bean Festival, Wilbraham Park, West Cape May; (609) 884–1005 (West Cape May City Hall). Country western music, games, crafts, food (lots of limas, of course), and the crowning of Miss Lima Bean. The locals absolutely love this one!

**Late November–New Year.** Christmas in Cape May, throughout the city; (800) 275–4278 or (609) 884–5404. Celebrate an old-fashioned Victorian Christmas in beautiful Cape May with candlelight tours, a wassail party, caroling, arts and crafts, parade, band concerts, food and wine tastings, and other holiday festivities.

## OTHER RECOMMENDED RESTAURANTS AND LODGINGS

## Cape May

The Abbey, 34 Gurney Street at Columbia Avenue; (609) 884–4506. Once two summer retreats owned by a wealthy Pennsylvania coal baron and his son, the striking gothic Villa with its 60-foot tower, stenciled and ruby glass arched windows, and shaded verandas has been combined with the cottage next door to create one fabulous bed-and-breakfast. Rates range from $100 to $275 per night double occupancy. Open April–December.

Virginia Hotel, 25 Jackson Street; (800) 732–4236 or (609) 884–5700. Established in 1879 as a small, elegant inn, the Virginia Hotel continues its tradition of excellence in this restored gingerbread building with its graceful two-story veranda and impeccably appointed rooms. Open year-round, rates range from $80 to $155 weekday and from $130 to $210 weekend in winter to $120–$225 weekday and $180–$295 weekend during peak summer season. Special rates and packages may be available. The hotel's Ebbitt Room restaurant is renowned for its fresh seafood and new American cuisine specialties.

Union Park Dining Room, Hotel Macomber, 727 Beach Drive; (609) 884–8811. Innovative twists on American and seafood dishes include lobster shepherd's pie and polenta-crusted sea bass. Expensive.

Waters Edge, Beach and Pittsburgh Avenues; (609) 884–1717. The internationally and seasonally inspired menu changes daily. Expensive.

La Patisserie, 524 Washington Mall; (609) 884–7107. Exquisite cookies, cakes, and pastries—especially the jewel-like fruit tarts and the melt-in-your mouth almond, cheese, or chocolate croissants. Give twenty-four hours notice and you can adopt one of the fantasy breads made in the shapes of giant crabs, turtles, alligators, birds, and other local marine inhabitants.

Mad Batter Restaurant, Carroll Villa Hotel, 19 Jackson Street; (609) 884–9619. This charming restaurant has long been famous for its fabulous moderately priced breakfast/brunch batter selections, including specialty pancakes, waffles, blintzes, and orange and almond French toast. Lunch and dinner, too.

## West Cape May

Daniel's on Broadway, 416 South Broadway; (609) 898–8770. Currently one of the hottest spots at the Jersey shore, this handsome restaurant housed in a restored 1870s mansion takes classic American regional cuisine to new heights of elegance. Moderate to expensive. Open year-round.

Mangia Mangia, 110 North Broadway; (609) 884–2429. Moderately priced Italian pasta, seafood, and other specialties. Children's menu.

### FOR MORE INFORMATION

Greater Cape May Chamber; (609) 884–5508.

Cape May County Chamber of Commerce; (609) 465–7181.

Cape May Region Welcome Center, Ocean View Service Area, Garden State Parkway; (609) 624–0918. Open daily 9:00 A.M.–4:30 P.M. for information and brochures.

# Lewes and Cape Henlopen, Delaware

## THE OTHER SIDE OF THE FERRY

### 1 NIGHT

*Night Fishing • Dolphin Watching • Seas of Lavender
Oceans of Orchids*

Most Philadelphians know Lewes, Delaware, as the town on the other side of the Cape May–Lewes Ferry. You may have spent a few hours there yourself, strolling along the waterfront, visiting some of the charming shops, or enjoying lunch with a unparalleled view of the Delaware Bay. But if you think this kind of brief foray into Lewes means you've "been there, done that," you couldn't be farther from the truth.

Lewes and nearby Cape Henlopen State Park have shared an exciting, even tumultuous history: as an ill-fated Dutch whaling settlement in 1631, as target for late seventeenth-century pirate raids and cannon bombardment during the War of 1812; and as a crucial Atlantic coastline defense post during World War II. You can still see the remnants of those past years in the area's carefully restored homes (one with a cannonball still lodged in its wall), museums, and lookout towers—even on the rolling sand dunes of the cape. Fortunately peace now reigns over this lovely little town as well as over the adjacent miles of virtually unspoiled ocean and bay beaches, and the protected lands ranging from dunes to freshwater wetlands to pine forests.

Only 85 miles south of Philadelphia in Delaware's Sussex County, Lewes is not exactly an unexplored treasure, but it certainly is an underexplored one.

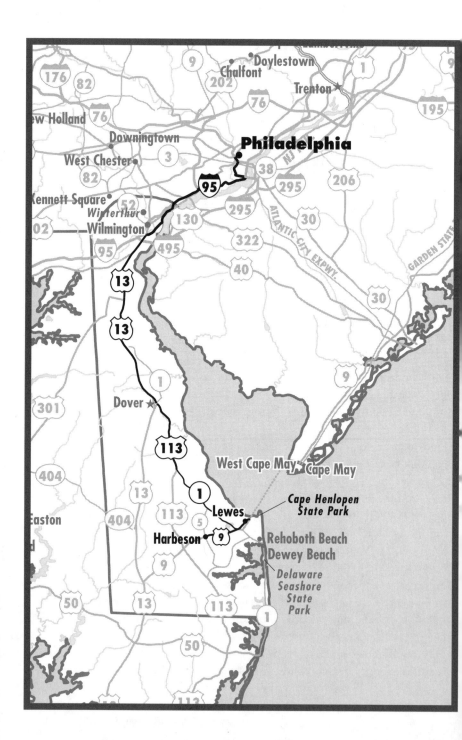

And here's a tip—if you want to endear yourself to the natives, keep in mind that Lewes is pronounced *loo*-iss, not looz as in youse.

## DAY 1

## *Morning*

It takes about 2½ hours to get to Lewes from Philadelphia. Take the Schuylkill Expressway (I–76) east to I–95. Take I–95 south for 28 miles to I–295. Travel north on 295 for 1 mile until you reach Route 13/Route 40; then follow Route 13 south for 66 miles to Route 1. Follow Route 1 south 18 miles to Route 9, then Route 9 for 2 miles into Lewes.

To get a hint of Lewes's earliest history, start at the **Zwaanendael Museum** on the corner of Savannah Road and Kings Highway; (302) 645–1148. Although its elaborate architecture and stonework facade are decidedly seventeenth-century European, this eye-catching building was actually built in 1931 to commemorate the 300th anniversary of the arrival of the area's—and the state's—first settlers. The original whaling colony quickly came to a tragic end, but this replica of the city hall that stood in their native city of Hoorn, Holland, in 1631 preserves and shares its history and artifacts. Other exhibits and displays tell the stories of the British bombardment of Lewes during the War of 1812, the town's long career as a major port of trade, and the DeBraak, a captured Dutch-built ship sailing under English flag that was sunk by a storm off Cape Henlopen in 1798. Open Tuesday–Saturday 10:00 A.M.–4:30 P.M., Sunday 1:30–4:30 P.M. Free.

A few steps away at 114 West Third Street, artist John Austin Ellsworth keeps the craft of blacksmithing alive while producing wonderful items for the home and garden at his **Preservation Forge** (302–645–7897). In this working shop and museum, you can see early blacksmith-made ironwork and watch Ellsworth create new items ranging from fireplace pieces to weather vanes to ornately crafted gates. If you have a particular design in mind, he also takes custom orders. Open summer months 8:00 A.M.–4:00 P.M. every day except Sunday and Wednesday. Hours vary other seasons so call first.

## *Afternoon*

**LUNCH: A Taste of Heaven,** 107 Savannah Road; (302) 644–1992. If the weather is good, you can dine on the outside patio with a view of the canal, but even if Mother Nature is being uncooperative, you can always find blue skies above your head in this transformed two-century-old house. Inexpensive lunchtime sandwiches are elevated to a new level with such innovative combinations as Granny Smith apple and brie with cilantro mango chutney, and shrimp roll-up with cream cheese, horseradish, and red pepper glaze. Even the potato chips are extraordinarily flavorful. Save some room for the house specialty dessert–key lime pie. Open Wednesday–Sunday in summer, Friday and Saturday beginning October 1.

It has long been believed that lavender has the power to heal the spirit and soothe the soul. So to really get you into the relaxation mode drive about 5 to 6 miles west on Route 9 to the village of Cool Spring (between Lewes and Georgetown). When you reach the railroad tracks, take a left onto Route 290 south. One mile down the road on your right you'll see **The Manor at Cool Spring Lavender Farm** (302–648–8325). Here Joe Palenik and his wife Pauline Pettitt-Palenik (known around town as "the Lavender Lady") grow about thirty varieties of lavender and blend them into a collection of fabulous products, including bath and massage oils, soaps, crafts, jelly, and hard candy. In season they also offer homemade jams, pickles, and fresh vegetables. Call ahead and Joe will take you on a tour of prized fields, where he'll explain the history and uses of lavender and show you his latest experimental plantings. The tours are free.

A few miles down the road near the small town of Harbeson, Bob Edelen and Nan Miller grow familiar and exotic varieties of orchids by the thousands in their greenhouses at **Hollyberry Orchids** (302-856-6653). To get there from Route 9 in Harbeson, head east on Route 5 for more than half a mile to County Road 293; turn right and continue about 2 miles. Open year-round, daily 10:00 A.M.–5:00 P.M., until 4:00 P.M. in winter. If you call ahead, Bob will be happy to show you around and answer any of your orchid-growing questions.

For some prime antiquing, head back to Lewes and take Route 9 east to Route 1. In the 3-mile stretch of Route 1 that extends north and south of Lewes, there are no less than 150 dealers in four warehouse markets offering all manner of antique, vintage, and collectible items. The furthest south is **Heritage Antique Market** at 1301 Highway One (302–645–2309) with fifty dealers. The furthest north is the **Antique Village Mall** at 221 Highway One (302–644–0842), with eighty dealers.

## *Evening*

Have an early dinner because you've got an appointment at 6:00 that's going to take up the rest of your evening.

**DINNER: Gilligan's Restaurant & Harborside Bar,** Front Street and Canal Square, Lewes; (302) 645–7866. If you feared that the fabled SS *Minnow* (the one that took Gilligan and company on their "three-hour tour") was lost at sea forever, you'll be glad to know that it has found a new life and a safe, secure home on the canal in Lewes. In addition to lots of atmosphere, this adorable seasonal restaurant also has a terrific menu specializing in American seafood and innovative regional cuisine. One particularly inspired selection is the Mofongo, a Latin bouillabaisse packed with shrimp, scallops, fish, and lobster in a just-spicy-enough tomato-cilantro broth ($21). Moderate to expensive. If the weather permits, ask to sit on the covered deck on top of the *Minnow* where you can watch the sunset and the boats as they return to the harbor.

Now that you've gotten your sea legs, it's time to take a real boat trip, namely a night fishing expedition offered in season at **Fisherman's Wharf** on Savannah Road by the drawbridge; (302) 645–8862. Full night excursions (6:00 P.M.–2:00 A.M.) are available Friday and Saturday from May 23 to August 30 and cost $35 for adults, $20 for children twelve and under. Half-night excursions, (6:00 P.M.–10:30 P.M.) cost $20 for adults and are available nightly from May 30 to September 1. Rod rentals are an additional $5.00 apiece. Daytime fishing and whale and dolphin watching trips are also available in season.

**LODGING: New Devon Inn,** corner of Second and Market Streets; (800) 824–8754 or (302) 645–6466. Two huge carved wooden elephant chairs (imported from Thailand and each carved from a single piece of wood, says the concierge) give the lobby of this circa 1926 inn an air of the exotic. While also impressive, the individually furnished, antique appointed upstairs guest rooms and suites have been decorated with a somewhat lighter touch. And the evening turndown service includes a cordial with your chocolate. Room rates range from $50–$90 weekdays, $65–$110 weekends during "sleigh bell season" to $95–$135 weekdays, $130–$170 during "seaside season." Continental breakfast is included in the room rate.

*Cape Henlopen State Park.*

## DAY 2

## *Morning*

**BREAKFAST: The Buttery,** New Devon Inn, (302) 645–7755. You can go with the complimentary coffee, juice, or muffins at the inn or treat yourself to a lavish Sunday brunch here at its lovely restaurant. For only $13.95 per person, you get a fresh fruit plate, bakery basket, choice of Champagne, mimosa, or bloody Mary, and one of nine entrees, including sirloin steak and eggs or New Devon Eggs topped with spinach, lump crab meat, and hollandaise.

Lewes may be a small town, but it is an absolute treasure trove of historic sites. For a single $6.00 admission price, you can tour a number of these significant sites, beginning with the **Lewes Historical Society Complex** at Shipcarpenter and West Third Streets (302–645–7670). For this ambitious and highly successful project, the society transported eighteenth- and nineteenth-century buildings, including an early Swedish log house, doctor's office, country store, and residences, from all over Lewes and its neighboring towns to this beautifully landscaped site. It then restored and accurately furnished them to give us a glimpse of the personal and working lives of their former occupants.

Also included in that $6.00 admission is the Historical Society-operated **Cannonball House Marine Museum** (118 Front Street, corner of Front and Bank) with its patched-over hole in the wall where a British cannonball from the War of 1812 remains lodged. (Appropriately enough, right across Front Street you'll find the **1812 Memorial Park,** then the site of an important defense battery, now a commemorative park marked by guns from that encounter (as well as one from an abandoned pirate vessel and another used during World War I.) You can also visit two other Lewes Historical Society sites, the **Ryves Holt House** (Second and Mulberry Streets), built in 1665, the oldest known house in the state, and the **Lightship Overfalls** (on Pilot-town Road on the Lewes & Rehoboth Canal), commemorating the ship that protected the entrance to Delaware Bay from 1892 to 1961. All of the sites are open Tuesday–Friday 11:00 A.M.–4:00 P.M., Saturday 10:00 A.M.–12:30 P.M. from mid-June until the Saturday before Labor Day.

Husband-and-wife entrepreneurs Gavin and Louise Braithwaite own two of the most fun shops in Lewes. Their traditional and contemporary handicrafts shop called the **Stepping Stone** (107 Market Street; 302–645–1254) offers the works of about 175 artists across the United States and includes an international collection of handmade musical instruments, such as a gourd piano and two different types of musical spoons. **Puzzles** (111 Second Street, 302–645–8013), another Braithwaite offspring, has everything from rustic handcrafted wooden designs to the latest Rubik's mind teasers. For jigsaw beginners there are two- or three-piece models and ones with 2,000–3,000 pieces for the pros. For crossword addicts, there are word games at every level of complexity and in just about every language. Best of all, there's a great baby-sitting area where impatient young ones (and spouses) can happily occupy themselves testing their puzzle-solving skills.

## Afternoon

**LUNCH: Second Street Grille,** 115 West Second Street; (302) 644–4121 or (302) 644–4122. For a seafood feast, get the spicy tomato Maryland crab soup and an order of crispy, greaseless calimari with chili mayonnaise at this casual, yet upscale spot. Moderately priced lunches, moderate to expensive dinners.

About 1 mile east of Lewes is **Cape Henlopen State Park** (302–739–4702), a naturalist's paradise with 4,000 acres of every type of terrain, including ocean and bay beaches, rolling dunes (such as the 80-foot-high Great

Dune), pine forests, salt marshes, and freshwater wetlands. These varied environments make the park the perfect habitat for a wide variety of plants and animals, including a number of rare and endangered species. During migrating seasons, it provides a much-needed resting place and feeding area for many types of birds. And for us it offers a place to swim, sun, fish, and explore the interpreted nature trails for hours without ever getting bored. You'll also find an unparalleled view of the Delaware Bay and Atlantic coastline from the top of the **World War II Observation Tower.** Open to the public; admission is included with your park entrance fee.

Before you begin your explorations, pay a visit to the **Nature Center** (open 9:00 A.M.–4:00 P.M. year-round), which has five 1,100-gallon marine aquariums, a touch tank, and interpretive exhibits. For a few extra dollars, you can participate in guided canoe trips, bird-watching expeditions, wetland explorations, and other educational and recreational programs that are available on a regular basis.

The park is open from 8:00 A.M. to sunset year-round. A $5.00 entrance fee is charged for out-of-state vehicles daily during the summer season and on weekends and holidays in the spring and fall.

## Evening

**DINNER: La Rosa Negra,** 128 Second Street; (302) 645–1980. Homemade pastas, including twenty types of ravioli, and other Italian specialties at moderate prices make this a popular spot year-round. Delectable signature dishes include red salmon with lump crab meat and seafood lasagna. Also not to be missed are the award-winning ice cream creations ranging from scoops of simple yet luxuriously rich vanilla to elaborate truffles and pies. Inexpensive to moderate.

To return to Philadelphia, reverse your original route. The trip should take about 2½ hours.

### THERE'S MORE

**Nassau Vineyards,** 36 Nassau Commons, Lewes; (302) 645–9463. Located about 2 miles (as the crow flies) and seven to ten minutes from downtown Lewes in the tiny, tiny borough of Nassau, Delaware's only winery is open for self-guided tours and free tastings. To get there, take Savannah Road

(Route 9) to Route 1 and go north for about ½ mile. Turn left at the Nassau overpass bridge onto Road 14B, and when you come to the farm equipment store turn left and follow the sign.

**Beach Plum Island Nature Preserve,** just north of Lewes; (302) 739–4702. A satellite of Cape Henlopen State Park, most of this 129-acre barrier island is protected to preserve the habitat for native plants. But you are welcome to stroll the beach, do some surf fishing (required permit is available at the park office), and listen to the sounds of nature. Open 8:00 A.M. to sunset year-round.

**Cape May–Lewes Ferry,** Cape Henlopen Drive, Lewes; (800) 64–FERRY or (302) 426–1155. Take a relaxing 17-mile (seventy minutes one-way) ride across Delaware Bay aboard newly renovated MV *Twin Peaks* or MV *Cape May,* state-of-the-art vessels with expansive passenger decks, cushy lounges, and fine restaurants. Fee: $18–$20 for passenger car and driver (other passengers are additional); $4.50–$6.50 for foot passengers six and over. Operates 365 days a year.

**Camping.** Cape Henlopen State Park, 42 Cape Henlopen Drive, Lewes; (302) 645–2103. From April 1–October 31, the park offers 159 campsites with water hookup for $18 per night for nonresidents.

## SPECIAL EVENTS

**April.** Great Delaware Kite Festival, Cape Henlopen State Park; (302) 645–8073. Held annually on Good Friday for more than 30 years, this event features kite-flying competitions, kite vendors, food, and entertainment.

**October.** Lewes Maritime Weekend, town of Lewes. Actually two events in one, this exciting weekend begins on Saturday with the Boast the Coast Festival (302–645–8073) celebrating the area's maritime history with exhibits and programs for the whole family, a crafts show and sale, food, schooner tours, and a spectacular lighted boat parade. On Sunday, the University of Delaware presents Coast Day (302–832–8083) to showcase educational programs and exhibits at the university's College of Marine Sciences in a festival atmosphere that includes entertainment, boat tours, arts and crafts, and a marine petting zoo.

**October.** Lewes Historical Society Craft Fair, Historic Complex, Shipcarpenter Street; (302) 645–7670. Held annually on the second Saturday in July and October.

**October.** Punkin' Chunkin', location to be announced; (800) 515–9095 or (302) 645–8273. For this somewhat off-the-wall event, recently brought to national attention by David Letterman on his late-night show, people bring some pretty elaborate homemade contraptions to compete for distance and accuracy in shooting, throwing, and/or catapulting pumpkins.

## OTHER RECOMMENDED RESTAURANTS AND LODGINGS

### Lewes

Inn at Canal Square. 122 Front and Market Streets; 800–222–7902 or 302–645–8499. Besides the spectacular views, Lewes' only waterfront B&B offers generously sized rooms (most with balconies overlooking the harbor) decorated in gracious eighteenth-century English style. Continental breakfast is included with the room rate of $85–$185 per night depending on the season.

Lighthouse Restaurant, Savannah and Anglers Road by the drawbridge on Lewes Harbor; (302) 645–6271. This unmistakably seashore dining spot offers well-prepared seafood specialties and lovely harbor views. Inexpensive to moderate. Open year-round.

Royal Zephyr Dinner Train/Queen Anne's Railroad; 730 King's Highway; (888) 456–TOOT or (302) 644–1720. 1940s vintage dining cars turn a 2½-hour journey through the countryside into a trip back in time. $54.95 per person. Seasonal; call for schedules. Murder Mystery Dinner Trains are also available Saturday June through November. Schedules vary the rest of the year.

Daily Market, 420 East Savannah Road; (302) 645–8284. This deli/convenience store has fresh sandwiches and great picnic snacks as well any last-minute beach necessities. Open 365 days a year.

King's Homemade Ice Cream Shop, 201 Second Street; (302) 645–9425. The best. Seasonal.

## Milton/Cool Spring

The Manor at Cool Spring Lavender Farm Bed and Breakfast, Route 290,
Cool Spring; (302) 648–8325. Along with their incredible lavender farm,
Joe and Pauline Palenik offer two (soon to be three) guest rooms in their
charming 1902 white clapboard house. Included is a sumptuous five-
course breakfast inspired by Pauline's native England. Rates from
$120–$140 per night.

### FOR MORE INFORMATION

Lewes Chamber of Commerce and Visitors Bureau; (302) 645–8073.

Southern Delaware Tourism Office; (800) 357–1818 or (302) 227–1818;
www.visitdelaware.com.

# DOWN THE SHORE

# Beaches of Southern Delaware

## REHOBOTH AND DEWEY

### 2 NIGHTS

*White Sand Beaches • Natural Hideaways • Family Days*
*Romantic Nights*

Although "down the shore" traditionally refers to the beaches of South Jersey, the Garden State certainly does not have a monopoly on fun by the sea. The Southern Delaware side-by-side beach towns of Rehoboth and Dewey have long been favored escape destinations for the people who live and work in Washington, D.C. And for good reason.

Rehoboth is the sister that likes to shine in the spotlight. By day it's an old-fashioned kind of place with lots of town-sponsored activities for the whole family. By night it takes on a more sophisticated personality, its streets sparkling with the lights of a myriad of eclectic shops, restaurants, and nightspots. Directly to the south of Rehoboth is Dewey, the quiet sister characterized by boundless natural beauty and a tranquillity that can soothe the most stressed-out soul.

Like most East Coast shore points, peak season at the beaches of southern Delaware is from Memorial Day to Labor Day. So if you want to miss the crowds, consider going in the late spring or early fall. The beaches are just as beautiful then and most of the shops are open.

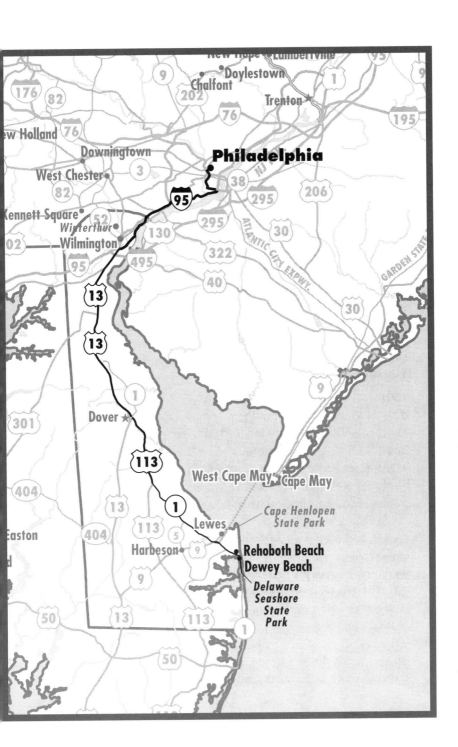

ESCAPE THREE

# DOWN THE SHORE

## DAY 1

## *Morning*

Rehoboth Beach is 118 miles (nearly three hours driving time) southeast of Philadelphia. To get there take the Schuylkill Expressway (I–76) east to I–95. Travel south on I–95 about 28 miles to I–295; going 1 mile north you'll come to Route13/Route 40. Stay on Route 13 south for about 66 miles until you reach Route 1. Then take Route 1 south for 18 miles to Route 9 north. Take Route 9 north for 1 mile until it intersects with Route 1; then take Route 1 another 4 miles or so into Rehoboth.

Go east on any street and you'll find yourself face-to-face with the white sands, natural dunes, and foaming surf of **Rehoboth Beach.** Don't fight the urge—kick off your shoes and dig your toes into the wet sand along the water's edge. Then take a leisurely walk and let the sounds of the waves and calls of the shorebirds melt your city stress away. Be sure to keep your eye on the horizon. If you're in the right place at the right time, you might even see dolphins frolicking right off the shoreline.

## *Afternoon*

**LUNCH: Nicola Pizza,** 8 North First Street (right off the boardwalk); (302) 227–6211 or (302) 226–BOLI. This is the home of the Nic-o-boli, a locally beloved variation of the stromboli ($4.75–$6.55) and its cousins the Nic-spin-oli with spinach ($4.75) and the "Nico e Bolito" with chicken and jalepeño peppers ($4.85). Open seven days from 11:00 A.M. until the "wee hours of the morning."

Then break out the heavy-duty sunscreen and head back to the beach for an afternoon of sunbathing, swimming, and sand castles. If the winds cooperate, you might even want to fly a kite. Don't have one? No problem! Just take a short walk over to **Chesapeake Flag, Kite, and Yo Yo Company** in the center of town at 122C Rehoboth Avenue (877–FLAGS–66 or 302–226–2193) where you'll find a fabulous collection of every kind of flyer from a two-line stunt kite to an 8-foot-long frog to a very Monty Pythonesque 12-foot-long pair of legs. (If you're into yo yos, the **Yo Yo House** (877–YOYO–NOW or 302–226–2197), a new addition to the store, features more than one hundred styles ranging from the nostalgic to state-of-the-art flash and dazzle. Open daily year-round except Christmas and New Year's Day.

# DOWN THE SHORE

## *Evening*

**DINNER: Back Porch Cafe,** 59 Rehoboth Avenue; (302) 227–3674. This real treasure of a restaurant located in a turn-of-the-century guest house features a savvy, sassy menu that belies its quaint, understated exterior. Locally grown ingredients give an extra intensity to such creations as pork with ancho chili crust and Thai green curry duckling. As for dessert, I have only one thing to say—bourbon pecan steamed pudding with bourbon hard sauce accompanied by a cup of coffee en flambé. If the weather is amenable, ask to sit outside on the upper or lower deck.

After dinner check out the sights and sounds on the **boardwalk,** a mile-long fun but not frantic promenade with miniature golf, arcades, and a small amusement park. If you're here at 8:00 P.M. on any summer weekend, you can gather round the **Rehoboth Beach Memorial Bandstand** (302–227–6181), right off the boardwalk at Rehoboth Avenue, for a free old-fashioned band concert.

**LODGING: Gladstone Inn,** 3 Olive Avenue; (302) 227–2641. From the age of five, Tom Mills grew up in the gracious white building with the green shutters and big porch three doors away from the beach. Now he and his wife Linda have opened their family home to guests. Their warm welcome extends to entire families, making the Gladstone the only child-friendly B&B in Rehoboth Beach. Upstairs in the circa 1910 home are light-filled, airy rooms furnished with Victorian touches ($75 per night). There are also three apartments with ample room for six ($100 per night) and a separate two-story cottage. In the evening, the view from the front porch is mesmerizing as the ocean shimmers in the dying light. *Note:* Rehoboth is a hard-core parking meter/parking pass town—even on residential streets—and there's no off-street parking at the inn. As a courtesy to their guests, Tom and Linda provide prepaid parking passes.

## DAY 2

## *Morning*

Wake up early so you can enjoy an early bike ride on the boardwalk (permitted 5:00–10:00 A.M. May 15–September 15). If you need a set of wheels, **Atlantic Cycles** (18 Wilmington Avenue, 302–226–2543) is open from 6:00 A.M. to 6:00 P.M. with a choice of standard one-seaters ($3.00 per hour, $10.00

per day); or, for some real togetherness, a bicycle built for two ($5.00 per hour, $15.00 per day). Off-season, the shop is open 9:00 A.M.–5:00 P.M.

**BREAKFAST:** Gladstone Inn. Sit out on the front porch, read the paper (if you must) or just admire the ocean view over a complimentary continental breakfast featuring Linda's delicious home-baked muffins and breads.

Pack your bathing suit, sneakers, and more sunscreen for an excursion to Delaware Seashore State Park. But first, take Olive Avenue to First Street and stop at 11 North First to pick up a picnic lunch of sandwiches ($2.00–$7.25) and homemade baked treats ($1.25 for a giant cookie, $2.25 for a brownie) from **Slides** (302–22–PARTY). Open seven days in summer from 8:00 A.M.

As you continue south, First Street becomes King Charles Street then, after bearing to the right, Lake Drive, which borders **Silver Lake.** The locals (including Tom Mills from the inn) insist that in the trees surrounding the lake live a dozen or a couple of hundred (depending upon your source of information) wild parrots, the descendants of a pair of runaway pets. The story also goes that the tropical birds survive the winter by sheltering by an electrical transformer on the lake's shore. I have never spotted any, but many of the town's visitors and permanent residents insist that they have.

When you have finished parrot-seeking, follow Lake Drive to Bayard Avenue, which will intersect with Route 1; then take Route 1 through Dewey to **Delaware Seashore State Park** (302–227–2800). This 2,000-acre recreational area and nature preserve has *everything.* There are two patrolled ocean swimming areas for challenging the waves and a family-friendly Rehoboth Bay bathing area with calmer waters for less strenuous dips. Just north of the inlet is one of the few designated surfing areas in the state, and other beaches are set aside for surf fishing. So that you don't have to go back to town all wet and sandy, the park has modern bathhouses with showers and changing areas.

## Afternoon

**LUNCH: Delaware River Seashore State Park** has two very nice pavilions where you can enjoy your picnic lunch.

After lunch, you can do some more bird-watching along the 1½-mile nature trail on **Burton's Island** in the park. The salt marshes here are a favorite summer nesting place for gulls and terns. If you would like to do some ocean fishing, the **Indian River Marina** (302–227–3071) offers excursions and a well-stocked bait and tackle shop. Delaware Seashore State Park is open seven

*Surf fishing on Rehoboth Beach.*

days a week from 8:00 A.M. to sunset year-round. A daily park fee of $5.00 for out-of-state-registered vehicles is charged Memorial Day Weekend–Labor Day, and Saturday, Sunday, and holidays in May, September, and October.

Back in town, in Henlopen Gardens bordering Rehoboth Beach on the north, see what's going on at the **Rehoboth Beach Art League** (302–227–8404). This cluster of four rustic buildings and lovely gardens is the setting for a wide variety of exhibits, programs, and special events all year long. It is also the site of the 1743 **Homestead House,** now a museum featuring restored rooms of period furnishings. Admission is free. Open 10:00 A.M.–4:00 P.M. Monday–Saturday, 1:00–4:00 P.M. Sunday.

## *Evening*

**DINNER: Cultured Pearl,** 18 Wilmington Avenue; (302) 227–8493. It's the big picture window filled with lively parakeets and canaries that initially captures your attention, but it's the food that keeps it. For the timid a section of the menu devoted to "East meets West" compromises pairings of shrimp and vegetable tempura with filet mignon and mashed potatoes. But for an authentic experience, stick to the sushi bar, hosomaki, and other Japanese specialties. Moderate to expensive.

Rehoboth Beach's shopping district, concentrated along Rehoboth Avenue and Wilmington Street, comes alive at night when locals and visitors alike come out to stroll, window-shop, and enjoy the cool ocean breezes. Many of these establishments have an international flavor that makes them fun to visit and their merchandise hard to resist. At the **Tideline Gallery** (146 Rehoboth Avenue; 302–227–4444) riveting deco blue swirl jazz art sculptures share shelf space with colorfully painted rolling pins (signed by the artists), adorably whimsical animal banks, and decorative yet practical cylindrical stoneware bread bakers.

It's hard to believe that the intricately detailed, ultra-delicate hanging sculptures at **Scandinavian Occasions** (125 Rehoboth Avenue; 302–227–3945) are actually paper cuts, a traditional Scandinavian craft. And the tiny shop called **I.M. Polish** (204 Rehoboth Avenue; 302–226–5225) offers unique imported items including green amber jewelry, hand-painted wooden friendship eggs, Polish Jell-O (called Kisiel), and intriguing Russian laser art that uses laser beams to create tiny explosions at varying depths in glass to form images of flowers, apples, even the Kremlin.

Stop in to **Dream Cafe** (26 Baltimore Avenue; 302–226–CAFE) for some freshly baked waffles and homemade ice cream, which you can enjoy inside or outside at the sidewalk cafe.

**LODGING:** Gladstone Inn.

## DAY 3

## *Morning*

**BREAKFAST: Victoria's,** Boardwalk Plaza Hotel, Olive Avenue and the Boardwalk; (302) 227–0615. If it's a summer Sunday, don't miss the renowned brunch. In addition to the traditional omelette and waffle stations, the buffet includes a full raw bar, carving station, bounty of fresh seasonal fruits, and unbelievably decadent dessert selection. Price is $24 per person. Out on the boardwalk patio with its ornate iron furniture and arched trellises, you can really dine like royalty as you enjoy the passing scene along with your breakfast.

# DOWN THE SHORE

If you want to get one more dip in at the beach, the innkeepers at the Gladstone Inn kindly provide an outdoor shower so you won't have to ride home with sand in your pants.

## *Afternoon*

**LUNCH: Jake's Seafood House Restaurant,** First Street, between Baltimore and Maryland Avenues; (302) 227–6237. You can't go to the shore without indulging in a traditional seafood feast and this has been one of the best places to find one since 1929. Open seven days for lunch and dinner 11:30 A.M.–10:00 P.M. Entree prices range from $8.50 for clam strips to $26.95 for lobster tail stuffed with crab imperial. Seafood sandwiches range from $4.50 for tuna salad to $7.75 for jumbo lump crab cake.

To return to Philadelphia, reverse your route from Day 1. The return trip should take about 2¾–3 hours.

### THERE'S MORE

**Rehoboth Outlets,** 1600 Ocean Outlets, Route 1; (888) SHOP–333 or (302) 226–9223. Save 20 to 60 percent off original retail prices at more than 150 name-brand outlets along this 2-mile stretch of Route 1. (Remember, shopping in Delaware is tax free!)

**Rehoboth Bay Sailing Association,** at Rehoboth Bay Marina, Collins Street, Dewey Beach; 302–227–9008. Half- and full-day rentals of pontoon boats (depending on size $150–$160 for four hours, $240–$250 for eight hours), and steerable skiffs ($65–$100 for four hours, $95–$185 for eight hours). Two-hour sightseeing cruises ($10.00 for adults, $8.00 for children twelve and under); or half-day crabbing or fishing trips ($20.00 for adults plus $5.00 rod rental fee; $15.00 for children–8:00 A.M.–noon or 1:00–5:00 P.M.) Marina is open Memorial Day–Labor Day seven days a week 7:00 A.M.–6:00 P.M.; April and October call for hours.

**Camping.** Delaware Seashore State Park, Route 1, south of Dewey Beach; (302) 539–7202. A variety of accommodations for everything from tents to large recreational vehicles. Three-point hookups for electricity, water, and sewer service are available on some sites. Campsites are available on a first-come, first-serve basis. $24 for nonresidents. Open mid-March to mid-November.

## SPECIAL EVENTS

**Easter.** Easter Promenade, Rehoboth Beach Convention Center, 229 Rehoboth Avenue, Rehoboth Beach; (800) 441–1329 or (302) 227–2233. Parades and other seasonal family activities. Free.

**August.** Annual Delaware State News Sand Castle Contest, Fisherman's Beach, north end of Rehoboth Beach boardwalk; (302) 741–8204 or (302) 741–8210. Amateur sculptors compete for cash prizes. Free.

**October.** Rehoboth Beach Autumn Jazz Festival, over thirty venues throughout Rehoboth and Dewey Beach areas; (800) 29–MUSIC. Three days filled with seventy-five events including a free midday concert, seminars, jazz brunches, club shows, and art exhibits. Call for ticket prices.

**October.** Annual Sea Witch Halloween & Fiddler's Festival, throughout Rehoboth Beach; (800) 441–1329 or (302) 227–2233. Costume contests, parades, hay rides, craft shows, entertainment, laser light show, and shop-to-shop trick or treating for the kids. At the Fiddler's Festival, musicians compete for $1,500 in cash prizes.

**November.** Rehoboth Beach Independent Film Festival, Atlantic Theaters in Rehoboth Mall; (302) 226–3257. Three days of critically acclaimed national and international films. Workshops and guest speakers.

## OTHER RECOMMENDED RESTAURANTS AND LODGINGS

## *Rehoboth Beach*

Blue Moon Restaurant, 35 Baltimore Avenue; (302) 227–6515. The look and personality of this fabulously renovated old beachhouse-turned-restaurant is constantly changing along with the menu, which features modern American cuisine using the freshest locally grown produce. Expensive. Open seven days year-round.

LaLa Land, 22 Wilmington Avenue; (302) 227–3887. There's nothing modest about this place with its almost psychedelic hand-painted blue, purple, and pink dining room. There's nothing shy about its menu either—the gnocchi is served with truffle oil and asparagus tips, the mahi-mahi with corn bacon salsa and guacamole, and the grilled pork chop with a cumin-chili rub. Expensive. Seasonal.

Sydney's, 24 Christian Street; (800) 808–1924 or (302) 227–1339. Located in one of the first schoolhouses in Rehoboth Beach, this sophisticated spot specializes in hot New Orleans–style cuisine and cool blues and jazz. Open year-round.

Crystal Restaurant and Lounge, 620 Rehoboth Avenue; (302) 227–1088. It doesn't look like much from the outside, but this unassuming little restaurant has endeared itself to the locals with breakfasts starting at $1.99, lunches from $4.95, and dinners from $5.95. Open year-round.

Eden, 122 Rehoboth Avenue; (302) 227–3330. Try the signature Going Nuts pasta with a pesto made from pine nuts, pecans, and walnuts! Moderate.

Boardwalk Plaza Hotel, Olive at the Boardwalk; (800) 33–BEACH or (302) 227–7169. Family-owned and -operated, this gracious Victorian hotel offers beautiful rooms furnished with antiques and period reproductions. One exquisite amenity is the indoor-outdoor spa pool where you can soak under the stars. Depending on time of month and week, rates range from $55 to $295 for a standard double. Ask about money-saving off-season package plans.

Sea Witch Manor, 71 Lake Avenue; (302) 226–WITCH. The painstaking attention to old-fashioned detail from the turrets to the wraparound front porch make it hard to believe that this dramatic bed-and-breakfast was built in 1994. For a romantic getaway, you won't find better. Memorial Day–Labor Day rates range from $135 to $170; off-season rates from $99 to $120.

## FOR MORE INFORMATION

Rehoboth Beach/Dewey Beach Chamber of Commerce, 501 Rehoboth Avenue, Rehoboth; (800) 441–1329 or (302) 227–2233; www.beach-fun.com.

Southern Delaware Tourism Office; (800) 357–1818 or (302) 227–1818; www.visitdelaware.com.

# Annapolis, Maryland

## MARITIME MASTERPIECE

### 2 NIGHTS

*Three Centuries of History • Harborside Feasts*
*Evening Races • Artistic Pursuits*

For more than three centuries, the Chesapeake Bay has been a primary source of commerce, culture, and cuisine for the people in Annapolis. Known as "America's Sailing Capital," it remains a city of sailors from the midshipmen of the U.S. Naval Academy to the after-work yacht racers.

Annapolis is also a great walking city, with streets that fan out from its centerpiece state capitol building. It's a good thing, too, because there's plenty to see here, including the nation's largest collection of surviving seventeenth-to-nineteenth-century buildings, ranging from humble early simple wood frame abodes to lavish English-style mansions.

And history is still being made—or at least being uncovered—at an archeological dig only fifteen minutes south of the city. There are even public dig days when you can try your hand at unearthing a few buried treasures yourself.

## DAY 1

### Morning

Annapolis is only about a 130-mile, 2½-hour drive from Philadelphia. To get there, take the Schuylkill Expressway (I–76) to I–95 and drive south on I–95 past Baltimore, about 120 miles to Route I–97. Travel south on I–97 for 21

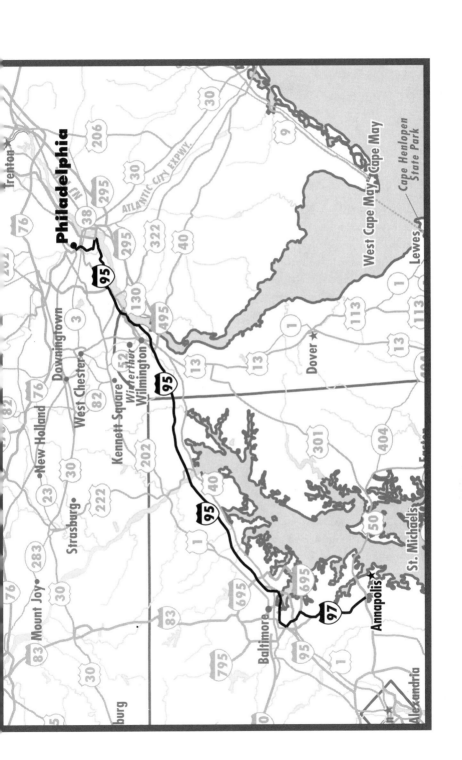

miles and you will come to Routes 301/50. Take Route 50 east to exit 29A (St. Margarets Road). Turn right at the light and go straight 2.3 miles. Make a left U-turn around the Uncommon Country Store onto Brownswood Road then take the first right onto Forest Beach Drive for a delicious introduction to Maryland's famous crabs.

## *Afternoon*

**LUNCH: Cantler's Riverside Inn,** 458 Forest Beach Drive; (410) 757–1467 At this inn, about 1½ miles down at the end of the road, you can feast on award-winning seafood specialties, including just about every preparation of crab from dip to soup to steamed (year-round) to cakes. You can even have your rockfish (striped bass) or New York strip stuffed with Maryland's treasure from the bay. Oysters served in a variety of ways are also available in season.

Reverse your tracks back to Route 50 west, which will take you across the Severn River Bridge. Take exit 24A Rowe Boulevard/Route 70. Follow Rowe Boulevard to State Circle, crowned by the Maryland State House. Bear right on Rowe Street to Northwest Street, then left. Turn right into **Gotts Court Garage,** which is located next to the **Visitors Center,** 26 West Street (410–280–0445). At Gotts, your first hour is free; then it's $1.00 per hour, maximum $8.00.

The **Maryland State House** (State Circle; 410–974–3400) sits on a hill at the hub of the city. The state capitol—and, for nine months in 1784–85, the nation's capitol as well—this impressive structure has a remarkable history and split personality . . . literally. A broad black line on the floor divides the original 1770s wood and plaster section from the early 1900s marble addition.

One of the many highlights of your tour is the room where, in 1783, George Washington resigned his commission as commander in chief of the Continental Army and where, less than a month later, the Treaty of Paris officially ending the Revolutionary War was ratified. Open Monday–Friday 9:00 A.M.–5:00 P.M., Saturday and Sunday 10:00 A.M.–4:00 P.M. Tours are given at 11:00 A.M. and 3:00 P.M.

In the eighteenth century Maryland Avenue was the most fashionable residential street in the city. Stretching from State Circle to the gate of the U.S. Naval Academy, it is still the epitome of style with its diverse collection of exclusive galleries and shops. At **Annapolis Pottery** (40 State Circle; 410–268–6153) you'll never find anyone asleep at the wheel, especially on Tuesday, Wednesday, and Thursday mornings when you can watch the artisans handcraft original stoneware vases, pots, and other decorative items. You'll find more local arts and crafts at the **Maryland Federation of Art Gallery On the Circle** (18 State Circle; 410–268–4566) and the **League of Maryland Craftsmen** (54 Maryland Avenue; 410–268–1277). If your heart—and taste—still dwells somewhere in the sixties, you'll love **Third Millenium Designs** (57 Maryland Avenue; 410–267–6428), a virtual shrine to all things pop, retro, and cool.

From Maryland Avenue, turn right onto Prince George Street. At No. 186 is the **William · Paca House & Garden** (410–263–5553), the private residence of one of the four Annapolitans who signed the Declaration of Independence. The five-part restored structure is a splendid example of eighteenth-century architecture. Particularly beautiful is the two-acre terraced Eden out back where you can admire the brilliant colors of the flowers, the clever fish-shaped pool, and the air of absolute serenity. Open daily 10:00 A.M.–4:00 P.M., Sunday noon–4:00 P.M. Call for January and February hours. Admission $7.00 for combined house and garden tour.

## Evening

**DINNER: Carrol's Creek Cafe,** at 410 Severn Avenue, Eastport; (410) 263–8102.

Continue south on Prince George Street until you come to Randall Street; turn right. Straight ahead is **City Dock**. At the head of the dock on the sidewalk is the **Kunte Kinte** plaque commemorating the arrival in 1767 of the African slave who was immortalized in his descendant Alex Haley's book *Roots,* as well as all of the others who were brought here in bondage. The dock is also one of the stopping points for **Jiffy Water Taxi** (410–263–0033), which you'll be taking for the five-minute excursion ($1.50) across Spa Creek to Eastport for dinner.

In addition to its spectacular bayfront view, Carrol's Creek is renowned for its Maryland-accented American cuisine. Yes, there are crab cakes, and oysters raw and fried, as well as a killer pecan-and-coconut crusted mahi-mahi. But spring for the specialty of the house, the Carrol's Creek Bay Dinner, a feast of cream of crab soup, salad, local rockfish, and dessert for $24.95.

After dinner in season you can sit out on the restaurant's deck/lounge and watch the yachts returning to the neighboring Annapolis Marina from the Wednesday evening races. Better yet, the Kaye family will take you for a two-hour sunset sail aboard their 74-foot *Schooner Woodwind* (410–263–7837), a replica of the luxury "yachts" of the early twentieth century. *Woodwind* departs from Pusser's landing at the Annapolis Marriott Waterfront Hotel next to City Dock Tuesday–Sunday at 6:30 P.M. mid-May to Labor Day weekend (5:30 P.M. in early May and September). Cruises are $27 per person for adults, $25 for seniors, and $15 for children. (Daytime cruises $3.00 less.) From May to the end of September, the Kayes also offer an overnight boat and breakfast package for two ($200) that includes a double stateroom, two-hour sail, and breakfast.

**LODGING: Historic Inns of Annapolis,** 58 State Circle; (410) 263–2641. This is really three eighteenth-century inns, **Governor Calvert House, Robert Johnson House,** and **Maryland Inn,** all centrally located across from State Circle and adjacent to Church Circle. Each of the three is distinctive in personality, and all are delightfully furnished with period antiques and reproductions. If you have a favorite among the inns, you can make a request to stay there when you make your reservation. Innkeeper Peg Bednarsky, who happens to be the very soul of hospitality, will try to accommodate your request, subject to room availability. Double occupancy rates range from $155 to $245, suites from $180 to $285.

## DAY 2

## *Morning*

**BREAKFAST: Treaty of Paris Restaurant,** 16 Church Street at the Maryland Inn; (410) 263–2641. Here you can enjoy a real Maryland-style breakfast in an authentic eighteenth-century setting. The moderately priced breakfast menu includes the traditional morning fare, but for some genuine local flavor, try a smoked salmon or lump crab omelette, or the eggs Maryland—poached eggs and sliced fresh tomatoes with backfin crabmeat and Old Bay hollandaise.

Head east on Maryland Avenue until it dead-ends at King Charles Street; turn right on King Charles, keep going straight, and you will find yourself at Gate 1, the main visitors entrance of the **United States Naval Academy.** One of Annapolis' best known landmarks for the past 150 years, this 338-acre campus—officially known as the Yard—is home to a brigade of 4,000 and a faculty of 580. Right inside the gate is the **Armel-Leftwich Visitor Center** (410–263–6933), where you can arrange for a guided tour of the Yard's many attractions. Guided tours are offered year-round, seven days a week. From

June–Labor Day, hours are Monday–Saturday 9:30 A.M.–3:30 P.M. and Sunday 12:15–3:30 P.M. Hours vary slightly during other months.

At precisely 12:05 P.M. every weekday, the entire brigade assembles for noon meal formation, an impressive event complete with ceremonial swords and drums and bugles that takes place in front of **Bancroft Hall,** the largest dormitory in the world and home to the entire brigade. Close by is a statue of the famous Indian warrior **Tecumseh,** to whom the midshipmen send their pleas for benevolence prior to important football games and important tests.

One of the most prominent features of the Yard—and of the Annapolis skyline—is the **Chapel** with its magnificent Tiffany Studios-designed stained-glass windows. Beneath the Chapel is the elaborate and eerily beautiful "undersea" **Crypt of John Paul Jones** with its black and white marble sarcophagus supported by carved porpoises, covered with sculpted seaweed and surrounded by models, photos, and mementos tracing the career of this famed Revolutionary War hero.

**Preble Hall** houses the **U.S. Naval Academy Museum** (410–267–2108), with four galleries showcasing a collection of more than 35,000 artifacts and artworks spanning centuries of naval history. Among the exhibitions are 1,210 medals from thirty countries dating from 254 B.C. to A.D. 1936, and 600 historic American and captured flags, including some that have been to the moon. One of the most riveting exhibits is the **Class of 1951 Gallery of Ships** with its awe-inspiring selection of precision-carved ship models crafted from wood, gold, and bone by artisans from the sixteenth to the nineteenth centuries. By the way, the last mentioned were carved from leftover beef bones by French prisoners-of-war being held in England during the Napoleonic conflicts. The museum is open Monday–Saturday 9:00 A.M.–5:00 P.M., Sunday 11:00 A.M.–5:00 P.M. Admission is free.

## *Afternoon*

**LUNCH: Harry Browne's,** 66 State Circle; (410) 263–4332. This twenty-year lunch and dinner tradition for Annapolitans and visitors has a moderately priced menu full of delicious surprises. It offers homemade soups, pastas, and quiche that regularly change with the availability of fresh ingredients and the imagination of the chef. Always available are the excellent cream of crab soup, chili served in a sourdough boule, and, of course, signature crab cake.

During the warm weather, one Saturday a month is public dig day at **London Town** (839 Londontown Road, Edgewater; 410–222–1919), Maryland's largest archeological dig. Take Route 50 west to Route 665/Aris T. Allen Boulevard. Get off at the second exit and make a right-hand turn onto Route 2. You'll go over the South River Bridge. The third traffic light is Mayo Road; turn left onto Mayo, then left again onto Londontown Road and continue to the end of the road. On those special Saturdays, you can get some very old dirt under your fingernails as you work alongside the pros who are searching for the lost forty dwellings, shops, and taverns that once comprised the bustling seventeenth-century tobacco port called London. On other days this site is still worth visiting for a tour of the one building that remains, an eighteenth-century mansion where you can learn about life in old-time London, and eight acres of gorgeous gardens. Open year-round, Monday–Saturday 10:00 A.M.–4:00 P.M., Sunday noon–4:00 P.M. House tours are available by appointment in January and February.

**DINNER: Rams Head Tavern,** 33 West Street; (410) 268–4545. Adjacent to State Circle is the second major focal point of the city, Church Circle. Go halfway around Church Circle to West Street to reach your destination for dinner. This lively tavern is conveniently located right next to (and, is in fact kin to) **Fordham Brewing Company,** Annapolis' first brewery established in 1703. So it's no surprise that the moderately priced menu is quite beer-friendly and that more than a few of its signature recipes include different incarnations of the brew. Nonspiked specialties include innovations like Jamaican Jerk Rasta Pasta and, of course, a signature version of the Maryland crab cake (market price). The Ram's Head offers diners free parking at Gotts Garage so if you're driving be sure to get your ticket validated.

Follow up your dinner with an evening of music from performers such as Livingston Taylor, Leon Russell, Jose Feliciano, and Arlo Guthrie at the **Rams Head On Stage** (410–268–5111), an on-premise 215-seat theater. Ticket prices vary per performer, but they tend to be in the mid-teens to mid-twenties range. The tavern offers a great dinner and show combo that gives you 10 percent off your entire meal check and a free beer nightcap (with ticket stub) after the show.

**LODGING:** Historic Inns of Annapolis.

## DAY 3

### *Morning*

**BREAKFAST: Cafe Normandie,** 185 Main Street; (410) 263–3382. There's nothing quite as romantic as savoring cups of cinnamon-laced coffee at a cozy table in a rustic French country bistro. Have a fresh croissant with your seafood or apple and cheddar omelette. Or try something a bit more exotic, perhaps eggs Basque with ratatouille or eggs Florentine with spinach and cheese. Moderate. This is also a great dessert stop either during the day or after dinner. The crepes are heavenly and the tarte tatin divine.

If you want to take home a piece of Maryland history, head for the City Dock area for a stop at the **Historic Annapolis Museum Store and Welcome Center,** 77 Main Street; (410) 268–5576. This extensive collection reflects the architectural, social, cultural, and maritime history of the city through eighteenth-century reproductions, hand-blown glassware, books, and other decorative and educational items. Open Monday–Saturday 10:00 A.M.–5:00 P.M., Sunday noon–5:00 P.M. For the best selection of U.S. Naval

*Annapolis Harbor.*

Academy and Annapolis clothing and accessories, go to **Peppers,** 133 Main Street; (410) 267–8722. They even have Navy-style gear for newborns!

To pick up the fixings for a fabulous picnic lunch, head to the **Market House** (410–269–0941) at City Dock. In operation since 1690, this market features nine merchants selling fresh seafood (there's even a raw bar), fried chicken, deli sandwiches, all kinds of cheeses, and heavenly breads and pastries. Open 365 days a year.

You can say a fond farewell to the waters of Annapolis at **Sandy Point State Park,** 786 beautiful acres along the Chesapeake Bay that you'll find at 1100 East College Parkway, off Route 50/301 at the Bay Bridge western terminus; (410) 974–2149. The park has lovely beaches for swimming and boating (boat rentals are available), a pier for fishing, and hiking and biking trails for exploring. Home to a wide variety of woodland and marsh birds and located on the migratory route of waterfowl, it is one of the premier bird watching spots on Maryland's western shore. Bathhouse facilities are available at the park so you can refresh before you hit the road for home. The park is open year-round, 6:00 A.M.–9:00 P.M. from Memorial Day to Labor Day and for daytime use only other months. Admission is $2.00 per person on weekdays, $3.00 on weekends; seniors (sixty-two and over) and children under four in car seats are free.

## Afternoon

**LUNCH:** Picnic tables are available on a first come, first served basis at **Sandy Point State Park.**

To return home, get on Route 50 heading west and retrace your route from Day 1. It should take about 2½ hours to get back into center city Philadelphia.

### THERE'S MORE

**Hammond Harwood House,** 19 Maryland Avenue; (410) 269–1714. This restored pre-Revolutionary War residence provides a look at Annapolis history from the perspective of a family who lived here. Open daily 10:00 A.M.–4:00 P.M., Sunday noon–4:00 P.M. Admission is $5.00 for adults, $3.00 for students (six to eighteen) and free for children under six.

**Three Centuries Tours of Annapolis,** 48 Maryland Avenue; (410) 263–5401. A Colonial-garbed guide will take you on a walking tour along the city's architecturally diverse and historically significant streets. Daily at 10:30 A.M. and 1:30 P.M. $8.00 per person.

**Annapolis Summer Garden Theatre,** 143 Compromise Street; (410) 268–9212. For thirty-three years this outdoor community theater has been performing Broadway musicals under the stars from Memorial Day to Labor Day. Performances Thursday–Saturday evenings.

**Maryland Hall,** 801 Chase Street; (401) 263–5544. The city's primary community arts center is home to the Annapolis Symphony Orchestra, Chorale, Opera, and Ballet Theater.

**Banneker-Douglass Museum,** 84 Franklin Street; (410) 974–2893. Open Tuesday–Friday 10:00 A.M.–3:00 P.M., Saturday noon–4:00 P.M. This museum of African-American arts and culture features changing exhibits, lectures, films, and publications. Free.

**Chesapeake Marine Tours' Ecotour;** (410) 268–7600. Learn about the issues affecting the Chesapeake Bay while exploring one of its most beautiful tributaries. Tours leave from City Dock and are available 10:30 and 11:30 A.M. Saturday and Sunday from Memorial Day–Labor Day. $13.00 for adults, $6.00 for children under 11.

## SPECIAL EVENTS

**May.** Annapolis Waterfront Arts Festival, City Dock; (410) 268–8828. This is a great place to bring the family if you want to shop—and they don't. They can enjoy the music and food while you admire the creations of craftspeople who work in traditional and some quite unusual media.

**May.** Chesapeake Bay Bridge Walk; (800) 541–9595. Lots of locals and visitors gather every year to take this 4.3-mile stroll. Why? Because it's there!

**June.** Annapolis JazzFest, St. John's College Campus; College Avenue; (410) 349–1111. Three days of nonstop music. Bring a chair and blanket.

**End of August–late October.** Maryland Renaissance Festival, Crownsville Road between Routes 450 and 178; (800) 296–7304. Held Saturday, Sunday, and Labor Day Monday, this bawdy, brawling and absolutely brilliant recreation of a sixteenth-century English village features 250 performers, Shakespearean and other productions, and combat jousting. More than 130 shops with crafts by artisans from all over North America, and lots of food (including those giant turkey legs said to be favored by King Henry VIII).

**September.** Maryland Seafood Festival, Sandy Point State Park; (410) 268–7682. A three-day seafood extravaganza starring crabs, shrimp, oysters, and clams in just about every possible form. Also Maryland crab soup cook-off, live entertainment, and crafts.

**September.** Anne Arundel County Fair, Route 178 (General's Highway), Crownsville; (410) 923–3400. The real old-fashioned kind with four days of carnival midway rides, agricultural and craft demonstrations, outdoor skills contests, livestock sale, live bands, tractor pulls, skunk races—even a watermelon eating contest.

## OTHER RECOMMENDED RESTAURANTS AND LODGINGS

## *Annapolis*

Charles Inn, 74 Charles Street; (410) 268–1451. With its period art and furnishings, fresh flowers and cozy feather-topped beds, this restored Civil War–era home combines comfort and history. A luxurious full breakfast is included. Rates range from $79 to $225.

Blue Heron Inn, 172 Green Street; (888) 999–1839 or (410) 263–9171. Romantic furnishings reflect the decor of the Federal era during which this home was built in 1839. Includes full breakfast. Rates are $150 per night, two night minimum, or $200 for a single night when available.

Magnolia House, 220 King George Street; (800) 293–3477 or (410) 268–3477. One of the longest operating B&Bs in Annapolis has only two guest rooms (each with private bath). All the better, because it gives the lucky ones lots of time to chat with host John Prehn, a Naval Academy graduate, and his wife Mary, both of whom have done extensive tour-guiding in Annapolis. Year-round room rate is $95, which includes a full breakfast.

McGarvey's Saloon and Oyster Bar, 8 Market Space, City Dock; (410) 263–5700. There's a twenty-five-year-old tree growing through the middle of the floor and real Blue Angels helmets above the long wooden bar at this jovial spot known for its award-winning burgers, uniquely flavored chili, steaks, and seafood. Moderate.

Middletown Tavern Oyster Bar and Restaurant, 2 Market Space, City Dock; (410) 263–3323. Home of the oyster shooter (a gulp of raw oyster followed by a short beer) and other bivalve delights. Prices on the primarily seafood and steak menu range from $19.95 to $30.95. Pastas and sandwiches begin at $6.95.

Potato Valley Cafe, 47 State Circle, Suite 100; (410) 267–0902. It's amazing how many personalities—and nationalities—a potato can have! Inexpensive.

## FOR MORE INFORMATION

Annapolis & Anne Arundel County Conference and Visitor Bureau; (410) 280–0445; www.visit-annapolis.org.

Anne Arundel County Economic Development Corporation; (410) 222–7410.

Maryland Office of Tourism Development; (410) 767–6298; www.mdisfun.org.

# Maryland's Eastern Shore

## FOLLOW THE DOTTED COASTLINE

### 2 NIGHTS

*Skipjacks and Yachts • Secret Seasonings*
*Street Music*

*"The mildness of the aire, the fertilitie of the soile, and the situation of the rivers are so propitious to the nature and use of man as no place is more convenient for pleasure, profit and mans sustenance."*
—Captain John Smith, 1612

It isn't only the Chesapeake Bay Bridge that separates Maryland's Eastern Shore from the rest of the world. It is an entire way of life.

Here, the last of the once extensive fleet of oyster-dredging skipjacks—and their rugged crews—still ply the bay and deliver their catch of the day directly to the kitchens of waterfront restaurants. And boat builders still practice their centuries-old craft to construct and restore majestic wooden sailing ships for work, display, and pleasure.

As you travel south, then east along the coast, you'll pass through little dots of towns only about fifteen to twenty minutes apart, some with names you know (such as St. Michaels and Tilghman Island), and others, such as Grasonville, Oxford, and Easton, that may not be quite as familiar. Along the way you'll become acquainted with beautiful rivers named Choptank, Tuckahoe, Wye, Miles, and Tred Avon.

Peak visitor time along the Eastern Shore is during the summer. But the early fall brings a back-to-normal tranquillity as well as awe-inspiring arrays of fall foliage for those who like to avoid the crowds.

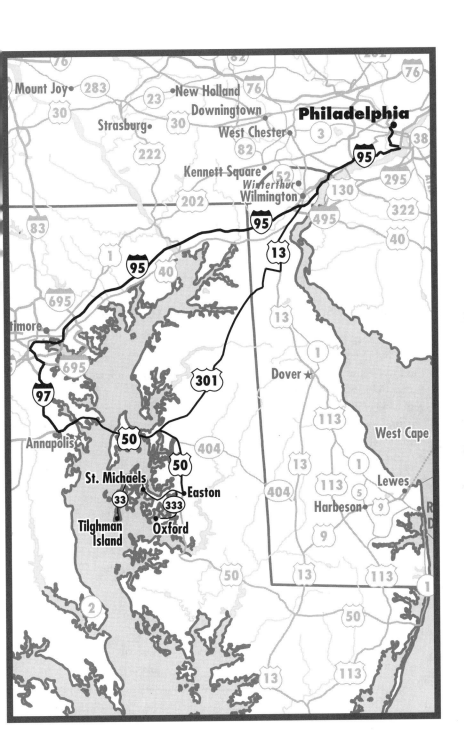

## DOWN THE SHORE

## DAY 1

*Morning*

Although there are shorter, more direct routes to St. Michaels from Philadelphia, this one allows you to have a taste of some of the Eastern Shore's best seafood and visit one of the area's most beautiful wetlands sanctuaries along the way. The trip will take about three hours and twenty minutes (about ½ hour longer than usual). Take I–76 (Schuylkill Expressway) to I–95 south past Baltimore. Just beyond the city follow signs for I–695 east toward Glen Burnie. This is a left exit. Follow I–695 until it merges with I–97 south (also a left exit). Take I–97 south until it merges with Route 50 east. Follow Route 50 past Annapolis and across the Bay Bridge to exit 42, Kent Narrows. Follow the blue directional signs to Harris Crab House in Grasonville.

*Afternoon*

**LUNCH: Harris Crab House,** Kent Narrows Way North, Grasonville; (410) 827–9500. You know the seafood is fresh because, as you eat, you can watch the local watermen deliver their day's catch of clams, crabs, and oysters right to the dock of the Harris family's processing plant next door. The Maryland vegetable crab and cream of crab soups are to die for. And the local catch combination platters ($17.95 for broiled, $18.95 for fried, and $22.95 for the deluxe signature model) are exquisite. Harris offspring Karen Oertel explains that the reason Maryland crabs are better than you can find anywhere else is the way they're cooked and the special secret seasonings that are used. If she has any of the Harris special blend available for sale, buy it. It spices up everything from chicken to vegetables. Open for lunch and dinner 11:00 A.M.– 10:00 P.M. 365 days a year. Sandwiches start at $3.25.

Go back toward Route 50, but instead of getting back onto the highway, turn left onto Route 18 and follow it for about 2 miles. Turn right at Perry Corner Road and go half a mile to the entrance of the wetlands center, which is on the right.

**Horsehead Wetlands Center** in Grasonville (800–CANVASBACK, 410–827–6694) is 500 acres of protected land, mostly salt marshes, where you can see Mother Nature at her wildest. Stop at the **Visitor Center** for a brief acquaintance with some of the types of butterflies, insects, and other forms of life that call this environment home. Outside the picture window is one of six ponds where you can watch the resident and visiting waterfowl in their natural habitat. For a panoramic view of the sanctuary and its inhabitants, take the Boardwalk two-thirds of a mile across the salt meadow and climb to the top of the 15-foot tower. Explore the beautiful trails that wind past the butterfly and hummingbird garden, wildflowers, and habitat ponds. You may even spot a bald eagle soaring overhead. Canoes are also available for self-guided water tours of the center. Open 9:00 A.M.–5:00 P.M. daily year-round. Admission is $3.00 for adults, $2.00 for seniors (fifty-five and over) and $1.00 for youths (eighteen and under).

Retrace your steps from Horsehead to get back onto Route 50 east. When the road divides into Route 301 and Route 50, keep following Route 50 east toward Ocean City. As you approach Easton, watch for signs for St. Michaels. Turn off Route 50 onto Route 322; you'll pass the Black and Decker plant on your right. At the light near the shopping centers, turn right onto Route 33 toward **St. Michaels.** Route 33 will turn into Talbot Street, the town's main thoroughfare lined with shops, restaurants, and other enticing places.

Make a right-hand turn from Talbot onto Mill Street at Navy Point and you'll come to the **Chesapeake Bay Maritime Museum** (410–745–2916). Highlights include a floating fleet of restored workboats and the three-story **Hooper Strait Lighthouse,** built in 1897, one of only three of the once typical cottage-style, screwpile lighthouses that formerly lined the bay. And you can pull up a crab or eel pot or tong for oysters at **Waterman's Wharf,** a recreated crabber's shanty. The museum is open seven days year-round. Hours are 9:00 A.M.–6:00 P.M. in summer, until 5:00 P.M. in spring and fall, and until 4:00 P.M. in winter. Admission is $7.50 for adults, $6.50 for seniors, $3.00 for youths six to seventeen, and free for children under six. Check out the Museum Store for Bay-inspired books, toys, gourmet foods, and other wonderful items.

## Evening

**DINNER: 208 Talbot Street** (410–745–3838). The flavors of the just-caught seafood are respected and served with imaginative accompaniments. Equally delightful chicken, beef, and lamb preparations are also available. Even if you don't usually order appetizers, try the baked oysters with prosciutto, pistachio nuts, and champagne cream, or the house-smoked bluefish taco. Expensive.

Most of St. Michaels' shops, historic sights, and galleries close up at around 5:00 or 6:00 in the evening, but the streets remain full of life long after, especially at the clubs along Talbot Street. One that is always guaranteed to be jumping with a busy bar, dartboard, pool tables, and live entertainment is the **Carpenter Street Saloon,** 2 blocks from the harbor, directly in the center of town at Talbot and Carpenter Streets; (410) 745–5111.

**LODGING: Hambledon Inn Bed & Breakfast,** 202 Cherry Street, St. Michaels: (410) 745–3350. There are a number of lovely bed-and-breakfasts along Cherry Street leading to the Harbour, but you won't find one that's more indicative of St. Michaels than this. Overlooking the marina and Honeymoon Bridge, this charming 1860 residence-turned-inn offers expansive water views from its spacious, individually decorated guest rooms; wicker-furnished waterfront porch, and sunny dining room. Rates range from $115 to $245 April–November and $85–$195 December–March. Full breakfast is included.

## DAY 2

## *Morning*

**BREAKFAST:** Hambledon Inn Bed & Breakfast. Here's when you can really appreciate the view from that waterfront dining room—over a hearty morning meal prepared by gracious innkeepers Kimberly and Steve Furman.

More than a century ago, many a waterman on the Eastern Shore made his living the hard way, even during the harsh winter months, dredging for oysters under sail on their skipjacks. Today you will find few of these sturdy craft working the Bay—and even fewer that will take visitors with them. One of these is the **Rebecca T. Ruark** (410–886–2176) at Tilghman Island. To get there, go east on Route 50 for about 14 miles and cross the Knapps Narrows Drawbridge onto the island. Go straight for about ½ mile and pass the fire hall and country store on your left. Continue another 100 yards to the entrance (on the left) of Dogwood Harbor. Built in 1886, the *Rebecca* is one of the oldest and fastest working skipjacks on the bay. Her captain, Wade Murphy Jr., is a third generation waterman with thirty-seven years' worth of knowledge and lore, which he is more than willing to share. During your two-hour adventure, you will have the opportunity to dredge for oysters—and enjoy them on the half-shell fresh from the water. A two-hour tour costs $30 per person. Captain Murphy's schedule is flexible, so call for sailing times.

Of all the towns in Talbot County, Tilghman Island is probably the one that has remained most untouched by change. There's plenty of water life and great eating on this 1½-mile wide, 3-mile-long stretch of land, but, as for shopping

*Unspoiled Tilghman Island.*

and other attractions, it's still pretty laid back . . . thank goodness. Two shops you shouldn't miss, however, are **Captain Dan Vaughan's** (410–886–2083) and the **Book Bank** (410–886–2230), both of which are located right off Route 33 on the island. Captain Dan's place, which is open all year, offers the kind of traditional hand-carved decoys for which Maryland is famous. And you could become a nautical expert at the Book Bank, which has more than 12,000 tomes on the subject as well as art inspired by it. Open April–December, Saturday and Sunday only from 10:00 A.M.–6:00 P.M.

## *Afternoon*

**LUNCH: Pescato's,** on the island just before the drawbridge; (410) 886–2126. Even though the Eastern Shore is renowned for its seafood, it's almost impossible to resist the delectable aromas wafting from the smoker at Pescato's. Among these incredibly fragrant and deeply flavorful home-smoked offerings are prime rib (priced per ounce at $1.30), chicken ($8.95), and beef barbecue ($5.95 for a sandwich). Also worth a taste are the menu's Mexican and Latin specialties.

Although there are a number of stores along the several blocks of Talbot Street that make up the center of town, they are mostly of the unique mom-and-pop variety and offer goods that range from fine to fun. Take the **Mind's Eye Gift Gallery** (103 Talbot Street; 410–745–2023), where you might see a giant totem pole/lighthouse, a bigger-than-life wire dragonfly, and who knows what else that might spring from the inspired minds and hands of the more than 200 American artists represented here. At the **Ship Shop** (211 North Talbot Street; 410–745–6268), you will find handcrafted model ships and other nautical art created by more than twenty artisans and artists, as well as model kits, books, and supplies so you can make your own.

Belly up to the tasting bar and sample some of the more than 4,000 salsas, hot sauces, and mustards at **Flamingo Flats** (100 South Talbot Street; 410–745–2053). They also have those wonderfully tacky pink flamingos and windup crabs you've been looking for. For crustaceans of the chocolate variety, head to **St. Michaels Candy Company,** 216 South Talbot Street (410–745–6060).

From St. Michaels, head east on Route 33 until it intersects with Route 329. Follow 329 south to the **Oxford–Bellevue Ferry** (410–745–9023). Established in 1683 and believed to be the oldest privately operated ferry in the nation, this charming reminder of the past takes the scenic route over the Tred Avon River to the lovely little town of **Oxford.**

The ferry offers crossings every twenty to twenty-five minutes from June 1 to Labor Day, Monday–Friday 7:00 A.M.–9:00 P.M., Saturday and Sunday 9:00 A.M.–9:00 P.M. From Labor Day to June 1, the ferry runs until sunset.

At the dock, you'll see a replica of Oxford's first **Customs House** (410–226–5760), which was built in the late eighteenth century. Another Oxford landmark is the world renowned **Cutts & Case Shipyard** (306 Tilghman Street; 410–226–5416), where state-of-the-art technology and more than 450 years of craftsmanship combine to produce and renovate some of the finest yachts and other private wooden sailing craft afloat today. You can visit the shipyard and wander around at any time, but if you call ahead, you might be lucky enough to get a guided tour from owner Edmund A. Cutts, a man of many talents and fascinating stories.

# Evening

**DINNER: Robert Morris Inn,** 314 North Morris Street, Oxford; (410) 226–5111. Author James Michener must have sampled a lot of seafood during the research for his best-seller *Chesapeake* and, apparently, he was quite vocal about his preferences. The Carpenter Street Saloon in St. Michaels claims to serve his favorite crab soup, and here at the Robert Morris Inn, right by the ferry landing overlooking the beautiful Tred Avon River, you can find the crab cakes that he actually rated best on the Eastern Shore. The inn's tavern has a comfortable, Colonial-feeling. The mostly moderately priced menu also features such specialties as baked seafood au gratin cake, which you can also order atop a burger for a deliciously different combination. Make sure you order a side of the tavern's signature Chesapeake fries, seasoned and cooked using a five-step process to make them extra tasty and crispy. During strawberry season, the inn also makes a dynamite fresh fruit pie. Dinner hours are 6:00–9:00 P.M. in season (April–November). The inn also has a formal, white tablecloth restaurant on the premises.

It's only a 12-mile drive to the next town of **Easton** for an evening's entertainment at the **Avalon Theatre** (40 East Dover Street; 410–822–0345), a restored 1921 art deco movie/vaudeville palace that now features musical concerts, plays, films, and other wonderful stuff all year-round. To get there, head away from the water down Morris Street, which will become Route 333. Follow 333 all the way out to Route 322. Cross 322 and get onto Peach Blossom Road. At the light, past the schools and the church, take a hard left onto Washington Street and you will find yourself in the main part of Easton's downtown area. After the theater, head back to Oxford and the Robert Morris Inn for your night's lodging.

**LODGING:** Robert Morris Inn, 314 North Morris Street, Oxford; (410) 226–5111. The inn was constructed prior to 1710 by ships' carpenters using paneling made with hand-hewn beams, oak pegs, and handmade nails. If you're a history buff, ask for a room in the old part of the house, which features an Elizabethan staircase and white pine floors. The common rooms should also be of interest with their three magnificent murals, 280-year-old handmade wall panels, and a brick fireplace made in England around 1812. Open April–November, some weekends in winter. Rates in the original section range from $90 to $180. From Sunday–Thursday, the tariff includes a continental breakfast and a $20 per room deduction for each night you have dinner in one of the inn's dining rooms.

## DAY 3

## *Morning*

**BREAKFAST: Breakfast at Jacqueline's & Lunch, Too,** 202 Morris Street, Oxford; (410) 226–0238. This lively spot is the place to go if you want to run into lots of locals. Jacqueline's specializes in morning food, so expect to find anything your appetite desires from fresh fruit to Belgian waffles to eggs Benedict at inexpensive to moderate prices. Sit-down and box lunches are also available. Open in season on Saturday and Sunday, 7:00 A.M.–2:00 P.M.

Sunday is a relatively sleepy day on this part of the Eastern Shore. So, after breakfast, drive back to Easton where although many of the shops, restaurants, and other attractions are closed, there are still some wonderful things to see and do.

In recent years, the face, economy, and social dynamics of Talbot County seem to change as swiftly as the tides. To preserve the area's legacy, the museum of the **Historical Society of Talbot County** (25 South Washington Street, Easton; 410–822–0773) exhibits furnishings, pictures, paintings, and memorabilia that span pre-Revolutionary to modern times. The society also offers guided tours of three historic seventeenth- and eighteenth-century homes, one with the intriguing name the Ending of Controversie. Open Tuesday–Saturday 10:00 A.M.–4:00 P.M. Call for Sunday hours. Admission is $5.00 for the museum and house tours, $3.00 for the museum alone.

For more history, visit the **Third Haven Friends Meeting House** at 405 South Washington Street; (410) 822–0293. Erected in 1682, this building has the distinction of being the oldest religious building still in use in the United States, the oldest frame building in continuous use, and the earliest dated building in Maryland. Visitors are welcome any time.

## *Afternoon*

**LUNCH: Legal Spirits,** Avalon Theatre, Easton. Last night, you visited the historic theater to see a show. Today you'll be coming back for lunch at this restaurant located in a former pharmacy right off the theater's main lobby. The seafood-centered menu stars our old friend the crab in a number of delightful incarnations. For something different order the fried calamari, roasted vegetables, and feta cheese salad. Moderate.

At the intersection of Routes 50 and 309, just north of town is the Easton Airport, where pilot Hunter Harris of **Aloft Inc.** (410–820–5959) keeps his 300-horsepower, 1942 open-cockpit Stearman biplane. For prices ranging from $37 to $135, you can feel the wind in your hair as Harris takes you on a ten-minute "hop around the patch" over Easton or twenty-minute flight over St. Michaels; a thirty-minute tour of St. Michaels, Oxford, and Easton; or a forty-five-minute deluxe aerial tour of these three towns plus the Bay Bridge and Kent Island. Rides are available April–October. Call for hours.

Since you are heading back to Philadelphia from Easton following the most straightforward route, it should only take you a little more than 2½ hours to get home. Go west on Route 50 for about 20 miles until you come to Route 301. Take Route 301 north for 52 miles to Route I–95. Head north on 95 into Philadelphia.

## THERE'S MORE

**Academy of the Arts,** 106 South Street, Easton; (410) 822–0455. Exhibits in these two recently renovated historic buildings include works by such famous nineteenth- and twentieth-century artists as James McNeil Whistler and Grant Wood. Open year-round Monday–Saturday (except Wednesday) from 10:00 A.M.–4:00 P.M. Wednesday hours are 10:00 A.M.–9:00 P.M. Admission is $2.00 for adults; $1.00 for youths twelve and older; free for children under twelve.

**Hog Neck Golf Course,** Old Cordova Road, Easton; (410) 822–6079. One of the top twenty-five public golf courses in the country, according to *Golf Digest*, Hog Neck offers a par 71, eighteen-hole championship course, a par 32 executive nine, a driving range, and pro shop.

**Canton Row Antiques,** 216-C South Talbot Street, St. Michaels; (410) 745–2440. This eighteen-dealer antiques mall offers European, country, and Victorian furniture, jewelry, and collectibles. Open year-round, seven days a week, 10:00 A.M.–6:00 P.M.

**St. Mary's Museum,** off Talbot Street between Chestnut and Mulberry, St. Michaels; (410) 745–9561. Two nineteenth-century structures—a waterman's family home and a former town lockup/mortuary/barbershop—have been joined together and filled with furnishings and personal possessions of local families to offer a glimpse of life in St. Michaels in the 1800s. Open May–October, Saturday and Sunday 10:00 A.M.–4:00 P.M. A donation is requested.

**Island Kayak Inc.,** Mission Road, Tilghman Island; (410) 886–2083. Paddle silently through the waters and observe the resident herons, egrets, ospreys, and, perhaps, bald eagles. Rentals and guided tours are available. Call for seasonal hours and prices.

***Lady Patty,*** Knapps Narrows Marina, Tilghman's Island; (800) 690–5080 or (410) 886–2215. Veteran seaman Captain Mike Richards offers two-hour excursions aboard his 1935 classic bay ketch, winner of the prestigious St. Petersburg (Florida) to Havana (Cuba) race in 1951 and probable competitor in the fiftieth anniversary race in 2001. The price for a two-hour sail is $30 per person.

## SPECIAL EVENTS

**May.** Annual Mid–Atlantic Maritime Arts Festival, Chesapeake Bay Maritime Museum, St. Michaels; (410) 745–2916. Ship models, maritime paintings, crafts, fish carvings, music, and seafood are the highlights of this three-day event.

**October.** Tilghman Island Day, on the harbor; (410) 822–4606 or (410) 886–2677. A celebration of the Eastern Shore's maritime history and world-renowned seafood with a full schedule of waterman's games, workboat races, crab picking and oyster shucking contests, cruises, music, and, of course, oceans of clams, crabs, oysters, and other gifts from the sea.

**November.** Annual Waterfowl Festival, Easton; (410) 822–4567. More than 450 of the nation's premier wildlife artists and exhibitors are invited to participate in the eighteen exhibits spread throughout the town.

## OTHER RECOMMENDED RESTAURANTS AND LODGINGS

## *St. Michaels*

Inn at Perry Cabin, 308 Watkins Lane; (800) 722–2949 or (410) 745–2200. Built right after the War of 1812, this splendid English-style country house, owned by Bernard Ashley, cofounder of the Laura Ashley Company, is considered the height of luxury on the Eastern Shore. Rates for April–October range from $295 to $695; call for off-season rates. A full breakfast and afternoon tea are included. The inn also has a renowned fine dining restaurant that offers an open-to-the-public prix fixe gourmet dinner for $65 on weekends.

Parsonage Inn, 210 North Talbot Street; (800) 394–5519 or (410) 745–5519. The architecture of this 1883 brick Victorian is a real attention-grabber. Inside it's genteel in a cozy sort of way with Queen Anne-style furnishings, brass beds, shell pedestal sinks, period light fixtures, and Laura Ashley bed linens. Weekend room rates range from $130 to $160 April–October; $120–$160 November–March. During the week, all rooms are discounted by $20. A full gourmet breakfast is included.

Buttermilk Cafe, 306 Talbot Street; (410) 745–5224. Bring your sense of humor and your ability to enjoy the unexpected at this cottage-like restaurant located right before the sidewalk ends. There's no set menu here; chief-cooks-and-bottle-washers Louise and Douglas Taylor prepare whatever's fresh and whatever they're in the mood for and post their selections on a blackboard that changes three meals a day. Open daily from 8:00 A.M. until "whenever" for breakfast, lunch (both inexpensive), and dinner (moderate). The Taylors like to be off Monday, but say "if you really want to eat here on a Monday, we'll open, even if it does screw everything up."

Suddenly Last Summer, 106 North Talbot Street; (410) 745–5882. The decor may border on imagination-gone-wild (in a fun way), but the seafood, steak, and poultry dinner menu is quite down-to-earth. Moderate to expensive.

## Tilghman Island

Lazyjack Inn Bed & Breakfast, 5907 Tilghman Island Road on Dogwood Harbor; (800) 690–5080 or (410) 886–2215. Magnificent harbor views from the sitting room and outside deck, home-cooked breakfasts, and guest rooms filled with unique architectural accents and antique furnishings are among the amenities that make this 160-year-old inn so welcoming. Midweek rates range from $120 to $175; weekends, from $135 to $195.

## Easton

Coffee East, 5 Goldsborough Street; (410) 819–6711. Fresh-brewed coffee drinks and teas, pastries and muffins, soups, quiches, sandwiches, gourmet pizzas, and sushi (on Wednesday). Inexpensive to moderate.

Columbia, 28 South Washington Street; (410) 770–5172. One of the hottest new dining spots on the Eastern Shore, Columbia's "contemporary innovative American menu" is deliciously influenced by the cuisines of France, Portugal, Italy, and other romantic locales. Expensive.

## FOR MORE INFORMATION

Maryland Office of Tourism Development; (410) 767–3400; www.mdisfun.org.

Queen Anne's County Office of Tourism, Grasonville; (410) 604–2100.

Talbot County Chamber of Commerce (St. Michaels, Tilghman Island, Oxford, and Easton); (888) BAY STAY or (410) 822–4606.

Easton Business Management Association; (410) 822–0065.

# ESCAPES

## BETWEEN AND BEYOND

*A view of the Washington Monument at cherry blossom time.*

# Greater New Hope, Pennsylvania

## ROMANCE AND ADVENTURE ON THE RIVER

**1 NIGHT**

*History • Antiques • Ghost Tours • Fine and Fun Dining*

Follow the meandering course of the Delaware River about 50 miles north out of Philadelphia and you'll come upon a cluster of charming little villages, towns, and hamlets, some in Pennsylvania, some across the river in New Jersey, collectively referred to as Greater New Hope. Each location has its own distinctive personality and its own special place in history. Some offer the atmosphere of a local marketplace at festival time, lively with visitors strolling, shopping, sight-seeing by day and enjoying music and theater by night. Others have a more laid-back, country-village feel, perfect for morning breakfasting in a hidden garden, an afternoon of serious antiques hunting, or an evening in romantic seclusion.

It is said that ghosts from Revolutionary and Civil War times roam these villages at night. But the locals assure you that the spirits mean no harm. They explain that, like everyone else who visits the area, once they experienced New Hope they simply never wanted to leave.

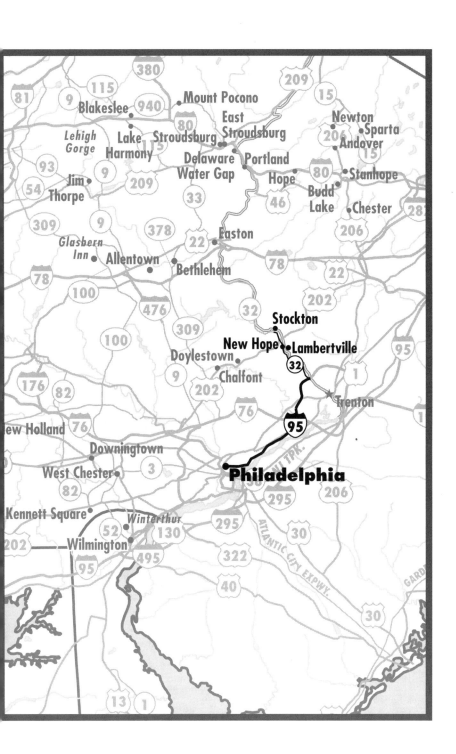

## DAY 1

### Morning

The quickest route from Philadelphia is to take I–95 north to New Hope exit 31. Turn left at the stop sign onto Taylorsville Road, go 5 miles and pass two stoplights. At the stop sign after the second light, turn left onto Route 32 north. Take Route 32 north 4 miles into the Village of New Hope.

Founded in 1700, **New Hope** has 118 structures over one hundred years old still in use. One of them is the post-Revolutionary War mansion of mill owner Benjamin Parry. At the **Parry Mansion Museum** (45 South Main Street; 215–862–5652), fine displays of original furnishings and possessions accurately reflect the fashions and tastes of the eighteenth and nineteenth centuries, when Parry and his descendants lived there. Open 1:00–5:00 P.M., Friday, Saturday, and Sunday from late April through early December. Admission is $5.00 for adults, $4.00 for seniors and students, and $1.50 for children under twelve.

Park ($5.00 for the day) at the **New Hope & Ivy Land Railroad Station** at 32 West Bridge Street (215–862–2332). There you'll hop on a vintage circa 1920s passenger steam train bound for a relaxing twenty-five-minute trip through the magnificent Bucks County countryside to the nearby village of Lahaska. ($9.50 adults, $8.50 seniors, $5.50 children). At Lahaska, you can board a free shuttle that will take you to within steps of the popular shopping meccas of Peddler's Village, Penn's Purchase, and the Lahaska Antique Courte.

**LUNCH: Buckingham Mountain Brewing Co. & Restaurant,** 5557 Route 202, Lahaska; (215) 794–7302—actually, this is where the shuttle leaves you off. Take a tour of Bucks County's first microbrewery and sample the eight handcrafted brews available. Then relax and enjoy a moderately priced lunch with a breathtaking view of the countryside.

### Afternoon

Of course, all this good food has worked up an appetite for shopping. So it's on to the colorful self-contained forty-two-acre shoppers' paradise of **Peddler's Village**. There's a lot to see here, so make your first stop the **Hospitality Booth on the Village Green** or the **Guest Services** office (215–794–4000) to the left of the entrance to the Cock 'n Bull Restaurant for maps and information. At the **Village Green**, there's always something interesting to see. It might be a giant sculpture made out of 150 tons of sand or displays of handcrafted patriotic topiary, quilts, or gingerbread houses.

You'll find everything from fine to folk art and from clothing to dollhouses and miniatures in the village's boutique shops. One of the most colorful is the **Village Toy Shoppe** (215–794–7031) with its animated polar bear and giant Wizard of Oz figures outside and an extensive selection of puppets, marionettes, toy trains, and other kid-stuff inside. For a bit of nostalgia, there's the **Grand Carousel** (215–794–8960), where you can take a ride on the 1922 vintage carousel for $1.50 and browse the antiques arcade attractions. For a quarter you can sneak a peak at some bathing suit-clad "Coney Island Cuties" from a hundred years ago.

If you're into factory outlet shopping, cross the road to **Penn's Purchase** (5861 York Road; 215–794–0700), another self-contained shopping complex where fifty shops bearing famous names in clothing, art, furniture, sporting goods, electronics, and other items offer 20–50 percent off retail prices every day. And if it's antiques you're after, the **Lahaska Antique Courte** (Route 202; 215–794–7884) has fifteen shops selling all kinds of treasures including fine and folk art, primitive Americana, Civil War artifacts, and hand-carved music boxes.

When you're ready to return to New Hope, walk back over to the Buckingham Mountain Brewing Co. & Restaurant (5557 Route 202) and board the free shuttle back to the train station.

Back in New Hope, be sure to stop for a cone, cup, or sundae at **Gerenser's Exotic Ice Cream** (22 South Main Street; 215–862–2050), a fifty-year-old parlor specializing in homemade one-of-a-kind flavors such as African violet, Magyar apricot brandy, and Ukrainian rose petal.

## *Evening*

**DINNER: Inn at Phillips Mill,** 2590 North River Road; (215) 862–9919. From the beginning of New Hope, cruise along River Road for about 1.5 miles (keep an eye on your odometer) until you see the big red barn on the right-hand side of the road. Don't blink or you might miss the inn, which is right next door. Dinner here is one you'll definitely remember. If the weather permits, ask to be seated outside in the magnificent garden amid a profusion of wild flowers. Otherwise, you'll be just as happy in the downstairs or upstairs dining rooms inside. In the warm weather, the restaurant specializes in seafood; in the cooler seasons the fragrant rack of lamb will chase away any chill. BYOB. Expensive. No credit cards.

For a spirited end to your evening, drive back to Main and Ferry Streets and wait at the cannon. At 8:00 P.M. a lantern-bearing figure from **Ghost Tours** (215–957–9988) will lead you on a sometimes hair-raising one-hour walk through the village. Your guide will regale you with "true" stories of restless spirits who walk the night. If you're lucky (?), you might have a close encounter with the ghost of the phantom hitchhiker or catch a glimpse of Aaron Burr staring with sightless eyes from the window of a historic inn. Call for prices.

**LODGING:** The Inn at Phillips Mill (215–862–2984). Built in 1750, this old stone barn turned bed-and-breakfast has been owned since 1972 by architect Brooks Kaufman and his wife Joyce. It is obvious that the Kaufmans lavished a great deal of love and attention to restoring the structure with its five charming bedrooms, each with private bath, which range from $86 to $97. All of the rooms are furnished with antiques, quilts on four-poster beds, and dried-flower bouquets. Two-night weekend visitors can also rent what looks exactly like an enchanted cottage from an old fairy tale for $135 per night. No credit cards.

## DAY 2

## *Morning*

**BREAKFAST: Miele's,** corner of Bridge Street and Route 29, Stockton, New Jersey; (609) 397–8033. Although the Inn at Phillips Mill offers a light continental breakfast for an additional $4.50 per person, you might want to stoke up on heartier fare for the day ahead. For that, you'll need to drive into New Hope to Bridge Street and cross the no-toll bridge over the Delaware into Stockton, New Jersey. Right across the bridge you'll find Miele's, a cute old-timey restaurant where breakfast can range from moderate to expensive, but the generous portions and on-premise baking make it well worth the price. No credit cards are accepted. Before you leave, be sure to pick up a couple of their oven-fresh peanut butter or oatmeal cookies for the road.

After breakfast, take a less than 5-mile drive south on Route 29 to **Lambertville, New Jersey,** a peaceful eighteenth-century town of tree-lined streets, Victorian houses, and Federal row homes on the Delaware Raritan Canal. If you're looking for laid-back, you've found it. And if you're serious about antiques, you've struck gold . . . as well as silver, furniture, textiles, art,

*The Teddy Bear's Picnic in Peddler's Village.*

and glass from England, France, Holland, and eighteenth- and nineteenth-century America. Grab a guidebook at the local **Chamber of Commerce** (4 South Union Street; 609–397–1530) and begin your treasure hunt.

Don't miss the **Antique Center at the People's Store** (28 North Union Street; 609–397–9808), a forty-shop co-op that is Lambertville's oldest and largest antiques dealer. Then there's the **5 & Dime** at 40 North Union Street (609–397–4957), a real relic from the past that boasts of having the East Coast's largest selection of antique and collectible toys dating from the turn of the century through the baby boom era—all for sale. To watch a local artist in action, visit oil painter and tile maker **Betsy Love** in her working studio at 26 Bridge Street, open by appointment (609–397–8838) or catch-as-catch-can.

## *Afternoon*

Cross the bridge back into New Hope and take Route 32 north to **Bucks County River Country,** "the World's Tubing Capital," located in **Point Pleasant, Pennsylvania** (215–297–8823). When you reach Point Pleasant, you'll cross a bridge in the middle of town. At the foot of the bridge, make an immediate right onto Byram Road. Cross another bridge and you're there. From May through late October the scenery along the banks of the Delaware is spectacular from the vantage point of a canoe, kayak, tube, or leisure raft. If you prefer your thrills a bit more on the wild side, you can also challenge the river's white waters. Expect to pay $15 for four hours of tubing.

**LUNCH:** For lunch, pay a visit to the resident Island Hot Dog Man.

## Evening

**DINNER: Havana Restaurant,** 105 South Main Street; (215) 862–9897. On your way back to Philadelphia, stop in New Hope and join the locals here for dinner. You can dine alfresco or in the dining room decorated in a style that can only be described as fun and funky. Compared to the decor, the creative, mostly moderately priced "contemporary world cuisine" menu is relatively tame.

After dinner, head south on Route 32 and drive about 3 miles until you come to Taylorsville Road; bear right onto Taylorsville Road; continue south about another 3 miles until you intersect I–95 south, which you'll take all the way to Philadelphia. The trip home should take you about one hour.

### THERE'S MORE

**Coryell's Ferry Historic Sightseeing Boat Rides/Gerenser's Exotic Ice Cream,** 22 South Main Street, New Hope; (215) 862–2050. Cruise the Delaware aboard the *Major William C. Barnett,* a 65-foot Mississippi-style stern-wheel riverboat. Tickets are $5.00 for adults, $3.00 for children under twelve, and free for infants with two paying adults.

**Rice's Sale & Market,** 6326 Greenhill Road, New Hope; (215) 297–5993. Country market established in 1860 with more than 850 vendors. Open Tuesday and Saturday only.

**Bucks County Playhouse,** 70 South Main Street, New Hope; (215) 862–0220. Professional theater presenting musicals and plays from April through December. Children's theater presentations all season long as well.

**New Hope Canal Boat Company,** 149 South Main Street, New Hope; (215) 862–0758. Board a mule-drawn canal boat just like the ones that plied this canal in the 1800s for a one-hour ride while a costumed guide describes the life of the people who lived and worked along the canal at that time. $6.95 for adults, $6.50 for children under twelve.

**John & Peter's,** 96 South Main Street, New Hope; (215) 862–5981. For more than twenty-six years, this renowned showcase for new artists (many have gone on to become national headliners) has been serving up an eclectic blend of music ranging from folk to rock to jazz to rhythm and blues. Cover charge ranges from $3.00 to $5.00, except on Monday open-mike nights, when admission is free.

**Prufrock Coffeehouse,** 75 South Union Street, Lambertville; (609) 397–4397. The name alone is enough to make you want to go there. Relaxed atmosphere, board games, reading material, art exhibits, poetry readings, espresso, ice cream, and desserts.

## SPECIAL EVENTS

**July.** Teddy Bear's Picnic, Peddler's Village; (215) 794–4095. Parades, pageants, an auction, and a workshop for teddy bear owners and buffs of all ages. There's even a Bear Care Clinic offering repairs and tender loving care for your fuzzy friends. Free.

**Mid-November–January 2.** Gingerbread House Competition and Display, Peddler's Village; (215) 794–4095. Artistic bakers compete for more than $5,700 in cash prizes. Winning entries are displayed in the village gazebo throughout the holiday season.

**December.** Coryell's Ferry Militia, New Hope; (215) 862–2050. Reenactments of historical events and an enchanting Colonial Christmas Ball.

## OTHER RECOMMENDED RESTAURANTS AND LODGINGS

## New Hope

Odette's, River Road (just outside New Hope); (215) 862–2432. Built in 1794 as a tavern for river boatmen, the well-known dining establishment housed in a beautifully restored stone inn offers innovative continental cuisine and delicious river views. It's also a great after-dinner spot for music and entertainment.

Wedgwood Inn, 111 West Bridge Street; (215) 862–2570. Victorian-style personality and charm. Antiques, hardwood floors, fresh-cut flowers, two acres with gazebos, pool and tennis club privileges, complimentary continental breakfast and afternoon tea. Rates range from $75 to $165 weekdays, $100 to $199 weekends.

## Peddler's Village

Golden Plough Inn, Route 202 and 263, Lahaska; (215) 794–4004. Individually appointed rooms and suites, many featuring gas-lit fireplaces and double-sized whirlpools. Breakfast at the Spotted Hog Restaurant included. Rates range from $105 to $325.

Spotted Hog, Route 202 and Street Road; (215) 794–4030. Once a hotel and eighteenth-century public house, this adorable restaurant offers moderately priced, family-friendly fare with a great view of the village.

## Lambertville

David's Yellow Brick Toad, 149 South Highway 179; (609) 397–3100. Lambertville's longest operating restaurant. Lovely setting; creative, moderately priced menu.

## Stockton

Stockton Inn, 1 Main Street; (609) 397–1250. This romantic circa 1710 inn inspired Rodgers and Hart to write one of their biggest hit tunes, "There's a Small Hotel." It features distinctive suites, many with fireplaces and canopy beds, and complimentary continental breakfast. Rates range from $65 to $130 weekdays, $90 to $170 weekends. Its restaurant, Colligan's Stockton Inn (same phone), was a favorite of F. Scott Fitzgerald, Oscar Hammerstein II, and Clark Gable. In warm weather, dine in the magnificent garden with its waterfalls and trout pond. Expensive.

### FOR MORE INFORMATION

New Hope Information Center, Corner of Main and Mechanic Streets, New Hope; (215) 862–5880.

Bucks County Conference & Visitors Bureau; (215) 345–4552; www.buckscountycvb.org.

# BETWEEN AND BEYOND

# Brandywine Valley, Pennsylvania

## MEMORIES OF WAR, IMAGES OF PEACE

### 1 NIGHT

*River Walks • Scenic Railway Rides*
*Historic Reenactments*

In the valley of the tranquil Brandywine River, south of Philadelphia, lies a place where Pennsylvania and Delaware come together, united not by bridges, but by miles of rolling green hills, history, and a common spirit. As a result, many people tend to combine the Brandywine Valley into one getaway experience. But there's really too much to see and do to try to cram everything into one trip.

For convenience, I have split the region into two parts, using the state borders as my dividing line. In this chapter we'll stay on the Pennsylvania side of the valley; in Chapter 3 of Between and Beyond Escapes, we'll visit the Delaware side. And because both sides of the Brandywine Valley are only about an hour south of Philadelphia on Route I–95, we have the advantage of being close enough to return again and again to savor the particular delights of each area and each season.

## DAY 1

### Morning

**BREAKFAST: Hank's Place,** intersection of Routes 1 and 100, Chadds Ford; (610) 388–7061. This modest-looking roadside luncheonette has a not-so-modest sign: HOME COOKING AT ITS BEST. But the locals—and even *Gourmet*

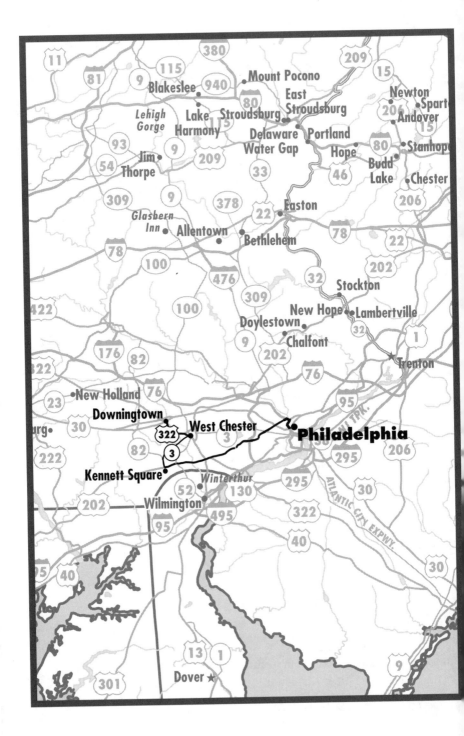

magazine—agree that Hank's Place has every right to make that boast. Grab a table or a stool at the counter where you might find yourself seated next to the local plumber, stockbroker, or artist-in-residence (native son Andrew Wyeth often stops by for breakfast). The prices are terrific, ranging from a low of $1.25 to a high of $5.95. But the real draw is the food, which includes buttermilk pancakes, Belgian waffles, Southern-style biscuits, and one incredible shiitake omelette.

After breakfast, get back on Route 1 and resume your drive south. About 4 miles ahead you will enter another world, a world of gracious living, dazzling colors, and intoxicating perfumes. This is **Longwood Gardens,** once home to the area's Native Americans, to generations of one Quaker family, and to a wealthy, powerful industrialist named duPont.

The adventure begins before you even enter the gardens themselves. Located at the entrance is the former **Longwood Meeting of Progressive Friends,** which was established in 1855 as a meetinghouse for a group of socially and politically radical Quakers and which would eventually become a local hub of the Underground Railroad. Now the **Brandywine Valley Tourist Information Center,** it houses displays and exhibits depicting the building's history and also offers brochures, maps, and personalized tour assistance. Open daily 10:00 A.M.–6:00 P.M., April through October; 10:00 A.M.–5:00 P.M., November through March (610–388–2900).

Outside is the **Progressive Meeting Cemetery,** where members and other prominent community members from the era rest.

For generations, the land that is now known as Longwood Gardens was home, hunting, farming, and fishing grounds to the Native Americans who lived in the area. In 1700, a Quaker family named Peirce turned it into a working farm and nationally renowned arboretum. Over the years the property changed hands several times until it was purchased by a company with a sawmill intent on turning the historic trees into just so much timber. However, in 1906, local industrial and financial giant Pierre S. duPont rescued the property, built himself a weekend retreat there, and designed a paradise of plants and flowers inspired by the pleasure gardens of Europe.

Today Longwood Gardens features 1,050 acres of gardens, woodlands. and meadows; 11,000 different types of plants; twenty indoor gardens; and spectacular illuminated fountains.

Make your first stop the **Visitors Center,** where a brief orientation film will help you get your bearings. From there, follow the well-marked paths and trails past the outdoor gardens of roses, topiary, and wildflowers to the conservatories with their creative year-round displays. For green thumbers, the Idea Garden offers creative inspirations for home gardens. Climb the Chimes Tower for a bird's-eye view of the gardens and fountains.

Also on the grounds is the **Peirce–duPont House,** originally built by the Peirce family in 1730 and used as a weekend retreat by the duPont family. The house now tells the story of life on the property through artifacts (dating back to the Leni Lenape tribe), photographs, home movies, and personal posses-sions of the Peirce and duPont families. Many of the original trees are still standing in **Peirce's Arboretum** adjacent to the house. The house is open daily from 10:00 A.M.–6:00 P.M. (5:00 P.M. in winter.). The outdoor gardens open daily at 9:00 A.M., the conservatory at 10:00 A.M. Closing times are gen-erally between 5:00 and 6:00 P.M. from January 2 to late November, and at 9:00 P.M. from Thanksgiving to January 1. Admission is $12 for adults ($8.00 on Tuesdays), $6.00 for youths ages 16–20, $2.00 for children ages 6–15, free for children under six. Call 610–388–1000.

## *Afternoon*

**LUNCH: Terrace Restaurant–Cafeteria,** located right on the grounds; (610) 388–6771. If you're hungry, yet don't want to tear yourself away from all of these natural wonders, grab yourself an outdoor table or window seat. The atmosphere is quite nice, the food is fresh and kind to the budget, and the view is terrific. A "value meal" that includes soup, sandwich, and soda costs only $6.95. (Kids can get a hot dog, chips, and soda for $3.95). After all today's walking, go ahead and splurge on a big, chewy oatmeal raisin or chocolate chip cookie. There is also a full-service white tablecloth restaurant adjacent to the cafeteria.

For a quick roadside treat, turn right onto Route 1 (in this neck of the woods it soon becomes Old Baltimore Pike) and travel less than ½ mile to the town of Kennett Square and **Phillips Mushroom Museum** (909 East Bal-timore Pike), a veritable shrine to the noblest and most lucrative fungus of all. As producer of more than half the mushrooms grown in the United States, Kennett Square has long held the title "Mushroom Capital of the World." Life-size dioramas let you see how these fabulous fungi grow and a surprisingly interesting video traces international mushroom history, legend, and lore. Admission is $1.25 for adults, 75 cents for seniors, 50 cents for children seven to twelve, free for children six and under. There's no admission fee for the attached gift shop where you'll find all sorts of farm-fresh familiar and exotic mushrooms as well as fungus-inspired kitchen accessories, cookbooks, patio furniture, and even decorative birds cleverly carved from you-know-whats. The museum and shop are open daily 10:00 A.M.–6:00 P.M.

## *Evening*

**LODGING: Meadow Spring Farm Bed & Breakfast,** 201 East Street Road/Route 926, Kennett Square; (610) 444–3903. This B&B offers the best of everything—central location, rural setting, and historic structure. To get there from the museum, head back in the direction of Longwood Gardens and keep going 1–1½ miles until you reach Route 82; turn right. Go about 2 miles north on 82 to Route 926; turn right again. About ½ mile up the road start slowing down so you won't miss the modest sign announcing that you have arrived at your destination . . . well, almost anyway—you still have to drive up a long, windy dirt road, past wheat fields, outbuildings, livestock, and wildflowers to get to the building.

Now, if you've left the kids with grandma and you're looking for a quiet secluded love nest, find somewhere else to stay. But if what you want is country charm, a warm welcome from a soon-to-be friend, and a lively family atmosphere, you've come to exactly the right place. When you arrive at this circa 1836 farmhouse, you'll be greeted like visiting family by owner Anne I. Hicks and/or her daughter Debbie and maybe a grandchild or two.

Anne's fun-loving spirit is reflected in her beloved collections of dolls, cows, and Santas that are displayed throughout the house. The guest rooms offer nice views of the gardens, swimming pool, or pond, and all are furnished with family antiques, Amish quilts, and lots of pillows. Open year-round, $85 for room with private bath; $75 for room with shared bath. Full breakfast and afternoon tea with Anne's home-baked goodies are included in the room rate. No credit cards are accepted.

**DINNER:** Ask Anne to pack you a light supper and to arrange an early evening ride through the beautiful Brandywine Valley countryside in a horse-drawn carriage. The two-hour ride costs $50 for up to a family of four.

## DAY 2

## Morning

Hit the road before daylight so you can greet the sunrise from the basket of a hot air balloon. **Lollipop Hot Air Balloons** (610–827–1610), headquartered in Chester Springs, has a convenient launch site only about twenty minutes away in Eagle, Pennsylvania. To get there, take Route 926 east less than 2 miles to where it intersects Route 52. Follow Route 52 north—about 3 miles up the road Route 52 will become Route 100. Drive north on Route 100 about 10 miles until you reach Little Conestoga Road at the Eagle Tavern in the town of Eagle. Head toward the yellow blinking light, and turn right onto Park Road. Turn left into the first driveway at the real estate office. The balloon launch site is inside the white picket fence.

Like most hot air balloon companies, Lollipop offers flights at sunrise and sunset. The daybreak flight allows you to enjoy an aerial view in the cool of the morning when the only wildlife to be seen is of the four-legged variety. Lollipop offers flights lasting one-half hour ($95 per person) or a full hour ($160 per person). The entire experience will take about 2½ to 3 hours because, true to the centuries old tradition of balloonists everywhere, every flight ends with a champagne (or soft drink) toast.

**BREAKFAST: Cadillac Diner,** 81 West Lancaster Avenue, Downington; (610) 873–9032. Take Route 113 south for 8 miles to Route 30 (Lancaster Avenue). The Cadillac Diner earned its place in history in 1957 when a young actor named Steve McQueen starred in a low-budget sci-fi movie shot right on the premises. Recently restored to its original stainless steel and neon glory, this proud "Home of *The Blob*" serves up fifties' movie lore along with the kind of down-home hearty fare you'd expect from an authentic diner. Prices are inexpensive, so you can afford to spend the extra $15 for your own personal copy of *The Blob* on video (available at the cashier's station).

Back at the intersection of Routes 1 and 100, slowly begin to work your way through scenic, historic Chadds Ford. On Route 1, just south of Route 100, is the **Brandywine River Museum** (610–388–2700), a structure that began life as a nineteenth-century gristmill and is now a showcase for paintings by the Wyeth family—father Newell Convers (N.C.) and sons Jamie and Andrew—as well as other American artists. One of the most beloved paintings in the museum is Jamie Wyeth's tongue-in-cheek portrait of a pig. The popular porker is also the subject of a bronze statue that stands outside on the riverbank.

Exit the museum and walk through the cobblestone courtyard to a path that winds through the wildflowers to the beginning of a 1-mile-long river walk. In a nearby meadow you'll see a painstakingly authentic reproduction of a Colonial era barn that houses the headquarters, small museum, and gift shop of the **Chadds Ford Historical Society**. From "The Barn," continue along the path until you come to the **John Chads House** (610–388–7376), the wonderfully preserved eighteenth-century stone home and springhouse that belonged to the local ferryman, farmer, and innkeeper for whom the town was named. (If you're wondering where the extra "d" in Chadds Ford came from, the Historical Society surmises that it was simply a Victorian-era flourish added when the town was named.) On weekends in May through September from noon to 5:00 P.M., Colonial-costumed guides bring history to life with demonstrations of domestic skills of the era, including baking in a beehive oven. Admission is $3.00 for adults, $1.00 for children.

Right across the street is **Chaddsford Winery** (610–388–6221), the largest (in terms of volume) winery in Pennsylvania and one of the top ten on the East Coast. Located in a renovated seventeenth-century barn, the winery is open for tours, tastings, and sales seven days a week from noon to 6:00 P.M.; special events, including concerts, barrel tastings, and festivals, are held throughout the year.

## *Afternoon*

**LUNCH: Chadds Ford Tavern,** Route 1 (1 mile south of the intersection of Routes 100 and 202), Chadds Ford; (610) 459–8453. When it was first built in the 1770s, this roadside tavern provided respite and refreshment to many of the famous generals who fought in the Battle of Brandywine. Beautifully restored, it is now a popular haunt for area artists (yes, that includes Wyeths) and other creative types. The inexpensive menu selections are eclectic and interesting, based mostly in American cuisine, but influenced by the spiciness of Mexico, the elegance of France, and the gusto of Italy.

Up and down Route 1 in Chadds Ford, you'll find all kinds of unique shops tucked in between the historic sites. Only a few yards apart are the **Pennsbury–Chadds Ford Antique Mall** (at the White Barn), with 120 dealers on two levels, and the **Brandywine River Antiques Market,** both of which offer a wide assortment of antiques, furniture, and accessories. Across the street at the Brandywine River Hotel (Routes 1 and 100) are the **Chadds Ford Barn Shops** (610–388–7682), a tiny garden village featuring country shops (including Jim Case's irresistible Brandywine fudge), working artisans, and the **Chadds Ford Gallery** (610–459–5510), which offers investor-collector quality art, including the largest collection of Wyeths anywhere.

## *Evening*

**DINNER: Chadds Ford Cafe,** Route 1 and Heyburn Road, Chadds Ford; (610) 558–3960. Situated literally back-to-back with Chadds Ford Tavern, this lively dining spot has an attitude and menu that will transport you straight to Jimmy Buffet's Florida Keys. Moderate. Children's meals for $4.99.

To get home, take Route 1 north. The return trip should take you a little over one hour.

### THERE'S MORE

**Brandywine Battlefield Park,** Route 1, Chadds Ford. On this battlefield, General George Washington and the Marquis de Lafayette took a united stand against the British. Although the battle was lost, a powerful alliance was forged, one that would eventually turn the tide of the war. You can tour General Washington's headquarters and Lafayette's quarters (for a nominal charge) and see the interpretive exhibits at the Visitor Center (free). Open Tuesday–Saturday, 9:00 A.M.–5:00 P.M.; Sunday, noon–5:00 P.M.

**Barns-Brinton House,** Route 1 and Chandler Road, Chadds Ford; (610) 388–7376. This restored eighteenth-century tavern and residence is open on weekends May through September and features reenactments of domestic life in the Brandywine Valley during the Colonial era. Admission is $3.00 for adults, $1.00 for children ages six to twelve, and free for children under six. Throughout the year special weekend demonstrations conducted by experts in eighteenth-century cooking are also held at the house.

### SPECIAL EVENTS

**May.** The Willowdale Gold Cup, Willowdale Steeple Chase, 101 East Street Road, Kennett Square; (610) 444–1582. Leaping horses, racing Jack Russell terriers, an antique carriage parade, vendor and food tents, and children's activities. General admission $8.00 in advance, $10.00 day of event; $5.00 for seniors and students; children twelve and under free. Proceeds benefit local environmental conservation efforts.

**September.** Chadds Ford Days, on the grounds of the Chadds Ford Historical Society, Rte. 100, ¼ mile north of Rte. 1; (610) 388–7376. A two-day open-air colonial fair sponsored by the Chadds Ford Historical Society. Colonial crafts for sale and show, local art, food, games, and live music.

## OTHER RECOMMENDED RESTAURANTS AND LODGINGS

### Chadds Ford

Brandywine River Hotel, Routes 1 and 100; (610) 388–1200. Located in the heart of the historic district, this upscale country hotel features fireside Jacuzzi suites. Rates range from $125 to $169.

The Gables, Route 1, (610) 388–7700. This restaurant's intriguingly innovative, globally inspired menu is a surprising contrast to its minimalist decor. Expensive. The bar is a popular local after-dinner hangout, too.

Pennsbury Inn Bed and Breakfast, 833 Baltimore Pike; (610) 388–1435. A beautiful historical home with a structure that spans the eighteenth and nineteenth centuries. Rates range from $140 to $450.

### Kennett Square

Half Moon Restaurant & Saloon, 108 West State Street; (610) 444–7232. Nineteen beers on tap and an adventurous menu that includes buffalo, elk, and venison, as well as traditional burgers. Mostly moderately priced.

### West Chester

Dilworthtown Inn, 1390 Old Wilmington Pike; (610) 399–1390. For classic American steaks and chops, you won't find better. Alfresco dining available. Live music on weekends. Expensive.

Faunbrook Victorian Bed & Breakfast, 699 West Rosedale Avenue; (610) 436–5788. Gorgeous ironwork, porches, fountains, gardens, walks, fireplaces, brass beds, fireside gourmet breakfast. Rates range from a low of $85 to a high of $115.

## FOR MORE INFORMATION

Chester County Tourist Bureau, 601 Westtown Road, Suite 170, West Chester, PA; (800) 228–9933 or (610) 344–6365; www.brandywinevalley.com.

Chester County Historical Society, 225 North High Street, West Chester, PA; (610) 692–4066.

# BETWEEN AND BEYOND

# Brandywine Valley, Delaware

## SEAT OF AN EMPIRE

### 1 NIGHT

*Glorious Gardens • Family Mansions • Riverfront Resurrection*
*Thoroughbred Racers*

Not to interfere with anybody's romantic aspirations, but in some cases, I think, separate vacations are best. Take, for instance, the Brandywine Valley. A great many people insist on combining the Pennsylvania and Delaware parts of this scenic and activity-packed area into one getaway. Admittedly, my initial impulse was to do the same thing. But, after visiting Wilmington and the surrounding area, I realized that there's enough to see and do here to make it a wonderful escape destination of its own.

This is the heart of the empire built and ruled by the powerful duPont family. It is where they built a company that was destined to become a world giant and family mansions and exquisite gardens that were destined to become historic landmarks.

But even in Wilmington, there was life before the duPonts. And there are still many colorful reminders of the city's pre-duPont past.

Of course, sight-seeing alone, even when the sights are as magnificent as these, does not a great escape make. Fortunately, Wilmington has a wealth of fun, games, and entertainment—ranging from golf to horse racing to opera—to keep sports aficionados, thrill seekers, and culture buffs happy, too.

Only 32 miles (forty to forty-five minutes driving time) south of Philadelphia on I–95, Wilmington is the nearest destination included in this book. But despite its proximity—or, perhaps, because of it—this small wonder right over the border is all too often underexplored and, as a result, underappreciated.

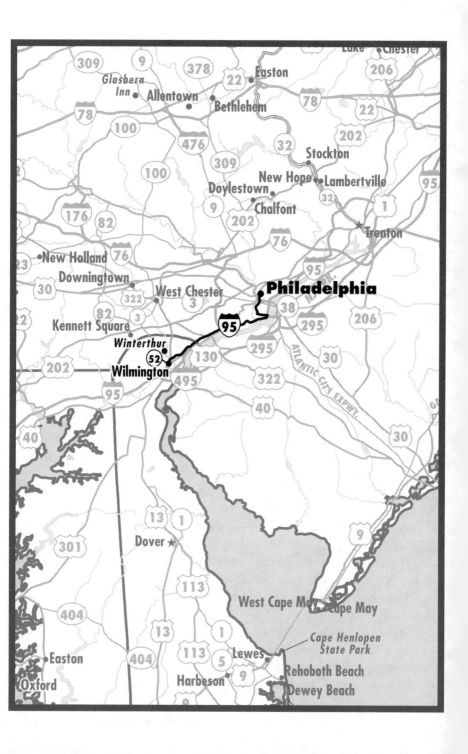

## BETWEEN AND BEYOND

## DAY 1

# Morning

For your first stop, get off I–95 at exit 7B, get onto Route 52 north and follow the signs 6 miles northwest of Wilmington to Winterthur.

One of the Brandywine Valley's premier attractions, **Winterthur** (800–888–3883 or 302–888–4600) is a magnificent country estate set on 965 acres where, almost half a century ago, Henry Francis duPont lived and indulged in his two greatest passions—horticulture and collecting early American decorative art. No matter what the season, duPont's sixty-acre garden of native and exotic plants will take your breath away. So will the period rooms and exhibition galleries that hold his collection of more than 89,000 objects, including Chippendale furniture, silver by Paul Revere, paintings by Gilbert Stuart, and a sixty-six-piece dinner service made for George Washington. General admission is $8.00 for adults, $6.00 for seniors and students, $4.00 for children (five to eleven), and free for children four and under. For an extra $5.00 per person, first-time visitors would do well to take the hour-long guided highlights tour. Open Monday–Saturday 9:00 A.M.–5:00 P.M., Sunday noon–5:00 P.M. Last tickets sold at 3:45 P.M.

# Afternoon

**LUNCH: Crossroads Cafe,** at Winterthur. One of the three very good dining options available at Winterthur, the Crossroads features individually themed food stations that offer everything from hearty hot stews and chilis to traditional deli fare to regional American down-home cookin'. The prices are inexpensive so you can splurge a little on dessert, which usually includes homemade mousses, pies, cobblers, gourmet crepes, and chewy cookies.

For some insight into Wilmington's pre-duPont days, head down to the riverfront to the **Kalmar Nyckel Shipyard and Museum,** 823 East Seventh Street; (302) 429–7447. Go east on Route 52 to I–95 south; get off at exit 6. Turn left onto Fourth Street and continue east under the railroad bridge to your first left-hand turn, which will be Swede's Landing Road; continue to the dead end at Seventh Street.

The newly constructed tall ship *Kalmar Nyckel* is a replica of the largest of the two Dutch warships that brought Delaware's first permanent settlers to the banks of the Christina River from Sweden in 1638. Crew members in period garb describe shipboard life in those early years. The shipyard and museum recall Wilmington's days as a major seventeenth-century shipbuilding center with exhibitions and live demonstrations. All attractions are open daily 10:00 A.M.–4:00 P.M. Sometimes the ship visits other cities and participates in tall ship races, so to be sure it's in town when you are, call first. Admission is $8.00 for adults, $6.00 for seniors, $4.00 for children seven to twelve.

Continue your tour of Wilmington's Swedish past with a visit to **Fort Christina** at the foot of Seventh Street adjacent to the shipyard; (302) 652–5629. You can read the history of the first Swedish settlers on brass plaques on the brick walls on either side of this historic park, then see The Rocks, the spot where the passengers of the *Kalmar Nyckel* disembarked in their new homeland. Some of their early log cabins remain as well. Nearby is **Old Swede's Church,** built in 1698, one of the oldest churches in America still used regularly for religious services. Famous and not-yet-famous artists from all over the country have painted the church, and many of their renditions are exhibited next door in **Hendrickson House.** Built in Pennsylvania in 1690 by settlers from the *Kalmar Nyckel* and relocated here in the 1950s, this old stone farmhouse also displays authentic furnishings and other artifacts from the period. A $2.00 admission covers all three sites. Open Monday–Saturday 10:00 A.M.–4:00 P.M.

Only blocks away from the waterfront, located in a Woolworth's Five & Ten from the 1940s, the **Delaware History Museum** (504 Market Street, 302–656–0637 or 302–655–7161) is as much fun on the inside as it looks on the outside. Three art deco galleries featuring changing interactive exhibits trace the history of Delaware through artifacts and relics such as costumes, toys, and decorative arts. Children will have a great time poking around in Grandma's Attic. A whimsical 9-foot-tall statue of George Washington makes sure you don't miss the gift shop, which offers a fine selection of Delaware handcrafted items. Open Tuesday–Friday noon–4:00 P.M., Saturday 10:00 A.M.–4:00 P.M. Free.

## *Evening*

**DINNER: Krazy Kat's,** Route 100 and Kirk Road at The Inn at Monchanin Village (about six miles northwest of Wilmington); (302) 888–2133 or (800) COWBIRD. From Wilmington take Route 141 north until it intersects with Route 100; go north on 100 to Kirk Road. To name a fine dining restaurant Krazy Kat's takes either a great sense of humor or a really good reason. The owners of this very, very hot spot have both. If the outrageous decor with leopard skin chairs and jaguars on the charger plates don't make you smile, the portraits of the goofy military-clad cats (and a few dogs) that adorn the peach-colored walls will. According to owners Dan and Nancy "Missy" Lickle, she a direct duPont descendant, the name came from her grandmother who used it as a term of affection when referring to a cat-adoring (and decidedly eccentric) tenant. Dinner entrees are priced mainly in the mid- to high-$20s, but the food is so superb and the setting so unique it's an experience not to miss. The menu changes regularly, but two standard favorites are Krazy Kat's Mixed Grille (with ostrich medallion, wild boar sausage, and a rack of lamb chop) and Jumbo Lump Crab Cakes and Shrimp Mousseline. Desserts . . . don't get me started.

For an after-dinner treat take in a show at the **Grand Opera House,** 818 North Market Street; (302) 658–7879 or (800) 37–GRAND. Located in a restored 1871 theater that once showcased the likes of "Buffalo" Bill Cody and John Philip Sousa, Delaware's center for the performing arts is now home to Opera-Delaware, the Delaware Symphony Orchestra, and the Russian Ballet of Delaware. Box office is open Monday–Friday 10:00 A.M.–5:00 P.M. or until 8:00 P.M. on performance evenings.

**LODGING: The Inn at Montchanin Village,** Route 100 and Kirk Road, Montchanin, DE; (302) 888–2133 or (800) COWBIRD. (For directions see Krazy Kat's.) The Lickles have transformed what was once a tiny nineteenth-century hamlet that was home to the workers at the duPont powder mills into an idyllic retreat that's close to all the city's attractions yet light years away from its busyness. A cluster of nine of the original stone, stucco, and wood buildings dating from 1840 to the 1900s has been painstakingly restored on the outside and updated on the inside to house thirty-seven guest units, each of which has been individually furnished with period pieces and reproductions. The independent spirit that makes Krazy Kat's so much fun is also very much in evidence here in the mixing of painted wooden wicker furniture with antiques and heirlooms. Room rates range from $150 to $170, suites from $180 to $375. A full breakfast at Krazy Kat's is included.

## DAY 2

## *Morning*

**BREAKFAST:** Krazy Kat's. Another chance to enjoy the decor and the marvelous food, this time at a breakfast as dainty or hearty as you like from a seasonal fruit plate to poached eggs Benedict.

To learn how and where the duPont legacy began, go 3 miles northwest of Wilmington via Routes 52 north to 100 north, then to 141 north and follow the signs to the **Hagley Museum** (302–658–2400). Situated on 240 acres of trees and flowering plants along the banks of the Brandywine River, this is where the duPont family built its first American home and started its business with a black powder mill. You can still visit the powder yards and Blacksmith Hill where working exhibits and live demonstrations colorfully illustrate nineteenth-century working and home life. To see how the other half lived, visit Eleutherian Mills, the palatial Georgian-style residence built in 1803 by E.I. duPont that now contains antiques and memorabilia of five generations of the duPont family. Open summer season (March 15–January 1) 9:30 A.M.–4:30 P.M., and winter weekends Monday–Sunday; winter weekdays there is a guided tour at 1:30 P.M. Admission is $9.75 for adults, $7.50 for seniors and students, $3.50 for children six to fourteen.

Adjacent to the Hagley Museum entrance is the **Delaware Toy & Miniature Museum** (302–427–8697). If this absolutely charming museum doesn't make you feel like a kid again, nothing will. More than one hundred eighteenth- to twentieth-century dollhouses, furnishings, dolls, trains, boats, and planes from Europe and America tempt the child (or grown-up collector) in you to come and play. Other miniatures in ivory, silver, and porcelain as well as a wonderful collection of more than 700 tiny vases dating as far back as 600 B.C. will dazzle you. Open Tuesday–Saturday 10:00 A.M.–4:00 P.M., Sunday noon–4:00 P.M. Admission is $5.00 for adults, $4.00 for seniors, $3.00 for children twelve and under. (Babes in arms are free.)

## Afternoon

**LUNCH: Buckley's Tavern,** 5812 Kennett Pike/Route 52, Centreville; (302) 656–9776. This rustic restaurant and bar in a tiny village 5 miles north of Wilmington has been a Brandywine Valley landmark since the 1950s. Housed in a former early-nineteenth-century residence, Buckley's decor is Colonial cozy and its moderately priced menu interesting, with handmade pizzas and freshly made sandwiches that include such surprises as Carolina pulled pork and smoked Cajun sausage with tomato, okra, and onions.

For year-round thoroughbred and harness racing, head for **Delaware Park Racetrack** on Delaware Park Boulevard in Wilmington; (302) 994–2521. To get there from Wilmington, take I–95 south to Exit 4B. Follow to second light and turn right onto Route 7 north. The entrance is 1½ miles on the left. From April–November you can enjoy live thoroughbred racing. Every day (and Tuesday through Sunday nights) throughout the year big screen televisions in Delaware Park's big theaters and even more comfortable Race Book lounge simulcast races from top tracks around the world. First daily post time is 12:45 P.M. Free admission and parking as well as a beautiful wooded picnic grove and dining options ranging from concession stand to elegant fare.

## Evening

**DINNER: Sienna,** 1616 Delaware Avenue; (302) 652–0653. If you were one of the many long-time fans of Philadelphia's wonderful La Truffe restaurant during its more than twenty-five-year run, you'll be pleased to know that owners Jeannine Mermet and Les Smith have not taken their talents far away. They have found a new home in Wilmington at this classy place offering a wide-ranging menu with Italian, French, Portuguese, Spanish, Israeli, Greek, and Moroccan roots. Moderate to expensive.

To return to Philadelphia, simply head north on I–95. The return trip should take less than one hour.

### THERE'S MORE

**Nemours Mansion and Gardens,** Rockland Road between Routes 141 and 202; (302) 651–6912. This Louis XVI-style chateau set on 300 acres of splendid gardens and trees belonged to Alfred I. duPont and houses antiques and art dating back to the fifteenth century. Open May–November, tours are offered every two hours 9:00 A.M.–3:00 P.M. Tuesday–Saturday; Sunday 11:00 A.M.–3:00 P.M. Visitors must be at least sixteen years of age. Admission is $10.

**Rockwood Museum,** 610 Shipley Road; (302) 761–4340. One of Wilmington's non-duPont mansions, this 1851 rural Gothic manor displays an impressive collection of American, English, and other European furnishings, costumes, and decorative arts dating from the 1600s to the 1800s. Open Tuesday–Saturday 11 A.M.–3:00 P.M. Admission $5.00 for adults, $4.00 for seniors, $1.00 for children. Guided tours are available for $1.00 extra.

**Delaware Art Museum,** 2301 Kentmere Parkway; (302) 571–9590. A permanent collection of works by leading nineteenth- and twentieth-century artists, including Winslow Homer, Thomas Eakins, Howard Pyle, and three generations of Wyeths; Pre-Raphaelite paintings and decorative arts. Open Tuesday, Thursday, Friday, and Saturday 9:00 A.M.–4:00 P.M.; Wednesday until 9:00 P.M.; Saturday and Sunday 10:00 A.M.–4:00 P.M. Admission is $5.00 for adults, $3.00 for seniors, $2.50 for students, free for children six and under. Every Wednesday evening from 5:30 to 9:00 is Art After Hours night with special programs and free admission.

**Delaware Center for the Contemporary Arts,** 103 East Sixteenth Street; (302) 656–6466. Changing exhibits of cutting-edge works using all media and multimedia. Open Monday–Friday 11:00 A.M.–5:00 P.M., Saturday 1:00–5:00 P.M. Admission is free.

**Delaware Museum of Natural History,** Route 52 (5 miles northwest of Wilmington between Greenville and Centreville); (302) 658–9111. Delaware's only dinosaurs and other exhibits take you back in time and around the globe to learn about the past, present, and future of native and exotic mammals, fish, and birds. Monday–Saturday 9:30 A.M.–4:30 P.M., Sunday noon–4:30.

**Delcastle Golf Club,** McKennan's Church Road; (302) 995–1990. Eighteen-hole par 72 public golf course in a country-club atmosphere. Adjacent are a driving range and facilities for tennis and miniature golf. Open seven days a week from daybreak until sunset. Greens fees are $19 weekdays, $14 for seniors, $13 for juniors; $24 Saturday and Sunday. Cart rental is $15 for one person, $25 for two.

**Brandywine Zoo,** 1001 North Park Drive, Brandywine Park; (302) 571–7747. A collection of about 150 animals from North and South America and temperate Asia ranges from river otters to Siberian tigers. Open daily year-round 10:00 A.M.–4:00 P.M. Admission is $3.00 for adults, $1.50 for seniors and children.

**Wilmington & Western Railroad,** Greenbank Station, Route 41; (302) 998–1930. Take a ride on an authentic turn-of-the-century steam train through the historic Red Clay Valley. For a lovely alfresco lunch, pack something yummy and take one of the regularly scheduled express trains to Mt. Cuba Picnic Grove. One-hour excursion tickets are $8.00 for adults, $7.00 for seniors, $5.00 for children two to twelve.

**First USA Riverfront Arts Center,** 800 South Madison Street; (888) 395–0005. Call for information on current exhibit. Scheduled shows include *Splendors of Meiji: Treasures of Imperial Japan* and the *History and Traditions of Scotland*.

## SPECIAL EVENTS

**July.** Delaware Handicap at Delaware Park Racetrack. The state's Grand Race of the Year, this more than century-old annual tradition features top horses and riders vying for a $500,000 purse.

**Labor Day weekend.** Annual Craft Festival at Winterthur. Held in association with the Pennsylvania Guild of Craftsmen, this two-day event features handmade jewelry, toys, stained glass, sculpture, furniture, wearable art, and other crafts created by more than 180 juried artisans from eleven states. Tickets are $8.00 per day in advance, $10.00 at the gate; children twelve and under are admitted free with an adult.

## OTHER RECOMMENDED RESTAURANTS AND LODGINGS

## *Wilmington*

Brandywine Brewing Company. 3801 Kennett Pike, Greenville Center; (302) 655–8000. Award-winning handcrafted microbrews and innovative menu touches, such as pumpkin cheddar ale soup, signature corn chowder, and Eastern Shore pizza with Maryland crab meat. Lunch and dinner prices are generally moderate.

PUFF, Rockland Road and Route 100; (302) 658–0100. The name is an acronym for "Pick Up Fine Foods." This highly regarded gourmet takeout establishment housed in an 1889 railroad station adjacent to the Inn at Montchanin Village offers great sandwiches, homemade a la carte items, and cookies called "Oh Gods" that are perfect for picnics.

Columbus Inn, 2216 Pennsylvania Avenue (Route 52); (302) 571–1492. When "Buffalo Bill" Cody and Annie Oakley ate here, black bean chili or the calypso spiced chicken breast stuffed with lobster, grilled corn, cabbage, and goat cheese probably weren't on the menu. What a shame. Moderate to expensive.

The Hop, 4542 Kirkwood Highway; (302) 633–1955. An inexpensive 1950s-style diner/restaurant that serves great homemade food, including a signature filet mignon sandwich and superbargain blue-plate specials, along with more than thirty soda fountain flavors.

Hotel du Pont, Eleventh and Market Streets; (800) 441–9019 or (302) 594–3100. Originally built in 1913, this historic 217-room hotel has recently undergone a $40 million renovation and, as a result, is more elegant than ever. Room rates range from $140 to $209 weekdays, to $239–$289 weekends. Special packages are also available. The hotel's Green Room fine dining restaurant has long been regarded as one of the Brandywine Valley's best.

### FOR MORE INFORMATION

Delaware Tourism Office; (800) 441–8846 or (302) 739–4271.

Greater Wilmington Convention & Visitors Bureau; (302) 652–4088; www.wilmcvb.org.

## BETWEEN AND BEYOND

*ESCAPE FOUR*

# Doylestown, Pennsylvania

## CULTURED PEARL

---
**1 NIGHT**
---

*Lakeside Serenity • Soaring Castles*
*Artistic Inspiration*

Doylestown has long been a hotbed of creativity. In addition to being the home of prolific author James A. Michener, renowned librettist Oscar Hammerstein II, and horticulturist W. Atlee Burpee, the unique beauty of this village situated directly in the heart of Bucks County has been a muse for generations of writers, sculptors, painters, and other artists.

And with its small-town charm and miles of carefully preserved natural splendor, it's no wonder. This is a place where one minute you can be marveling over the simple perfection of a wildflower and the next minute be awestruck by a thought-provoking piece of man-made art. It is a place where the day begins with the sweet sound of birdsong and ends with a stirring symphony.

There's an elegance and style here that is almost regal. In fact, one particularly inspired—and wealthy—local resident even built himself a kingdom of medieval-style castles (now superb museums) on a mile-long strip in the village.

Since its earliest days, when it was known as William Doyl's Tavern (after the local innkeeper who set up his business there in the early 1700s), Doylestown has graciously shared its abundance of cultural and natural wonders with visitors. Only about one hour north of Philadelphia, it is a quick escape that can have a long-lasting impact on both body and soul.

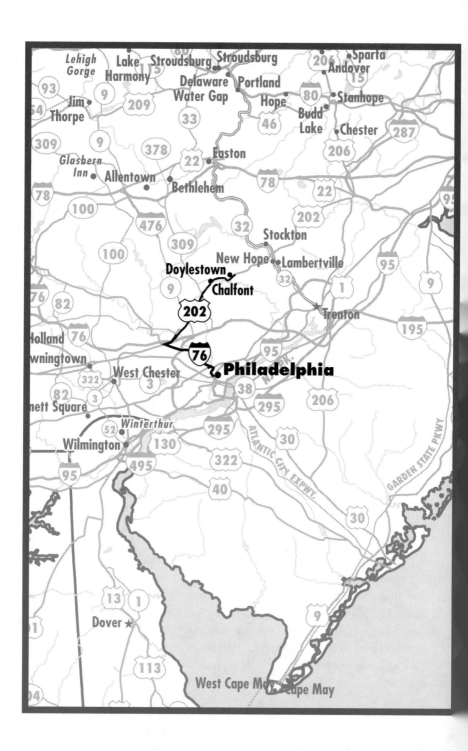

## DAY 1

*Morning*

From Philadelphia take the Schuylkill Expressway (I-76) west for 14 miles until you come to Route 23; take Route 23 west about 3 miles to Route 202. Take 202 east for about 18 miles straight into Doylestown. Driving time should be a little over 1½ hours.

In downtown Doylestown, make your first stop **Lilly's** (1 West Court Street; opposite the courthouse; 215–230–7883), a wonderful little gourmet takeout and catering establishment, for a memorable brown bag lunch. Owner Lilly Salvatore adds many thoughtful touches to her offerings, such as black bean salsa to a smoked turkey roll-up or horseradish mayo and roasted peppers to tender roast beef served on hand-sliced rye bread. Inexpensive. At night, Lilly's magically becomes a full-service white tablecloth bistro.

One of Doylestown's most illustrious and fascinating citizens was noted anthropologist, archeologist, historian, ceramist, writer, and collector Henry Chapman Mercer. A leader of the twentieth-century Arts and Crafts movement, his castlelike home, museums, and tile works are some of the area's most identifiable landmarks. To get to the stretch of Route 313 known as the **Mercer Mile,** follow Court Street about 5 miles to the first of Mercer's castles, **Fonthill Museum** (Route 313 and East Court Street; 215–348–9461). Unlike most structures, Mercer designed Fonthill from the inside out because, in addition to being his home, he intended it to house his vast collections of prints, decorative tiles, and other treasures gleaned from his travels around the world. Built entirely of hand-mixed concrete between 1908 and 1910, this dramatic structure now exhibits more than 900 of Mercer's personal treasures, has forty-four rooms, eighteen fireplaces, thirty-two stairwells, and 200 windows. Open year-round Monday–Saturday 10:00 A.M.–5:00 P.M., Sunday noon–5:00 P.M. Admission is $5.00 for adults, $4.50 for seniors, $1.50 for youths six to seventeen, free for children under six.

Right next door is Mercer's **Moravian Pottery & Tile Works** (130 Swamp Road, Route 313; 215–345–6722), where artisans still use original formulas and methods to handcraft magnificent decorative tiles and mosaics. From the time it was opened in 1912, this facility has produced tiles that adorn buildings throughout the United States (including the halls of the state Capitol) and around the world. Be sure to visit the adjacent **Moravian Tile Shop,** where the intricate works of art made on the premises are for sale. Open for self-guided tours daily year-round from 10:00 A.M.–4:45 P.M.

## Afternoon

**LUNCH:** Enjoy your lunch at one of the picnic tables situated in a grove of trees outside the Moravian Pottery & Tile Works.

The third castle along the Mercer Mile is aptly named the **Mercer Museum** (84 South Pine Street; 215–345–0210) and, like both of the other structures designed by this remarkable man, has an interesting story of its own. In 1897, Henry Mercer, always a collector of items that defined the everyday life of man through the ages, was searching in a junk dealer's barn when he came across a number of pre-1850 work-related implements that had been made obsolete by the Industrial Revolution. These items became the basis for a collection he called "The Tools of the Nation Maker," which grew to more than 50,000 antique objects representing sixty early American trades and Native American implements dating from 8,000 to 6,000 B.C. Open Monday–Saturday 10:00 A.M.–5:00 P.M., Tuesday until 9:00 P.M., Sunday from noon–5:00 P.M. Admission is $5.00 for adults, $4.50 for seniors, $1.50 for youths six and older, free for children under six.

If making—or drinking—wine is one of your favorite hobbies, take a ride out into the nearby countryside to **Peace Valley Winery** (300 Old Limekiln Road, Chalfont; 215–249–9058), where you can pick your own fruit or simply pick up a bottle of the winery's award-winning reds or whites. To get there, take Route 313 northwest to New Galena Road (Ginger Bread Square is on the corner). Turn left and go 2 miles to Old Limekiln Road. Turn right and go 1 mile to the twenty-acre vineyard where owner Susan Gross grows more than two dozen varieties of grapes. During harvest time (September to mid-October) you can pick your own blue (Fredonia) or white (Niagara) grapes for at-home winemaking. Susan also has a four-acre orchard of dwarf apple trees for making her—or your—spicy fall wines. Open Wednesday–Sunday noon–6:00 P.M. Hours are extended during harvest and Christmas seasons.

## Evening

**DINNER: Madam Butterfly,** 34 West State Street, Doylestown; (215) 345–4488. Back in downtown Doylestown, right off Main near the courthouse, you can enjoy the freshest sushi, sashimi, and other traditional Japanese delicacies. The authentically prepared food is wonderful, from the cracklingly crunchy tempuras to the tender-crisp hibachi stir-fries. Prices run the gamut from inexpensive to expensive, depending on how hungry you are and whether or not you prefer to order a la carte. The restaurant doesn't have a liquor license, so be sure to bring your own sake or other wine.

After dinner, check in with the **Bucks County Symphony Orchestra** (215–348–7321) to find out if they are having a concert tonight. These talented musicians, along with invited world-class guest soloists, have been bringing the classics to Bucks County for more than forty-five years. There are three subscription concerts in fall, winter (this is an afternoon concert), and spring, as well as various other events throughout the year. Most of the concerts take place at Central Bucks High School East, 2–3 miles southeast of Doylestown in the town of Buckingham. Ticket prices are $15 for adults, $12 for seniors, and free for children of all ages.

**LODGING: Inn at Fordhook Farm,** 105 New Britain Road, ½ mile from the center of Doylestown; (215) 345–1766. Take Court Street west to New Britain Road; turn right. There, surrounded by 200-year-old linden trees and nestled on 60-plus acres of woodlands and meadows, you'll find this jewel of an inn. Built in 1750 and restored and remodeled 200 years later, this former home of horticulturist and self-made businessman W. Atlee Burpee (founder of the seed company) is now an elegant getaway owned by his grandchildren Blanche Burpee Dohan and Jonathan and Carole Burpee. The inn's guest rooms are decorated with a mixture of English and American antiques and family mementos. Make special note of the living room fireplace inlaid with Henry Mercer's decorative tiles. Rates for rooms in the main house range from $100 to $135 per night weekdays, $150 weekends.

## DAY 2

## *Morning*

**BREAKFAST:** The Inn at Fordhook Farm. A full homemade breakfast is included with your room. Making the meal even more luxurious is the fact that you can savor it on heirloom china in the elegant dining room while admiring the view from the leaded bay windows.

Back to Peace Valley (see instructions for yesterday's trip to Peace Valley Winery, but instead of taking New Galena Road to Old Limekiln Road, turn left on Chapman Road) for a visit to the **Peace Valley Nature Center** (170 Chapman Road; 215–345–7860). Start at the Solar Building with its interesting displays of local wildlife and plants. There's a "please touch" section for

*The Mercer Museum.*

young ones, and you can pick up a map and schedules of guided nature walks. On this 300-acre protected property, you can find 14 miles of hiking trails through woods and fields filled with wildflowers, trees, butterflies, deer, and more than 250 species of birds. Open 9:00 A.M.–5:00 P.M. Tuesday–Sunday. The bird blinds and trails are open dawn 'til dusk.

Peace Valley Nature Center is actually part of 1,500-acre **Peace Valley Park,** where you'll find all-season water sports and activities tucked away in the wooded setting of **Lake Galena.** In season you can rent just about any kind of boat here, from paddle to sail. It is also a glorious spot for fishing and ice-skating. The park is open from dawn to dusk and there is no admission charge.

## *Afternoon*

**LUNCH: Ristorante Villa Capri,** 51 West Court Street; (215) 348–9596. An unassuming pizzeria in front, this restaurant has a back dining room reminiscent of the garden of a gracious Italian villa with white stucco walls, high arched leaded windows, imported wrought-iron work, and pink-toned marble. This generous taste of Italy also extends to the lunch menu, which features inexpensive hot and cold sandwiches, pizzas by the slice or pie, and moderately priced homemade specialties, such as spaghetti a la carbonara, cannoli Florentine, and eggplant rolatini.

Another famous Doylestown must-see is the **James A. Michener Art Museum** (138 Pine Street, across from the Mercer Museum; 215–340–9800). Housed in an 1884 former prison are exhibits that trace local art from Colonial times to the present, an outdoor sculpture garden and a 22-foot semicircular mural. Works of national and international scope are also exhibited on a changing basis. Open Tuesday–Friday 10:00 A.M.–4:30 P.M., Saturday and Sunday until 5:00 P.M. Admission is $5.00 for adults, $4.50 for seniors, $1.50 for students, and free for children under twelve.

Before you head back home, take a little time to stroll the historic streets of downtown Doylestown, with its beautifully maintained Colonial, Federal, and Victorian houses. The town also has some nice shops, including **Spirit Song** (17 West Court Street; 215–230–7311), a holistic gallery and shop featuring spirit-healing jewelry and art. Open Tuesday–Thursday noon–6:00 P.M., Friday and Saturday until 8:00 P.M., Sunday until 3:00 P.M. Tim and Robin Moyer sell their hand-carved Santas, birdhouses, pine mirrors, and other lovely furnishings at **Frog Pond Antiques** (70 West State Street; 215–348–3425), which is open Wednesday–Sunday noon–5:00 P.M.

To return to Philadelphia, follow Route 611 south all the way. The trip should take approximately one hour.

## THERE'S MORE

**National Shrine of Our Lady of Czestochowa,** 654 Ferry Road, Doylestown; (215) 345–0600. On exhibit at this Polish spiritual and pilgrimage center is a reproduction of a painting of the Virgin Mary that, according to legend, was created by St. Luke. Also on this 170-acre site is a church that can accommodate up to 1,800, and a smaller chapel with a seating capacity of 400. Open daily year-round, tours by request.

**Aldie Mansion,** 85 Old Dublin Pike, Doylestown; (215) 845–7020. This 1927 Tudor mansion was the home of William Mercer, brother of Henry and a talented sculptor in his own right. (He created all the fountains, benches, and wall plaques for the home's Italian garden.) In addition to being the headquarters for the Heritage Conservancy, this splendid old house also contains exhibits of works by local artists and craftsmen. Guided tours are available for an admission fee of $2.00. Call for days and hours.

## SPECIAL EVENTS

**July and August.** Brown Bag It With the Arts, Bucks County Courthouse Lawn, Doylestown; (215) 348–3913. Free music to eat lunch by every Wednesday at noon.

**July and August.** Free Concerts in the Park, Peace Valley Park, 230 Creek Road, New Britain; (215) 348–6114. Every Sunday.

**September.** Polish American Festival, National Shrine of Our Lady of Czestochowa, 645 Ferry Road, Doylestown; (215) 345–0600. Unlimited amusement rides as well as stage shows, polka party, arts and crafts, and lots of Polish and American delicacies (pierogies and hoagies do rhyme after all).

## OTHER RECOMMENDED RESTAURANTS AND LODGINGS

## *Doylestown*

B. Maxwell's Restaurant & Victorian Pub, 37 North Main Street; (215) 348–1027. Its proximity to the courthouse, clubby atmosphere, and all-American fare make this a favorite lunch spot of local lawyers and other movers and shakers. Menu prices range from inexpensive to moderate.

Black Walnut Cafe, 80 West State Street; (215) 348–0708. This popular bistro is a little bit country, a little bit modern, and totally warm and inviting. Entree prices on the imaginative dinner menu range from moderate to expensive.

Coffee & Cream, 6 East State Street; (215) 348–1111. The aroma of freshly roasted and ground coffee is intoxicating from the minute you walk in the door of this cute coffee/ice cream shop. Whether you take your brew hot or iced, make sure you also have a cookie, scone, or other freshly baked treat to wash it down.

Russell's, 96 West State Street; (215) 345–8746. Chef/owner Russell Palmer offers an innovative seasonal menu of "progressive continental cuisine" and an excellent wine cellar at this chic art-filled dining spot. You can dine outdoors if the weather permits and linger over an after-dinner drink at the intimate upstairs bar. Moderate to expensive.

Highland Farms, 70 East Road; (215) 340–1354. The views from this five-acre estate were said to have been the inspiration for some of the greatest hits written by its former owner, famed lyricist Oscar Hammerstein. In fact, each of the guest rooms in this eighteenth-century stone home is named for one of his musicals and contains lots of Hammerstein memorabilia as well as other classic antiques. A full country breakfast is included in the $135–$195 per night room rates.

Plumsteadville Inn, Route 611 and Stump Road, 4 miles north of Doylestown; (215) 766–7500. From its beginnings as a stagecoach stop in the mid-eighteenth century, this welcoming inn has been providing travelers with food, lodging, and boundless good cheer. Room rates begin at $95, full breakfast included. The inn also has a splendid country dining room that serves continental fare.

Sign of the Sorrel Horse, 4424 Easton Road; (215) 230–9999. During the Revolutionary War, this 1710 former gristmill supplied flour to General George Washington's troops and lodging to General Lafayette and his officers. Rooms range from $85 to $175, continental breakfast included. The inn also has a renowned fine dining restaurant.

Pine Tree Farm Bed and Breakfast, 2155 Lower State Road; (215) 348–0632. Fresh flowers, warm fires, and American Colonial antiques add extra charm to this 1730 Quaker farmhouse set amid sixteen acres of pine trees. There's a swimming pool, too. Rates range from $160 to $180 and include full breakfast.

## FOR MORE INFORMATION

Bucks County Conference and Visitors Bureau, (215) 345–4552; www.buckscountycvb.com.

Central Bucks Chamber of Commerce; (215) 348–3913.

# Lancaster County, Pennsylvania

## BACK ROADS THROUGH LONG AGO

### 2 NIGHTS

*Cultural Crossroads • Traditional Crafts • Farm Food*

Along Route 30, the main road that goes straight through the heart of Lancaster, you'll see lots of neon lights, a Pennsylvania Dutch–themed amusement park, just about every outlet store you can think of, and horse-drawn buggies filled with waving tourists. This Lancaster often surprises visitors who have come to experience a different culture, a more basic way of life, and a quieter getaway. However, you can still find the Lancaster you seek, tucked away on green and rolling back roads and in small towns with names like Mt. Joy, Lititz, Intercourse, and Bird-in-Hand that virtually radiate from the relative metropolis called Lancaster City.

If you choose to take these back roads, you will be immersed in another culture—actually, a variety of cultures. All of them have their roots in Switzerland where, in 1525, a group of Christians known as Mennonites, after their leader Menno Simons, broke away from the state church because of basic differences in their interpretation of Biblical teachings. In the late 1600s, a Swiss Mennonite named Jakob Ammann and his followers broke away and formed a separate sect, the Amish.

Persecuted in Europe, both groups sought religious freedom in Pennsylvania. And here they have peacefully coexisted ever since. But don't expect Lancaster to be a melting pot. Each group has retained its own strong and distinctive beliefs and customs (even though a third group called the Amish

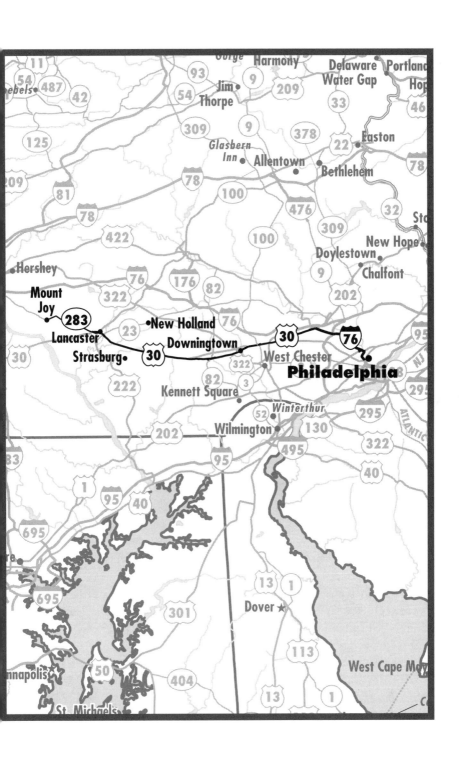

Mennonites has incorporated some of the teachings and practices of both). These differences give Lancaster County a character and flavor unlike any other place.

## DAY 1

## *Morning*

There are quicker ways to get to Lancaster County, which is about 1½ hours west of Philadelphia, but none so beautiful as via Route 30 with its gently rolling hills and cow-dotted farms. From Philadelphia, take the Schuylkill Expressway (I–76) to the King of Prussia/Route 202 south exit; go south on 202 to Route 30 west. Follow Route 30 west about 50 miles right into Lancaster.

Before you begin to explore the back roads of today's Lancaster County, a visit to the **Landis Valley Museum** (717–569–0401) will give you some insight into traditional Pennsylvania German (or Deutsch) life and culture. To get there, continue on Route 30 west until it intersects with Route 272 (Oregon Pike); take 272 north for about 2½ miles until you come to Landis Valley Road. The largest Pennsylvania German folk museum in the state, this open-air complex features eighteen historic buildings, tens of thousands of artifacts, costumed interpreters, working craftspeople, and living farmsteads. Guided tours are available, or you can simply stroll around at your leisure. There's also a great museum shop that specializes in handcrafted items. Open March–December, Monday–Saturday 9:00 A.M.–5:00 P.M., Sunday noon–5:00 P.M. Admission is $7.00 for adults, $6.50 for seniors, $5.00 for children six to twelve, and $19.00 for families.

## *Afternoon*

**LUNCH: J-M's Bistro & Pub,** 300 West James Street, Lancaster; (717) 392–5656. Take Route 30 east back into Lancaster and head to this contemporary lunch and dinner spot with an afternoon menu featuring some jazzy New Orleans-style sandwiches (including muffalettas and po'-boys) and an upscale roast beef sandwich starring chateaubriand. Light fare, too. Moderately priced lunches, moderate to expensive dinners.

To explore the back roads you could pick up a free map at the **Mennonite Information Center** (2209 Millstream Road, right off of Route 30 in

Lancaster; 717–299–0954). But it's a lot more fun, interesting, and educational to hire one of the center's guides to "backseat-drive" you in your own car to those off-the-beaten-tourist-path areas and sites.

As we rode past fruit orchards; fields of corn, tobacco and alfalfa; working windmills and waterwheels and one-room schoolhouses, our guide, a gentle Amish-Mennonite lady named Ada Fisher, described the customs, traditions, and daily routines that have defined the lives of the area's "plain people." She also asked us what our interests were so she could individualize our tour.

Whatever you do, request a stop at **Mascot Roller Mills** to see a 1760 mill that is still used to grind corn for the local Amish community (open weekdays and Saturday May–October, 9:00 A.M.–4:00 P.M. for free tours). As farmland has become increasingly scarce and expensive in Lancaster County, a number of the locals have become professional craftspeople and opened up workrooms and small businesses in the basements and barns of their homes. If you're interested, your guide will show you where to find the best furniture, toys, quilts, "quillows" (an ingenious combination quilt/pillow), and other beautiful handmade items. Then, of course, there are the multitude of roadside farm stands selling everything from fresh and pickled produce, to homemade root beer, to a mind-boggling array of baked goods.

Be sure to jot down the names and locations of any villages or shops you would like to revisit; it's easy to get confused when you're on your own. Remember, too, that almost all of the Amish-run businesses are closed on Sundays. Guided tours from the Mennonite Information Center are available Monday through Saturday and cost $7.00 for a setup fee plus $9.50 per hour (minimum two hours) for your guide. It is important to keep in mind that even the Amish who own businesses are very private people and that their faith does not permit them to be photographed.

## Late Afternoon/Evening

With all this wide open space and clean air, the sunsets are truly something to see, especially from the vantage point of a hot air balloon. The **U.S. Hot Air Balloon Team** (800–76–FLY–US) offers morning (during first two hours of daylight) and late afternoon (during last two hours of daylight) flights 365 days a year—weather permitting, of course. One of the most convenient departure points is at Rockvale Square (Routes 30 and 896). Go early and you can help the crew inflate your balloon and/or get some terrific preflight photos. $95 per half hour, $150 per hour.

**DINNER: East of Eden Pub,** 680 Millcross Road, extension of Eden Road; (717) 299–0159. For dinner and a good night's rest (tomorrow is an early day), take Route 30 east to Route 23 east toward New Holland. In less than 1 mile turn right onto Eden Road (at the firehouse) and, in a little more than ½ mile you'll come to a bridge. Right across the bridge is this wonderful little restaurant that specializes in Old World Austrian and German cooking. Be sure to try the sauerbraten, one of the schnitzel (veal) dishes, the spaetzle, or the Austrian bauernschmaus (roast pork, smoked pork, bratwurst, and smoked sausage with bread dumpling and sauerkraut). Mostly moderate prices. If the weather is nice, enjoy your meal in the riverside Biergarten.

**LODGING: Gardens of Eden,** 1894 Eden Road, Lancaster; (717) 393–5179. The name of this bed-and-breakfast would be just as appropriate even if it wasn't located on Eden Road. To get there from the pub, cross back over the bridge, then take a left onto the lane at the B&B sign and park below the stone wall. Situated on 3½ acres on the Conestoga River, the inn's lovingly landscaped exterior and antique, folk art and family heirloom-furnished interior make for a truly romantic setting. As soon as you meet innkeepers Bill and Marilyn Ebel, a historian/naturalist and floral designer, respectively, you can see that they have put a great deal of themselves into their home. In addition to three guest rooms in the 1867 main house, there is also a two-story cottage (actually a restored summer kitchen) on the grounds. Room rates range from $95 to $110 April–November; $85–$95 December–March. The cottage is $130 per night year-round. When you make your reservation at the Gardens of Eden, you can also ask the Ebels to arrange for a Dutch Country Tour with a guide from the Mennonite Center and/or a dinner at an Amish home (available on selected Saturday nights only).

## DAY 2

## *Morning*

If you are visiting the area on a Tuesday, Friday, or Saturday, rise and shine early so you can rub elbows with the locals and get the freshest goodies at the **Central Market** (right off of Penn Square; 717–291–4723) located right in the heart of Lancaster City. One of the oldest publicly owned farmers markets in the nation, Central Market has been a bustling center of commerce for local purveyors of produce, meats, cheeses, baked goods, and other foodstuffs since the 1730s. Open Tuesday and Friday 6:00 A.M.–4:00 P.M., Saturday 6 A.M.–

2 P.M. Have an eye-opening cup of cappuccino (yes, cappuccino) and a just-baked sweet, but don't fill up too much because there's a gourmet meal waiting for you back at your bed-and-breakfast.

**BREAKFAST:** Gardens of Eden. In her studio Marilyn Ebel uses her own home-grown herbs and flowers to make beautiful decorative items. She also uses many of them to create culinary works of art (such as a lovely lavender syrup for pancakes) in her kitchen. Breakfast here is a hearty affair that usually includes fresh fruit and homemade muesli, an egg dish or other entree, and oven-fresh muffins or breads. In nice weather you can eat out on the screened-in porch overlooking the back garden.

And, speaking of gardens, be sure to ask Bill for the grand tour of the ones that surround the inn. In spring and summer the Ebels' gardens are a profusion of colors and heady aromas from more than one hundred kinds of flowers, plants, trees, and shrubs, making this place a paradise, not only for guests, but for the more than sixty species of birds and other wildlife that frequently visit. And, if you can't resist the lure of the adjacent river, the Ebels offer their guests the use of a canoe and rowboat.

If you equate Lancaster solely with plain people, you might be surprised by some of the colorful, and sometimes even funky, local folk art and carved furnishings on display at the **Heritage Center Museum** (13 West King Street; 717–299–6440), a complex of five historic buildings in downtown Lancaster. Open April–December Tuesday–Saturday from 10:00 A.M.–5:00 P.M. Free.

## *Afternoon*

Now it's on to more backroad adventures in two charming towns by the names of Bird-in-Hand and Intercourse. Head east on Route 30 until you get to Route 340 (also called Old Philadelphia Pike). On Route 340 just ½ mile east of Route 30 is a must-stop for any aficionado of the fat, hard, salty twists we think of as Pennsylvania Dutch pretzels. Since 1888 Anderson has been a major player in the pretzel industry and at the **Anderson Pretzel Factory** (2060 Old Philadelphia Pike; 717–299–2321) you can watch from an overhead catwalk as your favorite snack food goes from dough to any of a wide variety of sizes, shapes, and flavors. If the free sample at the end of the tour only whets your appetite, you can stock up at the adjacent retail store. Open for self-guided tours Monday–Friday 8:30 A.M.–4:00 P.M. The retail store is open Monday–Friday 8:30 A.M.–5:00 P.M. year-round, and on Saturday 8:30 A.M.–3:00 P.M. April–December.

**LUNCH: Stoltzfus Farm Restaurant,** Route 772, Intercourse; (717) 768–8156. About 10 miles east on Route 340 you'll come to the village of Intercourse (you'll pass right through Bird-in-Hand along the way, but don't worry, you'll be back). If you would like to hazard any theories on how this area got its name, remember you're in Amish country. Actually, the name is a reference to the fact that the village sits at the intersection, or intercourse, of two famous old highways, the King's Highway (now Route 340) and New-port Road (now Route 772). For a true taste of Pennsylvania Dutch cooking, go 1 block east on 772 to Stoltzfus Farm Restaurant, which serves honest country fare in the Amish farm homestead where owner Amos Stoltzfus grew up. The family-style meals (priced at $12.95 for adults, $6.50 for children four to ten) include such local favorites as homemade sausage, chicken and ham loaf, chow chow, apple butter, pepper cabbage, and other traditional "sweets and sours." Of course, there are also lots of freshly baked desserts—don't miss the shoo-fly pie. If you like the homemade sausage, you can buy some to take home at the family's own butcher shop right across the street in Cross Keys Village Center. Closed December–March.

The **People's Place** (3513 Old Philadelphia Pike, Route 340, Inter-course; 800–390–8436 or 717–768–7101) is a complex of galleries, museums, and shops with answers to many of the commonly asked questions about Amish and Mennonite beliefs and practices. (Open Monday–Saturday 9:30 A.M.–5:00 P.M., June–August until 8:00 P.M.). One of its most popular features is the **People's Place Quilt Museum,** where creators, collectors, and admir-ers can check out the beautiful collection of pre-1940 quilts. Admission is $4.00 for adults, free for children. Downstairs at the **Museum Shoppe,** you'll find creations from more than 300 local crafters as well as an outstanding array of quilting fabrics, traditional and original patterns, and books. Open Mon-day–Saturday 9:00 A.M.–8:00 P.M. (November–May until 5:00 P.M.).

No visit to Lancaster County is complete without a cone, sundae, or shake from **Lapp Valley Farms Ice Cream.** If you don't have time to visit the actual farm (located in nearby New Holland), there's a Lapp Valley Farms shop at **Kitchen Kettle Village** (3529 Old Philadelphia Pike; 800–732–3538 or 717–768–8261) where you can indulge in any of their twenty incredible flavors.

Legend has it that the name **Bird-in-Hand** originated when two survey-ors laying out the Old Philadelphia Pike were deciding whether they would spend the night there or go on to Lancaster. "A bird in the hand is worth two in the bush," one supposedly said to the other. Whatever the derivation of its

*A local man and his son drive the back roads of Lancaster County.*

name, this picturesque village (about 3 miles west of Intercourse on Route 340) is renowned for its beautiful scenery. Another claim to fame is the **Bird-in-Hand Bake Shop** (542 Gibbons Road; 800–340–8558 or 717–656–7947). This family-owned and operated bakery is a little bit out of the way (Route 340 to Beechwood Road, right onto Gibbons Road, next to the little red schoolhouse), but the shoo-fly pies are the best, the cinnamon rolls irresistible, and the "whoopie pies" (two big moist cake-cookies sandwiched with thick white frosting) are the genuine article.

If you've been wondering how it feels to ride in the Amish family carriages you've been sharing the roads with throughout the county, take the twenty-five-minute, 2-mile tour offered by **Abe's Buggy Rides** (Route 340, ½ mile west of Bird-in-Hand; 717–392–1794). One of the oldest and most popular companies of its kind in the area, Abe's really does give you a unique backroads experience. Open year-round, closed Sunday. $10.00 adults, $5.00 children twelve and under.

**DINNER: Alois,** 102 North Market Street, Mt. Joy; (717) 653–2056. It's about 12 miles from Lancaster to Mt. Joy taking Route 30 west to where it intersects with Route 283; then 283 west to Route 230. Go west on 230 to where it becomes Main Street in Mt. Joy. One block off Main Street at 102 North Market Street you'll see a former brewery and Victorian hotel called Bube's. Inside are two beer-related museums, an art gallery, and three totally distinctive, absolutely wonderful restaurants. One of these is Alois, a truly romantic, fine-dining spot with hand-stenciled walls and ceilings, imaginative turn-of-the-century decor, and small intimate dining rooms. Chef Ophelia Horn, who has cooked for presidents and other heads of state, matches the elegance of the restaurant with a luxurious seven-course prix fixe feast, including cocktails, appetizers, desserts, and complementary wines, that goes on for at least 2½ hours. Incredibly, the price for the whole experience is only $26 per person (not including tax and gratuity). After dinner, ask for a tour of the complex— it's an evening's entertainment all by itself. Alois is open for dinner Thursday–Saturday.

**LODGING:** Gardens of Eden.

# DAY 3

## Morning

**BREAKFAST:** Gardens of Eden.

For railroad enthusiasts, the little village of Strasburg is a must-see. To get there, pick up Route 222 in Lancaster and drive south for 5 miles until you reach Route 741; take 741 east for 4 miles into Strasburg. Before you begin your excursion into railroading past and present, pick up a walking tour map of the town's historic district available at many of the shops or the information center located at Historic Strasburg Inn (One Historic Drive/Route 896; 717–687–7922) and take note of the many architecturally diverse eighteenth- and nineteenth-century log, brick, and stone houses and storefronts on its lovely tree-lined streets. Make sure you stop at **Eldreth Pottery** (246 North Decatur Street at Route 896; 717–687–8445) where you'll find salt-glazed pottery still being handcrafted and fired by a 400–500-year-old German process.

The first stop on your Strasburg railroading tour should be the **Railroad Museum of Pennsylvania** (Route 741 east of town; 717–687–8628). Colorful exhibits and illustrations follow the development of the railroad industry from the earliest steam locomotives to mid-twentieth-century technology. Open Monday–Saturday 9:00 A.M.–5:00 P.M., Sunday noon–5:00 P.M. (Closed Monday from November–April). Admission is $6.00 for adults, $5.00 for seniors, $4.00 for youths six to seventeen, free for children under six. If you're a collector of railroad and transportation memorabilia, go ¼ mile west of the Railroad Museum to **Depot Attic at Strasburg** (209 Gap Road, Route 741; 717–687–9300) where you'll find a large collection of authentic artifacts and books.

On a smaller but no less impressive scale is the **National Toy Train Museum** (Paradise Lane just north of Route 741; 717–687–8976), with five huge operating layouts and hundreds of locomotives and cars dating from the turn of the century to the present. Open 10:00 A.M.–5:00 P.M. weekends in April, November, and December; daily May 1–October 31. Admission is $3.00 for adults, $1.50 for children.

The main attraction here is the **Strasburg Rail Road** (Route 741; 717–687–7522), where an authentic turn-of-the-century steam train will take you for a narrated forty-five-minute ride through the countryside and back in time. At the 1882 Victorian station, passengers can purchase tickets to ride in the plush interior parlor car (called Marian), the open-air observation car, or the beautifully restored standard wooden coaches. Train rides are available pretty much year-round and run every hour daily from March 30 to October 30. Fares start from $8.00 for adults, $4.00 for children three to eleven, and free for babies through age two. Reserved seats (when available) are $1.00 extra. Parlor car Marian and dining car seats are additional.

**LUNCH: Lee E. Brenner Dining Car.** Add an extra dollar to your fare and you can ride in this restored wooden dining coach and order a lovely lunch from the inexpensive to moderately priced menu. Try the homemade chicken corn soup (a local specialty), and a sandwich, chicken salad platter, or chicken Caesar salad. A $3.99 children's menu features the ever-popular hot dog or peanut butter and jelly. You'll think you're in Paradise . . . Paradise, Lancaster County, that is, which is where you will be before the train turns around for the return trip to Strasburg. Lunch in the Lee E. Brenner is available on all regularly scheduled hourly trains from March–December. An elegant—and more expensive—dinner menu is also available seasonally.

For your return trip to Philadelphia, take Route 896 north about 3 miles to Route 30. Retrace your trail home going east on Route 30 until you reach the Schuylkill Expressway (I–76). The entire trip should take about 1½ hours.

### THERE'S MORE

**Covered Bridges.** At one time there were 1,500 of them in Pennsylvania. Today 219 of them remain, 28 of which are located in Lancaster County. The Pennsylvania Dutch Convention and Visitors Bureau (800–PA–DUTCH) offers a free Map and Visitors Guide to the area which gives directions to all the county's covered bridges.

**DeMuth House & Tobacco Shop,** 120 East King Street, Lancaster City; (717) 299–9940. If you're a fan of early twentieth-century American modernist Charles DeMuth, you won't want to miss the twenty-five original drawings and paintings displayed in his home. The building also houses the nation's oldest tobacco shop (circa 1770). Open Tuesday–Friday 10:00 A.M.–4:00 P.M., Sundays 1:00–4:00 P.M. Closed January. Free.

**Lancaster Museum of Art,** 135 North Lime Street, Lancaster City; (717) 394–3497. A contemporary art gallery with a global perspective. Open Monday–Saturday 10:00 A.M.–4:00 P.M., Sunday noon–4:00 P.M. Free.

**Fulton Opera House,** 12 North Prince Street (corner of Prince and King Streets), Lancaster City; (717) 394–7133. Built in 1852 and named after inventor Robert Fulton (who was born in nearby Quarryville), this magnificently restored Victorian structure is the nation's oldest theater in continuous operation. In the past George M. Cohan, Sarah Bernhardt, and Al Jolson played here. Today it is home to the Lancaster Symphony Orchestra, Fulton Academy Theatre, and the Lancaster Opera Company.

**Wheatland,** Route 23, 1120 Marietta Avenue, Lancaster City; (717) 392–8721. Built in 1828, this carefully restored example of Federal architecture was the home of James Buchanan, fifteenth president of the United States. Open seven days, April–November 10:00 A.M.–4:00 P.M. Admission: adults $5.50, seniors $4.50; youth twelve and up, $3.50; children six to eleven, $1.75.

**Hands-on House,** 2380 Kissel Hill Road just off of Oregon Pike (Route 272), Lancaster City (next to the Landis Valley Museum); (717) 569–KIDS. Otherwise known as the Children's Museum of Lancaster, this fun spot features eight play-and-learn areas including a corner grocery, a factory, a farm, and a spaceship designed for youngsters from ages two to ten and their parents to explore together. Open all year. Hours vary by day and season. Admission is $4.00 for children and adults.

**Dutch Wonderland,** 2249 Route 30 east, 4 miles east of Lancaster; (717) 291–1888. A family amusement park with rides, shows, and activities for all ages. Open June–August and selected days in April, May, September, and October. General admission (ages six to fifty-nine), $19.95; toddlers and seniors, $14.95.

**Wilton Armetale Store,** Plumb and Square Streets, 1 block south of Route 230, Mt. Joy; (717) 653–5595. The giftware, serveware, and accessories sold at this factory-direct store are made from a special alloy of ten different metals developed by the Wilton Company and handcrafted in its adjacent manufacturing complex. Open Monday–Saturday 9:30 A.M.–5:30 P.M.

## SPECIAL EVENTS

**March or April.** Annual Quilters' Heritage Celebration, Holiday Inn Lancaster Host Resort, 2300 Lincoln Highway East, Lancaster; (717) 854–9323. Dazzling displays of award-winning quilts from all over the United States attract quilt aficionados from over a dozen foreign countries.

**May.** Annual Rhubarb Festival, Kitchen Kettle Village, Route 340, Intercourse; (800) 732–3538. Celebrate spring and pay homage to this noble plant and food source at a fun-filled festival featuring food, music, family festivities, and games—all centered around rhubarb.

**July.** Annual Pennsylvania State Craft Show, Franklin and Marshall College Alumni Sports and Fitness Center, 929 Harrisburg Pike, Lancaster; (717) 579–5997. More than 250 juried members of the Pennsylvania Guild of Craftsmen offer exhibits and demonstrations during this three-day event that has been a tradition for more than fifty years.

### OTHER RECOMMENDED RESTAURANTS AND LODGINGS

## Lancaster

Kreider Dairy Farms Family Restaurant, Centerville Road and Columbia Avenue; (717) 393–3410. An inexpensive fun family restaurant known for its hearty home cooking and luscious homemade ice cream.

Willow Valley Restaurant, 2416 Willow Street Pike, 3 miles south of Lancaster on Route 222; (800) 444–1714 or (717) 464–2711. Smorgasbord-style meals featuring meats fresh from their own butcher shop, homemade soups, and excellent desserts. The country fried chicken is a classic. Moderate.

## Mt. Joy

Groff's Farm Restaurant, 650 Pinkerton Road; (717) 653–2048. Upscale Pennsylvania Dutch cooking has earned this restaurant national acclaim. You can order a la carte or family style. Moderate–expensive.

Rocky Acre Farm Bed and Breakfast, 1020 Pinkerton Road; (717) 653–4449. Kid-friendly 200-year-old stone farmhouse with generous size rooms, pettable animals, and lots of outdoor activities for families. Hearty farmer's breakfast included. Rates range from $75 per couple ($85 with children) for a room to $149 for an apartment.

## Strasburg

Iron Horse Inn, 135 East Main Street; (717) 687–6362. The sign outside the door says NO DYSPEPTICS ALLOWED. So bring a good appetite and sense of humor when you visit this rustic-on-the-outside, casually elegant-on-the-inside spot for lunch or dinner. Moderate to expensive.

Strasburg Country Store & Creamery, 1 West Main Street, Centre Square; (717) 687–0766. From the moment you step inside, you can smell the waffles that are constantly being baked for cones and bowls to hold the store's fabulous homemade ice cream.

Historic Strasburg Inn, Historic Drive, Route 896; (800) 872–0201 or (717) 687–7691. Colonial hospitality in a country setting with a long list of amenities including heated swimming pool, Jacuzzi, game room, and fitness center. Rates range from $79 to $149.

Limestone Inn Bed and Breakfast, 33 East Main Street; (800) 278–8392 or (717) 687–8392. The innkeepers, Richard and Denise Walker, are charming. And their 200-plus-year-old home with six guest rooms is a reflection of their personalities. Full breakfast is included. Rates range from $75 to $105 per night.

Red Caboose Lodge, Route 741 east; (717) 687–7522. Real railroad cabooses have been converted into motel rooms for couples and families. Prices vary by type of caboose, time of week, and time of year.

## FOR MORE INFORMATION

Pennsylvania Dutch Convention and Visitors Bureau; (800) 324–1518 or (717) 299–8901; www.padutch.com.

Downtown Lancaster Information Center, South Queen and Vine Streets. A convenient spot to pick up brochures and maps.

# BETWEEN AND BEYOND

# Harrisburg and Hershey, Pennsylvania

## STATE CAPITAL, WORLD CAPITAL

### 2 NIGHTS

*Handshakes • Kisses • Skating Bears • Senators at Bat*

Only 13 miles apart in Central Pennsylvania lie two capitals—one built on handshakes, the other on kisses. On weekdays, Harrisburg is a sea of suits bustling to and from meetings and sessions where laws are hammered out and enacted through processes that can run the gamut from filibuster to negotiation. In Hershey, the atmosphere seems much more laid-back, but the chocolate perfume that fills the air is a sweet reminder that this town is hard at work producing confections for the world.

As industrious as both these capitals are, they know how to play as hard as they work. No matter what time of year you go, there's never a lack of fun, whether your idea of a good time is riverside recreation, sky-high amusement rides, or sports on the green, diamond, or rink. You can also have some truly painless learning experiences as you follow a law from proposal to enactment and see the chocolate-making process from the perspective of a cocoa bean.

This is a great family escape, especially in these hectic times when everyone seems to be on a different schedule and time together is at a premium. And, who knows, the kids might be so moved by this family bonding experience that they may shower you with kisses even sweeter than those that come in the silver foil wrappers.

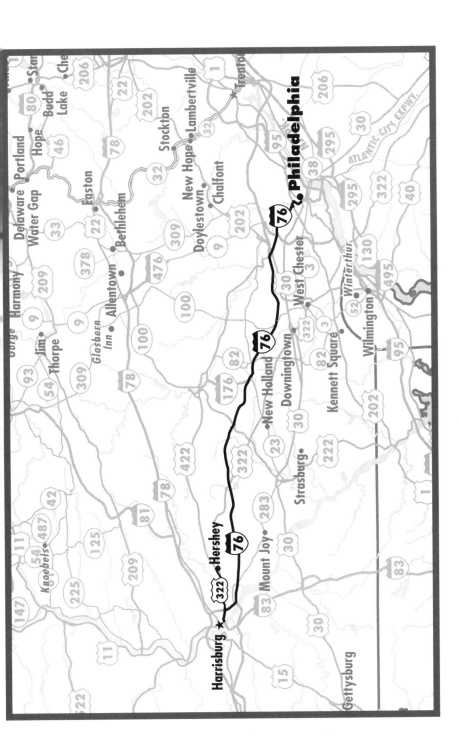

# BETWEEN AND BEYOND

## DAY 1

## *Morning*

**Harrisburg** is nearly two hours due west of Philadelphia. To get there, take the Schuylkill Expressway (I–76) west to the Pennsylvania Turnpike. You'll be on the Turnpike for about 81 miles when you'll come to I–283. Go north on 283, then north again on I–83 for a total of about 6 miles. Then go west on Route 22 for about 3 miles into Harrisburg.

You can't miss the **State Capitol Building** (800–868–7672); it's the magnificent Italian Renaissance-style structure on top of the hill. This is a must-visit site not only because of its significance as Pennsylvania's seat of government, but also because it is one of the most awe-inspiring structures in the state, with its soaring 272-foot-high vaulted domes modeled after St. Peter's Basilica in Rome and its sweeping staircase inspired by the one at the Paris Opera. At its dedication in 1906, President Theodore Roosevelt called it "the handsomest building I ever saw." There are also splendid collections of art and sculpture, including dramatic wall murals and ceramic tiles created by Henry Mercer of Doylestown depicting Pennsylvania history and significant symbols. Free forty-minute guided and self-guided tours encompassing the rotunda, senate, house, and supreme court are available every half-hour Monday–Friday, 8:30 A.M.–4:00 P.M., Saturday and Sunday at 9:00 and 11:00 A.M., 1:00 and 3:00 P.M. only. After the tour, be sure to stop by the **Capitol Welcome Center**, a worthy destination on its own with eighteen interactive audio-visual exhibits on the history of Pennsylvania and the operation of its state government.

## *Afternoon*

**LUNCH: Broad Street Market,** Third and Verbeke Streets in the downtown area; (717) 236–7923. From Tuesday through Saturday, you can join the locals for lunch at any one of the ethnic and eclectic food establishments housed in the two historic buildings that make up this complex. You'll find everything from Jamaican curried goat to Vietnamese soup, and from vegetarian and vegan specialties to a Pacific Rim cheeseburger! Prices are inexpensive, especially for a culinary trip around the world. On summer afternoons, there are free lunchtime music concerts at the market, too. Open Tuesday and Wednesday 9:00 A.M.–3:00 P.M., Thursday and Friday 7:00 A.M.–6:00 P.M., Saturday until 4:00 P.M.

# BETWEEN AND BEYOND

With four floors of exhibits and activities, the **State Museum of Pennsylvania** (Third and North Streets across the street from the capitol building; 717–787–4978) traces the state's history and heritage, literally from the earth's beginning to the present, through archeological artifacts, minerals, art, animal dioramas, and industrial and technological innovations. It has a wonderful planetarium, too. Open Tuesday–Saturday 9:00 A.M.–5:00 P.M., Sunday noon–5:00 P.M. Free.

In the spring, summer, and fall, the place to be on a beautiful afternoon is **City Island,** Harrisburg's playground located just offshore (1,000 yards) from the downtown area. You can get there by car over the Market Street Bridge or by foot or bike over the Walnut Street Bridge. Until 1987, this island in the Susquehanna River was merely sixty-three blighted acres of wasteland. Now it is a vibrant and growing recreation area with old-fashioned amusements, water sports, quaint shops, and fun-food concessions. Try the eighteen holes on the elaborately landscaped mini golf course at **Water Golf** (717–232–8533; open seven days a week from April–October and on weekends March, November, and December. Prices are $4.50 for adults, $3.50 for seniors and children five to twelve, free for children four and under).

At **Riverside Stadium** the **Harrisburg Senators** Class AA minor league baseball team (717–231–4444) plays from April to September. Box seats are $8.00, reserved seats are $6.00, and general admission is $5.00 for adults and $3.00 for children under twelve and seniors over sixty. You can rent a paddleboat or other small craft if you want to ply the river under your own power or you can board the *Pride of the Susquehanna* (717–234–6500), an authentic riverboat that offers forty-five-minute scenic cruises and two-hour dinner cruises from May to October. Cost for the forty-five-minute cruise is $4.95 for adults, $3.00 for children three to twelve, free for children two and under.

## Evening

Here's a bit of local wisdom—the best scenic overlook, with the most beautiful views of the capitol building, City Island, the parks, and other sites is from the seventh floor of the cafeteria at the Harrisburg Hospital on South Front Street. For dining, however, I would recommend the following spot:

**DINNER: Passage to India,** Holiday Inn Express, 525 South Front Street; (717) 233–1202. If you like Indian food—or even if you've been dying for a chance to try it–this easygoing restaurant is just the place to enjoy a wide selection of authentic delights. Succulent tandooris, heavenly vegetarian creations, saffron-scented rice and light-as-air native breads make it a delicious adventure. Prices are inexpensive to moderate. The all-you-can-eat lunch buffet ($6.99 weekdays, $7.99 weekends) is a great bargain.

**LODGING: The Hen-Apple,** 409 South Lingle Avenue, Palmyra; (717) 838–8282.

On to Hershey and your night's lodging. From Route 22 in Harrisburg, drive 3 miles east until you come to I–83; take I–83 south for another 3 miles until you come to Route 322. As you approach Hershey, Route 322 will bear off toward Ephrata. Keep going straight—the road will now be called Route 422 and will go directly into town. The total trip should take somewhere under twenty minutes.

When you get to Hershey (you'll be on Chocolate Avenue), roll down your window and take a deep breath. On warm summer nights, you can smell heaven. And while the streets may not be paved with chocolate, they seem to be illuminated by it as giant Hershey Kisses perch on top of the street lamps, their familiar white tags dancing in the breeze.

Your bed-and-breakfast is located in Palmyra, a tiny town right outside Hershey, so you still have about 2 miles to go before you sleep. Start counting the traffic lights when you get to the Hershey Motor Lodge on your right. At traffic light number six you will pass the Hershey Chocolate Factory on your left; keep going until you come to light number eight, where you will turn right onto South Lingle Avenue—there will be a mini mart with gas pumps on the opposite corner as you turn. Travel ½ mile on South Lingle until you come to a huge white house with a white retaining wall, a picket fence, and the welcoming glow of candles in the window.

The Hen-Apple, tucked away on a quiet residential street, is the home of Flo and Harold Eckert, and a wonderful, warm home it is. There's nothing stuffy about this 1825 Georgian-style farmhouse turned bed-and-breakfast with its lovely hand-stenciled walls and ceiling; light-hearted mixture of Victorian and country colors and furnishings; and mix of antiques, family heirlooms, and just plain fun stuff. The guest rooms range from whimsical to unabashedly romantic. The house is situated on two acres of greens and gardens—Flo's pride and joy—which explode in vibrant colors in spring and summer, and provide fresh herbs for her cooking all year-round. Room rates are $65 per night double occupancy on weekdays and Sunday, $75 on Saturday. A very special continental breakfast (really, like most people's full breakfast) is served weekdays; an even more lavish spread is served on Sunday.

## DAY 2

*Morning*

**BREAKFAST:** The Hen-Apple. Flo calls her breakfast continental, but don't expect merely toast and coffee. You can smell her fresh baking as soon as you get anywhere near the kitchen. She loves to whip up surprises (especially of the chocolate variety) so I won't give away any of her secrets. But come hungry. You won't want to miss a thing.

In 1894 a poor central Pennsylvania farm boy turned self-made businessman named Milton Snavely Hershey perfected a formula for smooth and creamy milk chocolate. From there he developed the Hershey bar, which became an American icon and international industry. To accommodate his growing work force he also built a town.

Today much of the town's employment and a great many of its attractions continue to be linked, in one way or another, to the chocolate factory with the words HERSHEY'S COCOA formed in shrubbery on its front lawn. So it is only fitting that this is where we begin today's activities.

Although the factory tour at the **Hershey Chocolate World Visitor Center** (Chocolate and Cocoa Avenues, 717–534–4900) is simulated, it's as close to the real thing as you're going to get. Like a theme park ride, it is creative and colorful as you ride along in your own automated craft, sharing the journey of a cocoa bean from harvest to Hershey bar and learning some of the secrets of chocolate-making along the way. You'll be impressed to learn that Hershey's is the largest chocolate factory in the world, capable of making more than twenty-five million of its famous kisses each day in its more than 2-million-square-foot facility. There's also a sweet little reward at the end of the tour. The largest part of the Visitor Center is devoted to sales of the products themselves, from the ubiquitous branded bars to the various members of the Reese's peanut butter branch of the family. Open seven days a week year-round, hours vary by month and season.

Once you've stoked up on your lifetime supply of chocolate, it's time to hit the teeth-clenching speed spirals, stomach-losing loops, and acrophobia-inducing heights of nearby **Hersheypark** (100 Hersheypark Drive, 800–HERSHEY or 717–534–3900). With more than fifty-five rides and attractions, including a 90-foot-high, 360-degree looping steel coaster; a 100-foot-tall Ferris wheel; and a superbig, superhigh water ride ominously named Tidal Force, there's plenty to keep the whole family amused for hours and dizzy for days. For kiddies (and those adults who find their rides more amusing), there are twenty just-the-right-size-and-speed rides, including one of the oldest operating carousels in America (circa 1919). Live entertainment; parades; seal, dolphin, and sea lion shows; and giant-sized schmoozing Hershey Bar and Kiss-costumed characters round out the impressive array of attractions spread throughout this 110-acre park. Open May–September, gates open at 10:00 A.M., days and hours vary by season. Regular admission (nine to fifty-four years old) is $29.95; for juniors (ages three to eight) and seniors (fifty-five and over) it is $16.95; free for children two and under.

## *Afternoon*

**LUNCH: Hershey Pantry,** 801 East Chocolate Avenue; (717) 533–7505. This is such a popular spot that lines frequently stretch out the door, so come early or late if you can. In this lace-trimmed tearoom environment you might expect dainty portions. Far from it. The breakfasts, lunches, and dinners are beyond generous, the desserts big enough for four, and the prices inexpensive for daytime meals, mostly moderate for dinner.

After the wild rides of Hersheypark, it's a good time to seek a little serenity at **Hershey Gardens** (717–534–3492). It's only a short drive east on Hersheypark Drive to Hotel Road, where you'll turn left and follow the signs to the gardens. The centerpiece for this twenty-three-acre Eden, which was begun in 1937 for Milton Hershey, is its collection of 7,000 roses representing 275 varieties. This and other seasonal flowering annual displays make the gardens an inviting retreat from mid-April to October. An exciting new addition is the **Butterfly House,** the largest indoor habitat of its kind in the state, featuring twenty-five different North American varieties of these colorful beauties (open mid-June to September). Open daily 9:00 A.M.–6:00 P.M.; Memorial Day–Labor Day hours are extended to 8:00 P.M. on Friday and Saturday. Admission is $5.00 for adults (sixteen and up), $4.25 for seniors (sixty-two and over), $2.50 for youths (three to fifteen), free for children under three.

A worthwhile side trip will take you a short distance from Hershey Gardens to the old **Session House of Derry Presbyterian Church** (248 East Derry Road), a glass-enclosed 1732 cabin of hand-hewn logs that housed the first school ever to be held in this part of frontier America. Adjacent is a cemetery where the earliest grave is marked 1735 and where at least forty Revolutionary War soldiers are buried. To get there, take a right as you exit Hersheypark onto Hotel Road, then a left onto Front Street. Front Street will intersect Hersheypark Drive, but keep going straight—the road will now be called Park Avenue. When you reach the intersection of Park Avenue and East Derry Road, turn left.

For an unforgettable antiquing foray (or, more accurately, marathon) visit the more than 250 dealers at **Ziegler's in the Country** (Route 743, right off of Route 322, 3 miles south of Hershey; 717-533-1662) and its sister **Ziegler's Antique Mall** (717–533–7990) 3.5 miles southeast on Route 743. No matter what age you are, you'll find lots of familiar collectibles from your childhood–and depending on what age you are, they may be classified as antiques or as "vintage" items. Visit both locations for maximum impact and selection of everything from home furnishings and garden fountains to matchbooks and Pez dispensers to baseball cards and Bobbsey Twin books.

**Dinner: Restaurant on Chocolate,** 814 East Chocolate Avenue; (717) 534–2734. For top-notch gourmet dining this is the best place in town. This is a romantic spot with an elegant decor and fine dining atmosphere, but you can come dressed in your nice casuals and still feel right at home. The New American Cuisine menu adds some innovative twists to such traditional fare as Atlantic salmon (with honey, lemon, and a walnut crust) and grilled pork tenderloin (marinated in Caribbean spices). Dinner reservations are required. Expensive

While some small towns roll up their sidewalks and go to sleep soon after dark, Hershey isn't one of them. From October through mid-April the **Hershey Bears,** one of the nation's oldest continuously operating American Hockey League teams, plays its home games at **Hersheypark Arena** (717–534–3911). Tickets range from $10 to $16.

From May first until the first week in September (or October if there are play-offs), the **Hershey Wildcats** professional outdoor soccer team plays its home games on the natural grass of **Hersheypark Stadium** (717–534–3911). Tickets range from $5.00 to $12.00. Games are generally played weekend evenings at 7:30 P.M. with a few weeknight games at 7:00.

**LODGING:** Hen-Apple.

# BETWEEN AND BEYOND

## DAY 3

## *Morning*

**BREAKFAST:** Hen–Apple.

Before you head back home, spend the morning visiting the more than 200 animals that live in the naturalistic habitats of **ZooAmerica North American Wildlife Park** at Park Avenue (Route 743), between Chocolate Avenue and Hersheypark Drive (717–534–3860). Originally begun in the early 1900s to display Milton Hershey's private animal collection to the public, this totally redesigned eleven-acre walk-through sanctuary brings together mammals, reptiles, birds, fish, and plants from all over the continent. Open year-round; 10:00 A.M.–5:00 P.M. September to mid-June; until 8:00 P.M. mid-June to August. Admission is $5.25 for ages thirteen to fifty-four; $4.65 for ages fifty-five and older; $4.00 for ages three to twelve; and free for ages two and under.

## *Afternoon*

**LUNCH: Breads N' Cheese of Hershey,** 243 West Chocolate Avenue; (717) 533–4546. This cozy European-style bakery and cafe serves great homemade soups, quiches, specialty pocket sandwiches, and salads, as well as oven-fresh desserts to die for. Take home some of the twenty-five styles of freshly baked breads, international cheeses, and pâtés, and did I mention pastries? Inexpensive.

To return to Philadelphia, take Route 743 for 1 mile south to Route 322; travel east on 322 for 14 miles until you come to Route 72. Go south on 72 for 2 miles until you come to the Pennsylvania Turnpike. Take the turnpike going east for 61 miles until you get to the Schuylkill Expressway (I–76); then head east on the expressway for 22 miles into Philadelphia.

### THERE'S MORE

**Art Association of Harrisburg,** 21 Front Street, Harrisburg; (717) 236–1432. Five galleries of rotating exhibits of regional and national artists plus a sixth gallery that displays and sells art by juried members. Open Monday–Thursday 9:00 A.M.–9:00 P.M., Friday until 4:00 P.M., Saturday 10:00 A.M.–4:00 P.M. and Sunday noon–3:00 P.M.

**Fort Hunter Mansion and Park,** 5300 North Front Street, Harrisburg; (717) 599–5751. Restorations, exhibits, and demonstrations bring the nineteenth century to life at this wonderful mansion situated on thirty-five acres of parkland on the banks of the Susquehanna River. Open May–November Tuesday–Saturday 10:00 A.M.–4:30 P.M., Sunday noon–4:30 P.M.; December Tuesday–Sunday until 7:00 P.M. Admission.

**Westhanover Winery,** 7646 Jonestown Road, Harrisburg; (717) 652–3711. You could visit this winery in the hills just for the scenery, but don't forget to taste some of owner George Kline's unique blueberry, sour cherry, berry, and apple varieties. Open Tuesday–Thursday noon–6:30 P.M., Friday noon–8:00 P.M., Saturday noon–5:00 P.M.

**Hershey Museum,** 170 Hersheypark Drive, Hershey; (717) 534–3439. Through photographs, artifacts, and colorful exhibits, this museum chronicles Milton Hershey's struggle to establish his chocolate business and build a town. Included are his extensive collections of Pennsylvania German and Native American art and artifacts. Open year-round 10:00 A.M.–5:00 P.M. Admission for adults (sixteen to sixty-one) is $5.00; for seniors (sixty-two and over), $4.50; for youth (three to fifteen), $2.50.

**Hershey Theatre,** 15 Caracas Avenue, Hershey; (717) 534–3415. From September through April, concerts, dance programs, Broadway musicals, and classic dramas starring national and world headliners perform in this exquisite venue with its sculpted, painted, gold, and tile ceilings; marble walls; Italian lava rock floors; and formal arches. The box office is open Monday–Friday from 10:00 A.M.–5:00 P.M. (10:00 A.M. to curtain time on performance days). Ticket prices range from $20 to $49 depending on day, time, and performance.

**Hershey Symphony;** (717) 533–8449. This excellent orchestra, which celebrated its thirtieth anniversary in March 1999, performs October through May at the Hershey Theatre. Tickets are $10.00 for adults, $8.00 for senior citizens, and $5.00 for students.

**Milton Hershey School,** Route 322 and Governor Road, Hershey; (800) 322–3248 or (717) 520–2100. Established and financed by Milton Hershey and his wife Catherine, who remained childless until their deaths, this educational institution, originally constructed for orphan boys, today provides tuition, housing, clothing, food, and medical and dental assistance for eleven hundred boys and girls. Founders Hall, the second largest rotunda in the world, is a magnificent tribute to the Hersheys' compassion and generosity. Open for self-guided tours year-round 10:00 A.M.–4:00 P.M. Free.

**Trolley Works,** Chocolate and Cocoa Avenues, Hershey; (717) 533–3732. See the sights of the town from an old-fashioned trolley complete with singing conductor. Tours depart every fifteen minutes from the front of Hershey's Chocolate World. Tickets are $6.75 for adults, $5.00 for children three to twelve, free for children two and under. Seating is limited so you might want to make advance reservations during peak summer and Christmas seasons.

**Golf.** Call 800–HERSHEY for information about the town's one eighteen-hole and two nine-hole public golf courses. The Hotel Hershey also has two eighteen-hole private courses for guests.

## SPECIAL EVENTS

**January.** Pennsylvania Farm Show, Farm Show Complex, Harrisburg; (717) 787–5373. Since 1851, this annual five-day showcase of farm animals, equipment, food, agricultural demonstrations, and hundreds of exhibits has been drawing visitors from all over the East Coast. Free.

**March.** Pennsylvania National Arts and Crafts Show, Farm Show Complex, Harrisburg; (717) 796–0531. Demonstrations and original contemporary and traditional crafts by more than 320 of the nation's finest juried artisans from more than thirty-five states.

**July.** Harrisburg Independence Weekend Festival, City Island; (717) 233–8275. The largest celebration of its kind in the region, featuring four days of food, rides, concerts, Jet Ski and boat races, Civil War reenactments, and a huge fireworks show. July 4th weekend.

**September.** Kipona Celebration, North and South Riverfront and City Island; (717) 255–3020. One of the oldest inland waterfront festivals in the nation, with race competitions, food, arts and crafts, theater, concerts, games, and rides.

**October.** Antique Auto Club of America Fall Meet and Flea Market, Hersheypark; 800–HERSHEY. This annual event attracts antique and classic car collectors and aficionados from all over the world.

**October.** Hersheypark Balloon Fest, near Hershey's Chocolate World; 800–HERSHEY. Dozens of hot air balloons fill the sky as the crowd below enjoys pay-as-you-ride amusement and hay rides, live entertainment, demonstrations, craft vendors, and lots of food. Free admission.

**October.** Pennsylvania National Horse Show, Farm Show Complex, Harrisburg; (717) 975–3677. One thousand horses and top international riders compete for prestigious titles and large cash awards.

**Mid-November to late December.** Hersheypark Christmas Candylane, Hersheypark; (717) 534–3900. No admission charge. Pay-as-you-ride amusements, live reindeer, and a million twinkling lights.

## OTHER RECOMMENDED RESTAURANTS AND LODGINGS

## *Hershey*

Carla's Cucina, 1144 East Chocolate Avenue; (717) 534–2099. Italian fare in a pretty and lively setting. Prices range from $8.95 for pizza to $21.95 for frutti de mer—mussels, slipper clams, lobster, and shrimp over pasta.

Spinner's Inn and Restaurant, 845 East Chocolate Avenue; (717) 533–9157. This newly renovated inn offers reasonable prices and some very nice amenities such as a heated pool, game room, and free continental breakfast. Rates range from $49 to $69 off-season, $69 to $89 peak season. There's also a casual upscale restaurant called Catherine's at Spinners (717–533–9050) right on the property.

Hotel Hershey, Hotel Road; (717) 533–2171. This is a beautiful full-service resort hotel with elegantly appointed rooms, indoor and outdoor swimming pools, whirlpool, sauna, exercise room, tennis courts, cycling and nature trails, tobogganing, and cross-country skiing. Room rates range from $178 to $258, depending on the season. Meal plans and special package plans are also available.

Milton Motel, 1733 East Chocolate Avenue; (717) 533–4533. This family-run operation is a very happy medium between the anonymity of a chain and the intimacy of a bed-and-breakfast. Heated pool, discounted Hersheypark tickets, and free coffee in the morning. Prices (double occupancy) range from $59 off-season to $109 in season.

Pinehurst Inn Bed & Breakfast, 50 Northeast Drive; (800) 743–9140 or (717) 533–2603. This beautiful brick home was built in 1930 by Milton Hershey. Summer rates are $52 per night, $75 in winter.

## *Harrisburg*

Raspberries, Harrisburg Hilton, 1 North Second Street; (717) 237–6419. Bountiful breakfast, lunch, and dinner buffets are real bargains at $7.95, $9.25, and $12.95, respectively.

Arches Restaurant, 4125 North Front Street (at exit I–81); (717) 233–5891. Casual breakfasts, lunches, and dinners with a river view. Continental dinner menu specializes in fresh seafood, veal, and prime rib. Inexpensive breakfasts, moderate to expensive lunches and dinners.

Zephyr Express, 400 North Second Street; (717) 257–1328. Casual California-style cuisine with gourmet pizzas, pastas, and specialty sandwiches. Inexpensive.

**Campgrounds.** Hershey Highmeadow Camp; (717) 566–0902. Nearly 300 open and shaded sites and rental cabins on fifty-five beautiful acres with many amenities. Free shuttle service to Hershey attractions, access to all Hershey golf courses, and other exclusive benefits. Prices vary by time of year and type of camping facility.

### FOR MORE INFORMATION

Harrisburg-Hershey-Carlisle Tourism and Convention Bureau; (800) 995–0969 or (717) 975–8161; www.visithhc.com.

Hershey Information Center; (800) HERSHEY (recorded message); www.800hershey.com.

# BETWEEN AND BEYOND

# Gettysburg, Pennsylvania

## ELOQUENT FIELDS,
## MEMORABLE ADDRESSES

### 2 NIGHTS

*Living History • Spirited Evenings • Civil War Antiques*

Before the summer of 1863, no one could have guessed that this little rural south-central Pennsylvania town would become a focal point and gathering place for generations of historians, students, military leaders, armchair generals, and visitors from around the world. It was a chance encounter that brought General Robert E. Lee's 75,000-man Army of Northern Virginia and General George Meade's 97,000-man Army of the Potomac together for three days of pitched battle that would decimate both forces and prove to be the turning point of the Civil War.

As a town, Gettysburg has accepted its permanent place in history—as well as in the international spotlight—with grace, dignity, and a commitment to preserving the memories and humanity of the people who lived, fought, and died here. With monuments, museums, reenactments, and the telling of stories that have been passed down through local families for as much as six generations, this town has prevented the events of those three days in July from becoming merely forgotten statistics in some dusty history book. But the most compelling storyteller of all is the battlefield itself. In speaking so honestly and accurately about war, it presents the most powerful argument for peace.

Peak tourist months for Gettysburg are April through October; it is quietest in January and February. Locals suggest coming in November, when most sites are open and a number of special annual events take place.

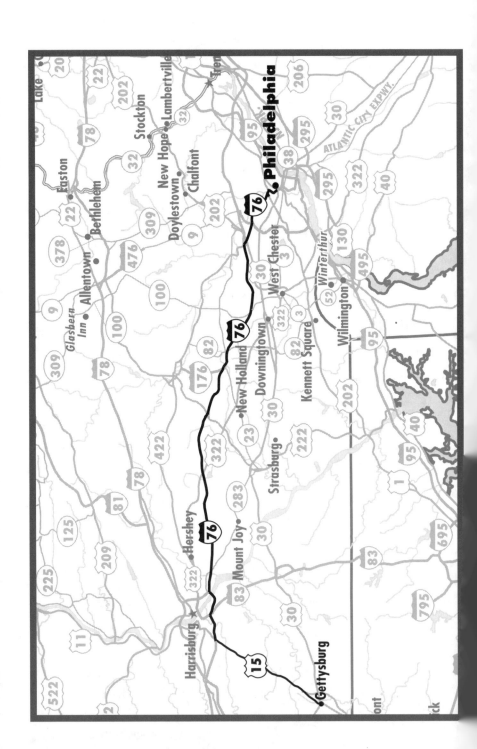

# BETWEEN AND BEYOND

*Helpful hint:* Unless you're a Civil War scholar, you may want to brush up on your history before your visit to Gettysburg. I recommend reading Michael Shaara's book *The Killer Angels,* or viewing the 1993 film *Gettysburg* or the Battle of Gettysburg segment of Ken Burns' *Civil War* series, both of which are available on video.

## DAY 1

## *Morning*

It takes about 2¾–3 hours to get to Gettysburg from Philadelphia. The quickest way is to take the Schuylkill Expressway (I-76) 22 miles west to the King of Prussia entrance to the Pennsylvania Turnpike. Travel west on the turnpike for about 92 miles to exit 17 (Gettysburg/Route 15); go south on Route 15 until you come to Route 30 west. Take Route 30 west for about 2 miles into Gettysburg.

Gettysburg is a great walking town. Once you identify its four main thoroughfares—York, Chambersburg, Carlisle, and Baltimore Streets, you can find your way just about anywhere. Making it extra easy is the fact that they all radiate from one focal point in the center of town. Called **Lincoln Square,** this point is right at the heart of the town's historic and commercial areas.

One block north of the square at 35 Carlisle Street is the **Visitor Information Center** (717–334–6274). In addition to being the place to come for brochures, walking tour maps, and other helpful stuff, this former railroad depot, built in 1858, has some interesting war stories of its own.

## *Afternoon*

**LUNCH: Pub & Restaurant,** southwest corner of Lincoln Square; (717) 334–7100. Grab a seat by a window so you can watch the action on the square as you enjoy one of the menu's many burger, chicken breast, or deli sandwich variations, salads, or soups. A favorite local spot for lunch or dinner. Inexpensive.

After lunch it's time to pay a call at some of Gettysburg's most famous addresses. In recent years more than one hundred buildings have been restored in the downtown historic district alone. One of them is on the other side of the square, right where President Abraham Lincoln seems to be offering directions to a tourist. Actually, these two whimsical life-size statues point the way to the **Lincoln Room Museum** on the second level of the historic **Wills**

## BETWEEN AND BEYOND

**House** (1 Lincoln Square; 717–334–8188), where Lincoln put the finishing touches on his Gettysburg Address and slept the night before he delivered it. A twenty-minute light-and-sound presentation includes a recitation of what is probably the most famous two-minute speech in American history. Open in season 9:00 A.M.–7:00 P.M. (until 8:00 P.M. Friday and Saturday). Call for off-season hours.

On the lower level of the Wills House is the **Antique Center of Gettysburg** (717–337–3669), one of the largest and most comprehensive antiques stores in the area with one hundred showcases displaying all manner of collectibles, including Native American and Western artifacts, militariana from all wars, and Abraham Lincoln memorabilia. Open Monday, Wednesday, Thursday, and Saturday 10:00 A.M.–6:00 P.M., Friday until 8:00 P.M., Sunday 11:00 A.M.–6:00 P.M.

From the square, travel 8 blocks west on Route 30 (Chambersburg Street) to **Lee's Headquarters and Museum** (717–334–3141), on the grounds of Larson's Quality Inn. From this strategically situated house (then a private home owned by noted statesman Thaddeus Stevens), General Robert E. Lee and his staff developed battle plans for the three-day struggle. Today it is filled with an extensive collection of Confederate and Union military and medical equipment, period artifacts, and rare photos and documents. If you really want to immerse yourself in history, the second floor is available for overnight accommodations. Open 9:00 A.M.–9:00 P.M. mid-March–November. Admission: adults $3.00; children six and older, fifty cents; free for children under six.

About 1 mile from Lincoln Square along Route 15 south is the entrance to the **Gettysburg National Cemetery** (97 Taneytown Road, adjacent to the National Park Service Information Center; 717–334–1124). Here rest nearly 7,000 of Gettysburg's esteemed dead spanning two centuries, including 3,500 from the Civil War and more than 3,300 American soldiers and dependents from subsequent wars. Stop by the information center for an excellent self-guided walking tour map and visit the site (marked by a monument) where President Abraham Lincoln delivered his famous address. The Soldier's Grand Monument, surrounded by its huge semicircle of graves, silently pays tribute to those who scrificed their lives. Open dawn to dusk.

For some of the finest Civil War art, visit **Gallon Historical Art** (9 Steinwehr Avenue; 717–334–0430), where the complete works of renowned Gettysburg artist-in-residence Dale Gallon are on display, and original oil paintings and limited edition prints are available for sale. Open 10:00

A.M.–8:00 P.M. Friday and Saturday, until 5:00 P.M. Sunday–Thursday in season; 10:00 A.M.–4:00 P.M. off-season.

## *Evening*

**DINNER: Blue Parrot Bistro,** 35 Chambersburg Street; (717) 337–3739. Enjoy continental fare in an easygoing setting at one of the hottest restaurants in town. One of the specialties on the moderately priced dinner menu is steak gilded with a choice of six sauces. Saturday night is prime rib, and Tuesday–Thursday evenings between 5:00 and 6:30 P.M. the daily Early Bird Special gives you an appetizer-to-dessert feast for only $12.95. Indoor and outdoor sidewalk cafe seating in season.

On summer evenings Monday–Friday at 8:00 P.M., "Mr. Lincoln Returns to Gettysburg," a forty-five-minute, one-man show is presented at the **Conflict Theater** (213 Steinwehr Avenue, Route 15; 717–334–8003). At first glance the Conflict looks like a well-stocked bookstore . . . and with 22,000 new, used, and taped volumes, it is indeed a great one. Owner Pauline Peterson, a descendant of the last survivor of the Seventy-second Illinois, is also a font of Civil War knowledge. But tucked away in the back of the store is the real treasure—an eighty-five-seat living history theater where, for a modest ticket price, you can take in a live musical or dramatic performance or one of several excellent film presentations depicting life and death in Gettysburg during the battle. Call for hours, performance information, and specific ticket prices.

**Lodging: Doubleday Inn,** 104 Doubleday Avenue; (717) 334–9119. To get to your lodging (the only bed-and-breakfast on the Gettysburg battlefield) from Lincoln Square, take Carlisle Street north to Lincoln Street; turn left on Lincoln. Make a right onto Cottage Street and take a left onto Mummasburg Road. From Mummasburg Road make a left onto Doubleday Avenue (National Park Service Auto Tour Stop No. 3). You'll drive past some monuments and the inn will be on your left. This beautiful 1929 home is situated on Oak Hill, where, during the first day of battle, a seriously outnumbered Brigadier General Abner Doubleday (the same man who, for many years, was believed to have invented baseball) held off Confederate forces, allowing the Union troops to regroup and gain a stronghold position in the field.

Today the inn offers a panoramic view of the town and battlefield. Innkeepers Charles and Ruth Anne Wilcox have furnished their home in an English country style accented with Civil War era antiques, art, and memorabilia. On selected evenings the Wilcoxes invite a local historian to entertain guests with historically accurate wartime accounts and lively discussions. Rates range from $89 (shared bath) to $99–$104 (private bath). A full breakfast is included. Note: Early-to-bedders should be aware that the floorboards in this charming old house tend to groan underfoot a bit, but the ambience, amenities, and warm hospitality more than make up for a few night noises.

## DAY 2

## *Morning*

**BREAKFAST:** Doubleday Inn. When was the last time you had breakfast by candlelight? The experience is delicious, just like the caramel (or apple) French toast, sausage and egg casserole, or other house specialties that are cooked up by your hosts.

There are many ways you can tour the **Gettysburg National Military Park** (aka the Battlefield). A number of them are discussed in the There's More section of this chapter. One great way is to ask your innkeeper to arrange for a tour in your own car with a licensed battlefield guide at the wheel ($30 for one to five persons in a vehicle, $45 for six to fifteen persons). I was lucky to get lifelong Gettysburg resident Terry Fox, who knows all the dates, names, and statistics you can handle, as well as the kind of colorful tidbits of information and local lore that add so much to a tour.

But before you embark on your field trip, I strongly recommend that you take advantage of the orientation activities and programs offered at the **National Military Park Visitor Center** (717–334–1124). For no charge you can see one of the world's largest collections of artifacts at the center's **Gettysburg Museum of the Civil War**. The 3-D Electric Map presents a thirty-minute light-and-sound show illustrating troop movement from the first volley to the final retreat. Shows every day, 8:15 A.M.–4:25 P.M. Admission: $3.00 for adults, $2.50 for seniors, $1.50 for youths six to sixteen, and free for children under six. At the nearby **Cyclorama Center** you'll see a 360-foot-long circular oil-on-canvas painting (circa 1884) depicting Pickett's charge, accompanied by a stirring sound-and-light show. Admission is $3.00 for adults, $1.50 for children six and up; under six free.

Gettysburg National Military Park looks very much like it did in 1863. So as you travel from site to site with such infamous names as Little Round Top, the Devil's Den, and the Angle, you will encounter the same farms, orchards, fences, and rock walls that the soldiers did on those three infamous days in

July. More than 51,000 soldiers were killed, wounded, or missing in action during the fighting, and today more than 1,400 monuments, markers, and memorials mark the spots on the 6,000-acre battlefield where they fought and fell. A particularly poignant stop is the **Eternal Peace Monument** where, in 1938, thousands gathered to watch a former Union soldier and a former Confederate soldier come together to light the symbolic eternal flame.

## *Afternoon*

**LUNCH: KrackerJack's Cafe & Spirits,** 610 Baltimore Street; (717) 334–5648. One of the lunch specialties here is barbecue—pulled pork, beef brisket, and a dynamite pulled sampler platter with hearty helpings of both. Moderately priced lunch and dinner menus, casual atmosphere.

Of course, the Battle of Gettysburg was not confined to the surrounding fields. Some of the heaviest fighting occurred right in the heart of town. At 309 Baltimore Street stands a former family residence that was occupied by Confederate sharpshooters during some of that fighting. Today the restored and authentically furnished **Schriver House** (717–337–2800) is an example of the powerful impact the war had on the everyday citizens who found themselves caught in the middle. Open April–October Monday–Saturday 10:00 A.M.–6:00 P.M., Sunday noon–6:00 P.M.; November–March Friday–Monday noon–5:00 P.M. Admission $5.00 for adults, $4.50 for seniors, $3.75 for children six to twelve.

Amazingly enough, the bloody fighting that raged throughout the town claimed only one civilian casualty—a 19-year-old woman named Mary Virginia "Jenny" Wade. As you tour the **Jenny Wade House** (758 Baltimore Street; 717–334–4100) with its hundreds of bullet and shell holes, the Talking Soldier tells of her tragic death after being hit with a stray bullet while baking bread for the Union Infantry. Jenny Wade is buried in Gettysburg National Cemetery. Open daily spring and fall 9:00 A.M.–5:00 P.M., until 9:00 P.M. in summer. Admission is $5.75 for adults, $3.25 for children.

While you're in the neighborhood, make sure you stop at **Dirty Billy's Hats** (430A Baltimore Street; 717–334–3200) where Hollywood comes when it needs authentic reproductions of historic headwear from any time in history. That's Billy's work you saw in the movie *Gettysburg*. If don't find what you're looking for at the shop or in his catalog, Billy can probably handcraft the hat of your dreams from a photo within four to six weeks. Open Friday–Monday 11:00 A.M.–6:00 P.M. And if you're interested in a head-to-toe

*Gettysburg is famous for its battlefield reenactments.*

Civil War makeover, you'll find historic reproductions of nineteenth-century military and civilian attire for men, women, and children at **Grand Illusions Clothing Company** (corner of Baltimore and Middle Streets; 302–386–0300). Call for hours.

## *Evening*

**DINNER: Dobbin House Tavern,** 89 Steinwehr Avenue; (717) 334–2100. Built in 1776 as a private family home, this building became one of the first stops north of the Mason Dixon Line on the Underground Railroad (the crawl space where the runaway slaves hid is part of the tiny free museum upstairs). It was also a hospital for soldiers from both the North and South after the nearby battle. Over 200 years later, the Dobbin House looks much the same, with its original native stone walls, seven fireplaces, and hand-carved woodwork. Even the china and flatware used in the restaurant exactly match fragments unearthed during reexcavation of the cellar. Entrees range from moderate to expensive, but you can get a real bargain—and a great meal—for a fixed price of $16.95 if you order the Colonial Fare of the Day, a four-course dinner.

Many of the locals believe that the spirits of those who died on the Gettysburg Battlefield still roam the streets and haunt the houses by night. The **Ghosts of Gettysburg Candlelight Walking Tours** (271 Baltimore Street; 717–337–0445) are based on generations-old accounts and tales dug up (so to speak) by Mark Nesbitt, author of the extremely popular *Ghosts of Gettysburg* series. Call for descriptions and times. $6.00–$6.50 for adults, free for children under seven. For hauntings of the indoor variety, head for the Farnsworth House (401 Baltimore Street; 717–334–8838). Descend the staircase into the stone cellar that is **Civil War Mourning Theatre,** where you will listen to ghostly storytellers speak of restless souls and unexplainable phenomena. Call for times. $6.00 for adults, free for children.

**LODGING:** Doubleday Inn.

## DAY 3

## *Morning*

**BREAKFAST:** Doubleday Inn.

Head back to the National Park Service Information Center, this time to catch the shuttle that will take you for a visit to the **Eisenhower National Historic Site** (19 Taneytown Road; 717–334–4474), the only private home ever owned by our thirty-fourth president and his wife Mamie. During his two terms as president, Dwight D. Eisenhower used his Gettysburg farm for weekend retreats (it sometimes even served as the temporary White House). After his retirement he and Mamie moved here permanently and stayed until their deaths. The preserved farm, furnishings, and personal belongings honor and offer insight into the lives of this renowned couple. Open daily April–October 9:00 A.M.–4:00 P.M., closed Monday and Tuesday November–March, closed four weeks in January and February. Admission is $5.25 for adults; $3.25 for youths thirteen to sixteen; $2.25 for children six to twelve.

Back in the downtown area, stop in at **Moonacre Ironworks & the Gettysburg Candle Shop** (62 Chambersburg Street; 717–337–9200) and try the devious little handmade wrought-iron puzzles ($12.95) with ominous names such as Satan's Stirrup and Blackbeard's Revenge. For something a little more traditional, see what seasonal delights crafters Dick and Carol Cole have whipped up for their **Fiddle Faddles Folk Art and Primitives** shop (54 Chambersburg Street; 717–334–8270).

**LUNCH: Camelot Coffee & Bakery Cafe and Restaurant,** 3 Steinwehr Avenue; (717) 338–9516. A very cute little breakfast and lunch place serving "London pub" entrees such as chicken Cornish pasty and "green knight" (broccoli, mushrooms, and cheddar cheese in puff pastry), as well as the standard soup/salad/sandwich fare. The desserts are outstanding—and, after all, you'll need the energy for the long ride home. Inexpensive.

To return to Philadelphia, reverse your route from Day 1. The return trip should take about $2\frac{3}{4}$–3 hours.

## THERE'S MORE

**Battle Reenactments.** Bushey Farm, 5 miles southwest of the Battlefield; (717) 338–1525. Major reenactments of encampments and battles, performances of period music, and demonstrations on domestic arts are highlights of these three-day events in July and September. Admission. Children get a reduced rate and youngsters under six are free. There are also numerous living history events and demos at various sites throughout the year.

**Historic Tours,** 55 Steinwehr Avenue; (717) 334–8000. Two-hour battlefield tours conducted by licensed guides in a classic 1930s Yellowstone Park bus. $12.00 for adults, $9.00 for children.

**Getttysburg Tour Center,** 778 Baltimore Avenue; (717) 334–6296. Take a trolley tour through the town with stops at many of the museums and other interesting sites along the way. Two package plans that include site admissions are available. Call for details and rates.

**Battlefield Bicycle Tour.** Tour originates from The Tannery Bed and Breakfast, 449 Baltimore Street; (800) 803–0236 or (717) 691–0236. A two-hour, 8-mile trip with professional guide, including bike, water, and helmets, is $27 single, $52 family, $45 couple. Call for seasonal hours.

**Battlefield Horseback Tour.** National Riding Stable, Artillery Ridge Camping Resort, 610 Taneytown Road, Route 134; (717) 334–1288. Two-hour tour on horseback with a licensed battlefield guide. One-hour trail rides with a trail master for accomplished riders or novices are also available. Call for times and prices.

**Gettysburg Scenic Rail Tours,** 106 North Washington Street; (888) 84–TRAIN. A variety of different options for seeing the countryside by rail. Particularly unique are the Fire Hall Dinner Trains that take you on a 34-mile trip through the Blue Ridge Mountains and conclude with a chicken barbecue or ham dinner in a local fire hall. Call for schedules and rates.

**Hall of Presidents,** Baltimore Street, next to the main entrance of the National Cemetery; (717) 334–5717. In this popular wax museum, all of our presidents from Washington to Clinton tell their own stories. The first ladies have their own hall, too. Open spring and fall 9:00 A.M.–5:00 P.M., summer until 9:00 P.M. Admission is $5.95 for adults, $3.25 for children.

**Land of Little Horses,** Knoxlyn Road, 3 miles west of Gettysburg on Route 30; (717) 334–7295. Animal lovers will find more than one hundred miniature horses and other fuzzy and furry friends to admire, applaud, and pet at this unusual attraction. Performances, nature areas, carriage museum, snack bar, petting farm, and menagerie. Open seven days, 10:00 A.M.–5:00 P.M. Memorial Day–August 30. Call for off-season hours. Admission is $6.50 for adults; $4.50 for children through age twelve; free for children under two.

**Magic Town,** 49 Steinwehr Avenue; (717) 337–0442. Amazing art and illusions make figures appear and disappear from the windows and alleyways of the realistic, three-dimensional street setting featuring holograms and the stunningly detailed sculptures created by artist Michael Garman. Open Sunday–Thursday 11:00 A.M.–8:00 P.M., Friday and Saturday until 9:00 P.M. Admission is $2.75 for all ages.

**Camping.** Gettysburg KOA Campground, 20 Knox Road; (717) 642–5713. Quiet wooded accommodations for tents and RVs with full hookup sites, laundry and game rooms, heated pool, playground, and other amenities.

Artillery Ridge Camping Resort, 610 Taneytown Road; (717) 334–1288. Tent and RV accommodations with hookups, free twenty-four-hour hot showers, laundry room.

## SPECIAL EVENTS

**May.** Annual Gettysburg Spring Bluegrass Festival, Granite Hill Campground, 6 miles west of Gettysburg on Route 116; (717) 642–8749. Nonstop music from some of the country's best bluegrass music performers in a beautiful country setting.

**May.** Annual Gettysburg Outdoor Antique Show, downtown Gettysburg; (717) 334–6274. More than 175 dealers from thirteen states line the downtown streets.

**May.** Annual Memorial Day Parade and Ceremonies; (717) 334–6274. One of the oldest (more than 130 years) Memorial Day observances in the United States with a big parade and ceremony in Gettysburg National Cemetery.

**June.** Gettysburg Civil War Heritage Days; (717) 334–6274. Held annually the last weekend in June and first week in July, this event commemorates the Battle of Gettysburg with living history encampments, battle reenactments, band concerts, Fourth of July program, and lectures series.

**June.** Gettysburg Civil War Collectors Show; (717) 334–6274. Sponsored by the Gettysburg Battlefield Preservation Association and held annually the last weekend in June, this event features original Civil War art, personal effects, weapons, documents, and books.

**August.** Gettysburg Annual Fall Bluegrass Festival; (717) 334–6274. Held annually the fourth weekend in August or the weekend before Labor Day. See Spring Festival in May.

**September.** Eisenhower World War II Weekend, Eisenhower National Historic Site; (717) 338–9114. A living history encampment featuring Allied soldiers, tanks, and military vehicles. Held annually the third weekend in September.

**November.** 136th Anniversary of Lincoln's Gettysburg Address, Gettysburg National Cemetery; (717) 334–6274. An annual observance with a wreath laying, celebrity speakers, brief memorial services, and other special programs sponsored by the Lincoln Fellowship of Pennsylvania.

**November.** Remembrance Day; (717) 334–6274. Held in conjunction with the Lincoln Observance, this event honors those who died in the Civil War and other American conflicts. The day is marked with a parade and other special events throughout the town. Sponsored by the Sons of Union Veterans.

## OTHER RECOMMENDED RESTAURANTS AND LODGINGS

## *Cashtown*

Historic Cashtown Inn, 1325 Old Route 30; (800) 367–1797 or (717) 334–9722. Commandeered by Confederate General A.P. Hill as his head-quarters during the battle, this 1749 inn now serves such specialties as bourbon walnut beef medallions, seafood trilogy, and pesto scallops. Moderate. Overnight accommodations are also available.

## *Gettysburg*

Herr Tavern Restaurant & Publick House, 90 Chambersburg Road; (800) 362–9849 or (717) 334-4332. Excellent American cuisine in a period setting. Moderate to expensive. Overnight accommodations are available.

Historic Farnsworth House Restaurant & Inn, 401 Baltimore Street; (717) 334–8838. Authentically restored circa 1810 dining rooms decorated with oil paintings of Generals Meade and Lee, photos by renowned Civil War photographer Mathew Brady, and artifacts. Specializing in period fare such as game pie, peanut soup, and spoon bread. Children's menu. Moderate. Overnight accommodations (some haunted) are also available.

James Gettys Hotel, 27 Chambersburg Street; (717) 337–1334. This restored 194-year-old hotel offers eleven amenity-filled suites from $115 to $135. Winter rates are also available.

Gettystown Inn, 89 Steinwehr Avenue; (717) 334–2100. An authentic Civil War–era home overlooking the site where Lincoln delivered his Gettysburg Address. Amenities include old-fashioned beds, hooked and Oriental rugs, and nineteenth-century antiques. Includes a full breakfast at the 1776 Dobbin House next door. Rates range from $85 to $105 double occupancy.

The Tannery Bed & Breakfast, 449 Baltimore Street; (717) 334–2454. Seven rooms with private baths in a nineteenth-century home and former tannery. Extended continental breakfast. Great front porch. Rates: $75–$125 per night double occupancy.

Gaslight Inn Bed & Breakfast, 35 East Middle Street; (717) 337–9100. Stately three-story brick house with elegantly appointed rooms (all with private baths, most with fireplaces) and old-fashioned front porch. Rates range from $110 to $150 per night.

## FOR MORE INFORMATION

Gettysburg Convention and Visitors Bureau, (717) 334–6274; www.gettysburg.com.

# New York City, New York

## DELICIOUS TO THE CORE

---

### 2 NIGHTS

---

*A Whole Lot of Everything . . . and More*

Like a huge Great Dane, New York City can bowl you over with its expanse and unbridled energy. From the moment you merge into the crush of humanity that, day and night, flows up and down its sidewalks and, at a decidedly slower pace, its streets, you become part of that energy, too, as you eagerly make your way to one adventure after another.

Thanks to a brilliant marketing campaign, many people have come to think of New York as "the Big Apple." But there's a tour group I know of that more aptly describes the city as "the Big Onion," made up of layers and layers of zesty flavors. Whether you choose to devour New York in big, random bites, or to methodically savor it one delectable layer at a time, a three-day escape to this fabulous town is just enough to whet your appetite.

### DAY 1

*Morning*

New York City is 98 driving miles and about two hours (due to almost certain traffic delays) northeast of Philadelphia. Quite frankly, the easiest and most efficient way to get to New York is by train, either on Amtrak (800–USA–RAIL) or the more economical SEPTA (215–580–7800). Once you arrive in the city, you can get around the way the locals do—on foot or via taxi (quick and reasonably priced) or by bus or subway (if you are comfortable with the

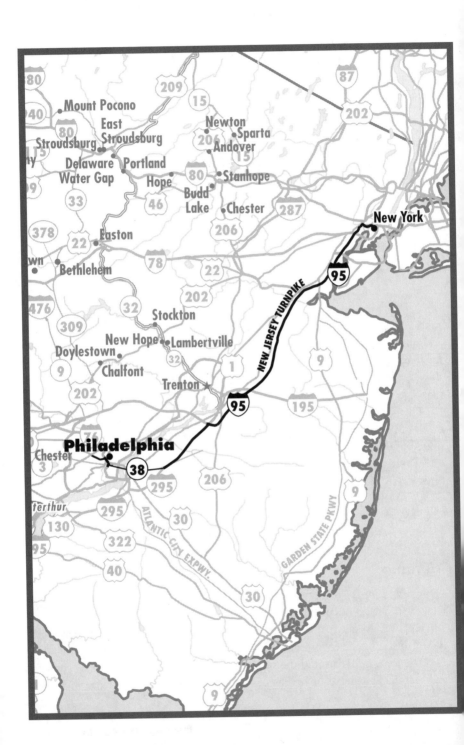

routes). If you truly can't bear to be without your car, go east on Race Street across the Ben Franklin Bridge; continue east for 4 miles on Route I–676. When you come to Route I–76 go east for two more miles to I–295. Go north on 295 for 1 mile and you'll come to Route 168; go east for 2 miles to the New Jersey Turnpike. Take the turnpike north 62 miles, which will take you back onto I–95. Travel 19 miles north on 95 to Route 1/Route 9, which will take you into Jersey City. Go east on Route 78 (Twelfth Street) to the Holland Tunnel.

The Holland Tunnel will let you out on Canal Street in New York, which you will follow south to West Broadway. At West Broadway, make a right-hand turn and go straight to Vesey Street, heading toward the 110-story twin towers of the **World Trade Center** (West-Church-Vesey-Liberty Streets; 212–323–2340). Take the elevator to the top of 2 WTC and marvel at the view from the glass-enclosed observation deck on the 107th floor (open daily 9:30 A.M.–11:30 P.M. June–August; until 9:30 P.M. September–May) or from the world's highest open-air observation deck above the one hundredth floor. If that's not thrilling enough, you can also take a simulated helicopter ride through the city streets. Admission is $12.00 for adults, $9.00 for seniors, $6.00 for youngsters six to twelve, and free for children under six.

## *Afternoon*

**LUNCH: TriBeCa Grill,** 375 Greenwich Street at the corner of Franklin; (212) 941–3900. About 1 block east of Vesey Street is Greenwich Street; head north on Greenwich until you come to Franklin Street. You are now in the heart of **TriBeCa** (Triangle Below Canal), bordered by Chambers and Lafayette Streets and the Hudson River, an interesting mix of old warehouses and new office buildings, artist lofts, and ultra-trendy eateries. This is one of the trendiest. Owned by actor Robert De Niro and renowned chef/restaurateur Drew Nieporent, this hot spot set in a converted coffee factory serves an ever-changing menu of American cuisine with pronounced international accents. Like many of the city's better-known restaurants, this one can be pricey, even at lunch, with entrees averaging $12–$16. For $20 you can get the prix fixe lunch, which includes salad or soup, one of two entree selections, and dessert.

If you travel east from the restaurant a few blocks, you'll bump into Broadway. Take Broadway down to **Battery Park,** located at Manhattan's southern tip, where you'll pick up the **Statue of Liberty/Ellis Island Ferry** (212–269–5755). Although there is no admission charge for either of these historic attractions, the ferry is the only way to reach them. One round-trip ticket price of $7.00 for adults eighteen and over, $6.00 for seniors, $3.00 for children three to seventeen (free for children under three) will take you to both.

Few pieces of art have touched as many lives and elicited as wide a range of emotions as *Liberty Enlightening the World,* the 151-foot-tall statue presented as a gift from France in 1886. You can see the world from Lady Liberty's perspective if you have the stamina to climb the twenty-two stories to her crown. Otherwise you can take the elevator and twenty-four steps 120 feet up to the observation level at the foot of the pedestal. Before you leave, be sure to visit the **American Museum of Immigration** in the statue's base. A couple of words of warning—the stairs are narrow and inside temperatures can be extreme, especially in summer. During peak visiting times (late spring to early fall) waits for your ascent to the crown can be as long as two hours.

Located a few hundred yards north of the Statue of Liberty is **Ellis Island,** the "island of hope, island of tears" where more than twelve million immigrants were processed during the largest human migration in modern history, between 1892 and 1954. Interactive displays and exhibits of artifacts and photos, taped reminiscences, films, graphic displays, oral histories, and music give a human face to the immigrant experience. Scan the more than 500,000 names inscribed on the **American Immigrant Wall of Honor** and you'll find George Washington's great-grandfather; Myles Standish and Priscilla Alden; and perhaps one of your own ancestors. Sometime in 2000, a new genealogy facility called the **American Immigration History Center** is scheduled to open to help families trace their own family trees through state-of-the-art computer technology.

Both the Statue of Liberty and Ellis Island are open seven days a week, 9:00 A.M.–5:00 P.M., with extended hours in summer. For recorded information call (212) 363–3200.

Monday–Saturday between 3:30 and 5:30 P.M., it's officially teatime on Manhattan's chic **Upper East Side** and, specifically, at **Payard Patisserie & Bistro,** 1032 Lexington Avenue, between Seventy-third and Seventy-fourth Streets; (212) 717–5252). If you like you can order your tea (or coffee) at the espresso bar and select a la carte from the dazzling array of single-serving pastries and other confections displayed in the glass cases out front. Or you can have the full royal treatment with a $16 fixed price extravaganza.

## *Evening*

On Friday and Saturday evenings, the **Metropolitan Museum of Art** (1000 Fifth Avenue at Eighty-second Street; 212–535–7710) stays open until 8:45 P.M., giving you plenty of time to tour its fabulous exhibits spanning 5,000 years and the world. Return to ancient times at the Egyptian Temple of Dendur and pass through the Moon Gate into a serene Chinese garden. Check out the knight-wear at the medieval armor exhibit and three centuries of fashion at the Costume Institute. The Roof Garden offers exhibits of contemporary sculpture along with a sensational view of the city. For the ultimate late-night experience, savor a cocktail and some wonderful live music on the balcony of the Great Hall. The museum opens daily (except Monday) at 9:30 A.M. Closing hours are Sunday, Tuesday–Thursday at 5:15 P.M. Admission is $8.00 for adults, $4.00 for seniors and students, free for children under twelve with an adult.

*The Metropolitan Museum of Art.*

**DINNER: Union Square Cafe,** 21 East Sixteenth Street; (212) 243–4020. You'd better have a reservation if you plan to dine here because this pretty spot seems to be everybody's favorite. The menu (which recently featured such offerings as organic herb-roasted chicken with pumpkin poppy spaetzle and "earth and turf" with butternut squash alla Parmigiana, potato artichoke bread, grilled eggplant, and Swiss chard) changes regularly with the availability of fresh ingredients and the imaginative impulses of the chef. Expensive.

**LODGING: Fitzpatrick Grand Central,** 141 East Forty-fourth Street at Lexington Avenue; (800) 367–7701 or (212) 351–6800. There's a little bit of Ireland in midtown Manhattan at this exquisitely intimate new boutique hotel. Everything from the bedspread fabrics to the little bottles of water in the minifridge is imported from the Emerald Isle. At the end of each day, you'll find on your pillow a bedtime story taken from the _Book of Ancient Legends._ Weekday room rates, double occupancy, begin at $295; weekends at $195.

## DAY 2

## _Morning_

**BREAKFAST: Chelsea Market,** 75 Ninth Street between Fifteenth and Sixteenth. Cross over Broadway to the west side of town; then head south on Ninth Avenue. Still revered as the site where the first Oreo cookie was made, this circa 1840 National Biscuit Company (Nabisco) factory is now home to a new generation of great cookie bakers as well as vendors of all kinds of other good stuff from live lobsters to Thai to pot pies. And since the market opens early (8:00 A.M. weekdays, 10:00 A.M. weekends), this is a great place to build your own breakfast feast. Start at **Ronnybrook Dairy Farm** (212–741–6455) for some rich organic yogurt. Next stop, **Manhattan Fruit Exchange** (212–989–2444) for some additional nutrients; and, finally, **Amy's Bread** (212–462–4338) for some oven-fresh scones, brioche, muffins, or a true Parisian repast of one-half baguette with butter, coffee or tea, and jam ($2.50). Chelsea Market closes at 7:00 P.M.

Go east to Fifth Avenue, then south until you come to **Washington Square Park** and the **Washington Arch,** a 77-foot-high George Washington inaugural bicentennial monument regarded as the official entrance to **Greenwich Village.** Bordered by the Hudson River, Houston (pronounced _How_-stun) Street, West Broadway, and Fourteenth Street, the Village has been a gathering place for artists and rebels for more than one hundred years. You can still experience some of that electricity today in the music clubs along **Bleeker Street** and in the multimedia exhibits at the **Guggenheim Museum SoHo,** 575 Broadway at Prince Street; (212) 423–3500. Open Sunday and Wednesday–Friday 11:00 A.M.–6:00 P.M., Saturday until 8:00 P.M. Admission is $8.00 for adults, $5.00 for seniors and students, free for children under twelve accompanied by an adult.

If Greenwich Village lit the spark of innovation, then **SoHo** has turned it into a bonfire. Beginning south of Houston Street (hence its name) and bounded by Canal, Lafayette, and Sixth Streets, this neighborhood of 1850s cast-iron warehouses is filled with galleries and small ethnic shops selling everything from Tibetan singing bowls to African tribal art and foods from crepes to go to Peruvian seven-flavor chicken. Come on a Saturday or Sunday between 9:00 A.M. and 5:00 P.M. to Broadway and Grand where more than one hundred dealers of everything from fine jewelry to vintage fashions set up shop at the outdoor **SoHo Antiques Fair, Collectibles, and Craft Market** (212–682–2000). One word of warning: SoHo shops and galleries generally don't open until 11:00 A.M. or later.

## Afternoon

**LUNCH: Zoë,** 90 Prince Street between Mercer and Broadway; (212) 966–6722. The weekend brunch at Zoë is great whether you're craving breakfast or lunch fare. Some samples from the a la carte menu recently included stuffed brioche French toast; house-smoked trout with truffled vinaigrette; and wood-oven baked white pizza. Moderate to expensive.

Head back up to Midtown for the grand tour (the one the natives take their friends on) of Manhattan Island, its three rivers, seven major bridges, five boroughs, and more than twenty-five famous landmarks on a three-hour, full-island **Circle Line Cruise,** Pier 83, West Forty-second Street at the Hudson River; (212) 630–8885. Tickets cost $22 for adults, $19 for senior citizens, and $12 for children twelve and under. Cruises are offered daily.

## Evening

**DINNER: Carmine's,** 200 West Forty-fourth Street; (212) 221–3800. Everything here is bigger than life, especially the blackboard menu with its close to forty entree selections of Italian and American specialties ranging from pasta served more than twenty different ways to four different preparations of porterhouse steak. The portions are gigantic, enough to feed a family of four. Take home a doggie bag to save room for dessert. Expensive.

With all those twinkling lights and architecturally compelling theater buildings, you simply can't ignore **Broadway's theater district**. Just on the Great White Way between West Forty-first and West Fifty-fourth Streets alone there are almost three dozen theaters featuring new and classic musicals, comedies, and dramas. To find out what's playing, call the Broadway Line toll-free at (888) 411–BWAY (locally 212–302–4111) or New York City on Stage hot line at (212) 768–1818.

For a little après theater sweet, go north on Broadway to 154 West Seventieth Street where **Cafe Mozart** (212–873–3428) is waiting to dazzle you with an unbelievable array of French, Italian, Viennese, and American-inspired desserts and soothe your spirits with live classical music. The choices are endless . . . and torturous. Prices are moderate.

**LODGING:** Fitzpatrick Grand Central.

## DAY 3

## *Morning*

**BREAKFAST: Parlour Cafe,** lower level of ABC Carpet & Home, 881 and 888 Broadway at East Nineteenth Street; (212) 473–3000, ext. 255. The cafe's interior is a mix-and-match of old and new, rustic and regal, wood and whatever tables and chairs with lots of dangly crystal gas chandeliers. It might be tacky if it wasn't so much fun (just like the store above it, a gargantuan, fascinatingly funky emporium of everything). Weekend brunch (9:00 A.M.–3:00 P.M.) is an a la carte affair with a menu that ranges from scrambled eggs with chorizo, jalepeño, and roasted tomatoes to "Elaine's" famous bottomless stack of pancakes. Prices are moderate to expensive.

On Central Park West and West Seventy-ninth Street is the **American Museum of Natural History** (212–769–5100), a collection of works by and about the world's premier and most prolific artist—Mother Nature. You can trace the evolution of vertebrate life through the world's largest collection of fossils, including dinosaurs (about one hundred), ancient fishes, and mammals, and discover the intricacies of our interdependence with our floral, furred, finned, and feathered planet-mates. A new air and space exhibition, including a planetarium, is due to open in 2000. The museum is open seven days, 10:00 A.M.–5:45 P.M. Sunday–Thursday and until 8:45 P.M. Friday and Saturday. Admission (which does not include IMAX presentations) is $8.00 for adults, $6.00 for seniors and students, and $4.50 for children.

## Afternoon

**Central Park** (212–794–6564) is where New York comes to play. Feeding time for the sea lions is only one of the many delights at the **Central Park Wildlife Conservation Center**—aka the zoo—at 830 Fifth Avenue, off Sixty-fourth Street; (212) 861–6030. Here more than two dozen species of animals live and play in natural habitats. Admission is $3.25 for adults, $1.25 for seniors, 50 cents for children three to twelve, and free for children under three. Open seven days 10:00 A.M.–4:30 P.M. You can also rent a rowboat for paddling ($10 per hour), a bike for pedaling ($10–$14 per hour), or even take a one-hour gondola ride at **Loeb Boathouse on the Lake,** Seventy-second and Fifth Avenue; (212) 517–3623. Available end of March–October, 10:00 A.M.–dusk seven days. One dollar buys a ride atop one of the antique carved horses on the 1908 **carousel.** And we haven't even touched on all the free stuff you can do at the park such as enjoying the free warm weather concerts (212–360–3444) and following the age-old tradition of climbing the statues of Alice in Wonderland and Hans Christian Andersen.

## Evening

**Late lunch/early dinner: Carnegie Deli,** 854 Seventh Avenue, Fifth-fourth and Fifty-fifth Streets; (212) 757–2245. Don't even think of leaving New York without a trip for one of this deli's world-renowned pastrami sandwiches or, perhaps, a bowl of matzo ball soup. Scan the wall of fame and see which celebrities share your devotion to deli. For dessert, there's real New York strawberry cheesecake. Moderate. No credit cards. Open seven days from 6:30 A.M. until 4:30 the next morning.

To return home, go south to Thirty-fourth Street, then west on Thirty-fourth through the tunnel. Continue to Route 495 until it intersects with I–95. Go south on I–95 for 25 miles until you come to the New Jersey Turnpike. Go southwest on the New Jersey Turnpike 52 miles and exit at Route 168. Retrace the rest of the route from Day 1.

## THERE'S MORE

**City Pass.** One ticket good for half-price admission to the Empire State Building, Metropolitan Museum of Art, Top of the World Trade Center, Intrepid Sea Air Space Museum, American Museum of Natural History, Museum of Modern Art. $26.75 for adults, $18.00 for seniors, $21.00 for youths thirteen to eighteen. Pick up at first attraction visited.

**TKTS,** Times Square and World Trade Center Building 2. Same-day discount tickets for evening performances go on sale at 3:00 P.M. and for matinees at 10:00 A.M. (Times Square) or 11:00 A.M. (WTC 2).

**New York Apple Tours,** Visitors Information Center, Eighth Avenue and Fifty-third Street; (800) 876–9868 or (212) 944–9200. Create your own tour of the city with a double-decker bus ticket good for two days of hop-on, hop-off sightseeing at more than sixty-five Manhattan and Brooklyn landmarks. Night tours are included. $35 per person.

**Big Apple Greeter,** 1 Centre Street; (212) 669–2896. New York volunteers will introduce you to little-known places and local favorites on personalized, one-on-one tours. Most incredible is the fact that this service is absolutely free

**Big Onion Walking Tours,** (212) 439–1090. Two-hour weekend ethnic neighborhood walking tours led by guides who hold advanced degrees in American history from Columbia or New York Universities. Every weekend and holiday year-round. Generally inexpensive tour prices vary with destination.

**Museum of Modern Art,** 11 West Fifty-third Street (Fifth Avenue); (212) 708–9400. Eye-opening creations from the 1880s to the present rendered in media ranging from painting and sculpture to architecture and film. Friday pay-what-you wish evenings from 4:30 to 8:30 P.M. Otherwise admission is $9.50 for adults, $6.50 for seniors and students, free for children under sixteen. Open daily 10:30 A.M.–6:00 P.M.; closed Wednesday.

**United Nations,** First Avenue at Forty-sixth Street; (212) 963–7713. Multilingual forty-five-minute guided tours offered daily (except Saturday and Sunday in January and February) 9:15 A.M.–4:45 P.M. Tours include the general assembly, council chambers, and works of art from member nations. Admission is $7.50 for adults, $5.00 for seniors, $4.50 for students, $3.00 for children grades one through eight.

**NBC Studio Tour,** 30 Rockefeller Plaza; (212) 664–4000. A one-hour guided behind-the-scenes sneak-peak at your favorite programs. Daily 9:00 A.M.–4:30 P.M. $10 per person; children under six not admitted.

### SPECIAL EVENTS

**June, July, August.** New York Shakespeare Festival, Delacorte Theater, Central Park; (212) 539–8500. Founded by Joseph Papp, these spectacular free summer productions of Shakespeare and other works are performed in an open-air amphitheater.

**November.** Annual Thanksgiving Day Parade. Begins at Central Park West at Seventy-seventh Street, continues down Broadway to Macy's Herald Square (Thirty-fourth Street), and finishes at Seventh Avenue.

**December.** Ice-skating at Rockefeller Center, Fifth Avenue between Forty-ninth and Fiftieth Streets; (212) 332-7654. Daytime and evening skating mid-October through April. Rentals available.

**December.** Lighting of the Christmas Tree, Rockefeller Center; (212) 698–2950.

### OTHER RECOMMENDED RESTAURANTS AND LODGINGS

## *New York City*

Hotel Wales, 1295 Madison Avenue (at Ninety-second); (212) 876–6000. This beautifully restored turn-of-the-century boutique hotel is located in the Carnegie Hall section of the Upper East Side. Continental breakfast each morning, tea and classical music recitals in the afternoon. Room rates range from $205 to $520.

Hotel Wolcott, 4 West Thirty-first Street, between Fifth and Broadway; (212) 268–2900. Ornate architecture, gilded and mirrored lobby, crystal chandeliers, and wrought-iron railings in a budget-priced hotel? Yes, and clean, comfortable rooms as well for $99–$140 double occupancy. Convenient midtown location makes the United Nations, Broadway theaters, shopping, and other major attractions easily walkable.

Grand Central Oyster Bar, Grand Central Station, Forty-second Street between Vanderbilt and Lexington Avenues; (212) 490–6650. A little pricey, but where else can you dine on more than thirty types of oysters and other fresh seafood in the rejuvenated splendor of one of New York's most famous landmarks?

Cowgirl Hall of Fame, 519 Hudson Street at Tenth; (212) 633–1133. Whimsical Western-style decor and good chuck-wagon grub (for example, Cajun fried chicken and catfish po'-boys) at moderate prices.

## FOR MORE INFORMATION

New York Convention & Visitors Bureau; (212) 484–1200; www.nycvisit.com.

Times Square Visitor Center, Broadway between Forty-sixth and Forty-seventh Streets. Open daily 8:00 A.M.–8:00 P.M.

# Baltimore, Maryland

## CITY OF FIRSTS

### 2 NIGHTS

*Visionaries • Good Sports • Star-Spangled Sites*

According to *The World Book Dictionary,* the word *rampart* is defined as a wide bank of earth, often with a wall on top, built around a fort to help defend it: *O'er the ramparts we watched. . . .*

OK, that's settled. I thought we should get that out of the way before visiting the home of Fort McHenry and the flag that inspired a certain lawyer named Key to wax poetic on a mid-September dawn almost two centuries ago. Well, the flag is *still* there, bigger than life (although with thirty-five additional stars and two less stripes), flying o'er the ramparts. And the city of Baltimore is still inspiring poets as well as painters, sculptors, and other artists, artisans, and innovators.

Perhaps that's why Baltimore's history is filled with so many firsts, including the first use of an umbrella in the United States (1772)—as well as the establishment of the first umbrella factory (1828). Baltimore also claims the building of the first passenger railroad train ("Tom Thumb" in 1830) and the manufacture of such necessities of life as ice cream (1851) and bottle caps (1892).

Baltimore is also a city of first-class historical, recreational, and cultural attractions. Ringing its lively harbor are some of the finest—and some of the funkiest—museums, shops, and dining spots you'll ever find in one place. But don't stop there. Beyond the waterfront are the city's distinctive neighborhoods, each with its own colorful personality, individual history, particular style of hospitality, and delicious flavors.

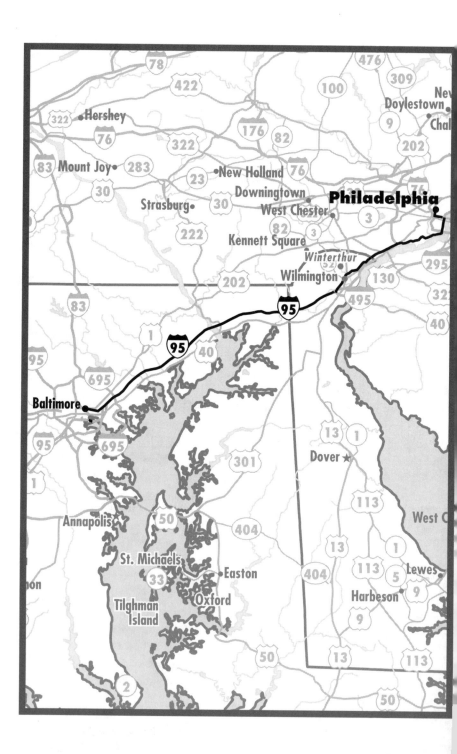

## DAY 1

## *Morning*

Baltimore is only 93 miles southwest of Philadelphia. But, realistically, the drive takes about two hours. The most straightforward route for getting there is to take the Schuylkill Expressway (I–76) to Route I–95. Travel south on 95 for 87 miles to Route 895 south and the Harbor Tunnel. From the tunnel, take Route 40 west straight into Baltimore. As most visitors do, follow the signs to the Inner Harbor and find a parking space nearby.

Shortly after Route 40 turns into Franklin Street, you will come to a fork in the road; take the right branch, which will put you onto Mulberry Street. From Mulberry, continue going east to Light Street. Turn right at Light Street and follow it down to Pratt Street, where you will make a left. Your first destination is the **Star-Spangled Flag House and 1812 Museum** at 844 East Pratt Street (410–837–1793). If you ask anyone from Philadelphia to name the most famous seamstress in American history, the answer would undoubtedly be Betsy Ross. In Baltimore, however, the answer would be Mary Pickersgill, whose flag may not have been the first one, but it certainly was a big (30 feet by 42 feet) and historically significant one.

In this restored and authentically furnished 1793 house, Pickersgill hand-stitched the star-spangled banner that flew above the ramparts of Fort McHenry the September night it was shelled by the British in 1814 . . . the same flag that stirred Francis Scott Key to pen the poem that became the lyrics of our national anthem. Be sure to go out in the garden to see the 18-foot-by-27-foot stone map of the United States in which each state is cut from stone native to it. Open Tuesday–Saturday 10:00 A.M.–4:00 P.M. Admission is $4.00 for adults, $3.00 for seniors, $2.00 for youngsters under eighteen.

## *Afternoon*

**LUNCH: Della Notte,** 801 Eastern Street (corner of President and Eastern); (401) 837–5500.

Continue east on Pratt Street and turn right on President. You are now entering the picturesque neighborhood known as **Little Italy** and you're just in time for lunch. Like warm, generous family homes, the restaurants of Little Italy welcome you with irresistible aromas and an abundance of Old and New World specialties. Della Notte's ornate Renaissance-style facade is the first thing to catch your eye and the giant faux tree "growing" out of the restaurant's center is hard to miss, but this is not one of those all theatrics no substance places. Order the crackling-crisp calamari fritti or polenta with a tomato, cream, and ground veal sauce; hearty minestrone soup; panini on freshly baked focaccia; or brick-oven pizzas and you'll know that under that somewhat glitzy interior beats a true Italian heart. Inexpensive to moderate.

On to the famous **Inner Harbor** to park your car for the day. One convenient spot is in the lot directly across from the main entrance to the American Visionary Art Museum (800 Key Highway), where you can park all day for $3.00. At the harbor, you'll spot signs for **Ed Kane's Water Taxi** (800–658–8947 or 410–563–3901), which, for a flat rate of $3.50 for adults, $2.25 for children under ten, offers an all-day ticket for transportation to fifteen landings and thirty-five of the city's major attractions.

Your water taxi ticket also covers ground transportation (which you'll pick up at Landing No. 4) to the **Fort McHenry National Monument and Historic Site** at the end of Fort Avenue (410–962–4290). Even if its ramparts hadn't been mentioned in America's most patriotic paean, this star-shaped brick fortress, originally built during the Revolution and in use through World War II, would be a site worth seeing.

Begin at the **Visitor Center,** where a film dramatization of the day- and nightlong bombardment by the British will prepare you for a tour of this formidable fort that includes restored powder magazines, guardrooms, officers' quarters, and barracks. The grounds are open daily 8:00 A.M.–5:00 P.M.(the Visitor Center until 4:45 P.M.) with extended hours in summer. Entrance fee is $5.00 for adults seventeen and over; children sixteen and under are admitted free.

Take the water taxi across the harbor to the **National Aquarium in Baltimore** (Pier 3, 501 East Pratt Street, 410–576–3800), where more than 10,000 creatures are on display in naturalistic habitats representing environments ranging from Maryland's own mountain ponds to the Atlantic coral reef to a tropical rain forest. In the Marine Mammal Pavilion, you can watch a dolphin show or come face-to-face with sharks. The upper level Rain Forest is home to all kinds of creatures from monkeys to brightly colored birds. Hours: July and August, 9:00 A.M.–8:00 P.M. every day; November–February, 10:00 A.M.–5:00 P.M. Saturday–Thursday (until 8:00 P.M. on Friday); March–June and in September and October, 9:00 A.M.–5:00 P.M. Saturday–Thursday (until 8:00 P.M. on Friday ). Admission is $11.95 for adults, $10.50 for seniors, $7.50 for children three to eleven, and free for children under three.

Back across the harbor is the **American Visionary Art Museum** at 800 Key Highway (410–244–1900). The 55-foot-high, multicolored, wind-powered whirligig outside in the central plaza should be your tip-off that this is not your traditional art museum. Inside its seven galleries are displayed the works of self-taught *visionary artists*—ordinary people from farmers to housewives to the homeless who are "inspired by the fire within" to express themselves in media ranging from painting and sculpture to tattoos and toothpicks. If you need some quiet time to adjust to this unusual experience, take a few moments to mellow out in the Wildflower/Sculpture Garden with its woven tree limb meditation chapel/nondenominational wedding altar. Open Tuesday–Sunday 10:00 A.M.–6:00 P.M. Admission for adults is $6.00; $4.00 for children, students and seniors.

## Evening

**DINNER: Joy America Cafe,** American Visionary Museum; (410) 244–6500. Just as the museum celebrates the individuality and imagination of the human spirit, the menu at its cafe showcases our cultural and ethnic diversity with its one-of-a-kind organic offerings, such as grilled shallot and black fig pizza with fontina and Parma ham or seared chicken roulade rubbed with blue corn tortilla dust and rolled with gorgonzola, black turtle bean salsa, and basil leaves. The views are impressive, too, whether they look out over the Inner Harbor or into the open kitchen. Pastry chef Elizabeth French has also established quite a following for her innovative desserts including the Whirligig, a sweet replica of the sculpture, and Spoons of Joy, a masterpiece of engineering involving crème brûlée. Moderate to expensive.

After dinner, walk over to the wooden finger piers in front of the Maryland Science Museum for one of the weekend calypso and reggae cruises aboard **Clipper City** (410–539–6277), a replica of one of the famous tall ships that plied the waters of the East Coast from 1854 to 1892. Not your ordinary sightseeing excursion, this is a three-hour floating party with live music, dancing, and a cash bar. Cruises are available April–November. The reggae cruise sails from 8:00 to 11:00 P.M. Friday and Saturday; tickets are $20 per person. Clipper City also offers two-hour sailing tours of the Inner and Outer Harbor daily ($12.00 for adults, $2.00 for children) and a three-hour brunch sail on Sunday ($30).

**LODGING: Celie's Waterfront Bed & Breakfast,** 1714 Thames Street, Fell's Point; (410) 522–2323. Celie's is located right across the water from Inner Harbor in the heart of one of the nation's oldest surviving maritime communities, the 1730 village of Fell's Point. To get there by car, take Pratt Street east to President Street; turn right onto President Street and follow it to Fleet Street. Turn left onto Fleet Street and go 8 blocks to Ann Street. Turn right onto Ann Street and travel 3 blocks to Thames Street. Make a left onto Thames Street to No. 1714 in the middle of the block; Celie's is the gray building with the rose trim.

Don't let the big iron gate at the door intimidate you. This three-story, seven-room B&B is a charmer. The cheerful antique-appointed rooms, some with fireplaces and/or whirlpools, are filled with sunshine from overhead skylights and windows that open onto the private garden, atrium, and harbor. There are flowers everywhere—from those growing in the colorful window boxes to the garden-fresh blooms that adorn each guest room. Double occupancy rates range from $115 for the courtyard room with two twin beds to $200 for the deluxe harbor front rooms. Continental breakfast is included.

## DAY 2

## *Morning*

**BREAKFAST:** Celie's Waterfront Bed & Breakfast. Not only does Celie's provide you with a hearty buffet spread of fresh fruits, breads, cereals, and gourmet coffees and teas, but it also offers a variety of beautiful settings in which to enjoy your repast. My favorite is the roof deck with its sweeping views of the Baltimore skyline and Inner Harbor. When the weather is cool there's usually a warming fire in the dining room.

Aside from its cobblestone streets and more than 350 original examples of eighteenth- and nineteenth-century architecture, Fell's Point is known for its wide array of art galleries and antique and specialty shops. **Angeline's Art Gallery & Boutique** (1631 Thames Street/Brown's Wharf; 410–522–7909) specializes in paintings, jewelry, curios, and sculptures by local and national artists, including owner Angeline V. Culfogienis herself. For something a little more exotic, visit **Japonaji** at 905 South Ann Street (410–522–1087), which features everything from ikebana to netsuke to sushi supplies. And if you want to know "who done it," ask at **Mystery Loves Company** (1730 Fleet Street; 410–276–6708), a bookstore specializing in new and used mysteries and first editions.

If you're a fan of the television series *Homicide*, you'll want to check out the **Waterfront Hotel** (1710 Thames Street; 410–327–4886), which has been prominently featured on the show since 1992. A hotel from the Civil War up through World War II, it currently operates as a tavern.

Take the car back to the downtown area. But instead of making your left-hand turn at Pratt Street, continue north to Fayette Street. Turn left on Fayette and take it to Amity Street. Turn right onto Amity.

Master of the macabre Edgar Allan Poe left a trail of houses and haunts that stretch from Boston to Richmond (including Philadelphia, of course). One of the most significant was his aunt Maria Clemm's house at 203 Amity Street, where he lived from 1832 to 1835 and began his writing career. Today the **Edgar Allan Poe House & Museum** (410–396–7932) has one of the most extensive collections of artifacts around, along with exhibits and a fine video presentation. Open Wednesday–Saturday noon–3:45 P.M. Admission $3.00 adults, $1.00 children twelve and under.

Two years after his 1847 death in Baltimore, Poe's permanent address became the **Westminster Burying Grounds & Catacombs** at Fayette and Greene Streets (410–706–2072). To get there from the Poe house, go south on Amity Street to the end of the block. Turn left onto Lexington to the first traffic light, which is Fremont. Turn right onto Fremont and follow it for 2 blocks south to Baltimore Street. Turn left at Baltimore and go 3 blocks to Paca. Make a left at Paca, go 1 block and turn left onto Fayette Street; the next street you will come to is Greene. Immediately on your left at the corner you will see Westminster Hall and the grave site of Edgar Allan Poe. Poe was originally buried in an unmarked grave behind the church until 1865, when a local schoolteacher organized a campaign encouraging children to donate their "pennies for Poe" to pay for his reburial in the family plot and a fitting monument to mark his resting place. The cemetery is open to the public from 8:00 A.M. until dusk.

## *Afternoon*

**LUNCH: Lexington Market,** Lexington and Eutaw Streets; (410) 685–6169. From the corner of Fayette and Greene, it's only 1 block north and about 2 blocks east to the oldest city market in the United States where more than 130 merchants sell all kinds of fresh produce, baked goods, and local meats. Monday–Saturday 8:30 A.M.–6:00 P.M.

You may have noticed that I haven't yet referred you to a place to feast on genuine Maryland crab cakes. Some of the best and most famous are served right here at **John W. Fraidley Seafood** (400 West Lexington Street; 410–

*Inside the B&O Railroad Museum.*

727–4898). An all-lump crabmeat cake with two sides is $14.95. Seafood sandwiches start at $3.95. Fraidley also sells uncooked and prebrowned crab cakes for take-home and can continually replenish your supply through its mail order service!

Turn left at the corner of Monument and Eutaw Streets, then right at Mulberry Street. Follow Mulberry east to North Charles Street; turn left. At North Charles and Mt. Vernon Place, you will see the 178-foot-high white marble column that was the first architectural monument (begun in 1815) built in honor of George Washington. At the **Washington Monument** (410–396–0929) there's a ground-floor museum and, for a $1.00 donation, you can climb the 228 steps to the top for a fabulous view of the city. Open Wednesday–Sunday 10:00 A.M.–4:00 P.M.

Aside from the monument, this urban oasis of nineteenth-century homes and beautifully landscaped parks called **Mount Vernon** is also a well-known cultural destination. The **Walters Art Gallery** (600 North Charles Street at

Mount Vernon Square; 410–547–9000) exhibits more than 30,000 objects, including Oriental art, Fabergé, and Lalique, spanning fifty centuries and four continents. Open Tuesday–Friday 10:00 A.M.–4:00 P.M., Saturday and Sunday 11:00 A.M.–5:00 P.M. General admission is free.

While you're in the neighborhood, you may want to check if there is a performance scheduled at the world-famous **Peabody Conservatory of Music,** 1 East Mt. Vernon Place (410–659–8124). The conservatory presents a free music series of operas, orchestra concerts, and recitals by students and instructors. If you would rather see a good play, **CenterStage,** the state theater of Maryland, at 700 North Calvert Street (410–332–0033) offers a six-play mainstage season series of original and classic comedies, dramas, and musicals from September to June for ticket prices ranging from $10 to $45.

## Evening

**DINNER: John Steven Ltd.,** 1800 Thames Street, Fell's Point; (410) 327–5561. Weather permitting, dine alfresco in the courtyard at this very, very charming restaurant. The internationally inspired menu contains some interesting surprises, such as the safari burger made from 100 percent ostrich meat; spicy Cajun crawfish pie; and seafood-packed Baltimore bouillabaisse. Light fare sandwiches and salads begin at $6.00 and heartier entrees range from $7.00 for a vegetable stir-fry to $21.00 for steak and crab cake.

**LODGING:** Celie's Waterfront Bed & Breakfast.

## DAY 3

## Morning

**BREAKFAST:** Celie's Waterfront Bed & Breakfast.

You'll be heading toward home today, but there are a few major stops you'll be making before your escape comes to an end. Take the car and head back toward the Inner Harbor. This time make your left-hand turn at Lombard Street, then a left onto Howard Street. Another left onto Camden Street will take you to **Orioles Stadium at Camden Yards** (333 West Camden Street; 410–685–9800), home of Baltimore Orioles baseball and one of the most famous ballparks in the country. If there's a home game scheduled for today or tonight, grab a ticket for a real old-fashioned "take me out to the ball game" experience at this natural Maryland bluegrass stadium modeled on the ones Babe Ruth and the gang used to play in. Ticket prices range from $9.00 for bleachers to $35.00 for a club box. By the way if you happen to miss baseball season, the Baltimore Ravens football team now has its own stadium at Camden Yards. For information call (410) 261–RAVE.

## *Afternoon*

**LUNCH: ESPN Zone,** 601 East Pratt Street at the Power Plant, Inner Harbor; (410) 685–ESPN. Can't get enough of sports? ESPN Zone features dining experiences in a simulated television studio set or in front of a 16-foot video wall that shows all sports all day. The menu features everything from burgers and ribs to Cajun fettuccine and cedar-planked salmon. Inexpensive to moderate. Indulgent yet irresistible desserts include the signature Zone Pancake, an "adult's only" skillet creation featuring a soufflélike pancake topped with homemade vanilla ice cream, fresh berries, and Chambord maple syrup.

To work off those calories (or at least try to fool your brain into thinking that's what you're doing), go score some points at the ESPN Zone's pay-as-you-play **Sports Arena.** This 10,000-square-foot entertainment area has more than 150 interactive baseball, football, basketball, and golf-oriented games and attractions, including state-of-the-art sports simulators and video games. Restaurant hours are Monday–Friday 11:30 A.M.–11:00 P.M.; weekends 11:00 A.M.–11:00 P.M. (until midnight Sunday). Arena hours are Sunday–Thursday until 11:30 P.M.; Friday and Saturday until 12:30 A.M.

Go west on Lombard Street, turn left at Schroeder Street, then left again onto Pratt Street and continue 1 block to the corner of Poppleton. It's a little out of the way, but for train and history buffs, the **B & O Railroad Museum** (301 West Pratt Street; 410–752–2490) is worth the effort. Many American cities have railroad museums, but only Baltimore is the home of the oldest station in the Western Hemisphere (Mt. Clare, which now serves as the entrance to the museum) and the origin point for the maiden voyage of the first passenger train (Tom Thumb). More than 200 pieces of full-size antique and replica locomotives, cars, and other equipment and artifacts are displayed in this thirty-seven-acre museum's five historic buildings and yard. At the hub is the 1884 roundhouse with its centerpiece wooden turntable that was used to repair the B & O line's passenger trains until 1953. Open daily 10:00 A.M.–5:00 P.M. Admission $6.50 for adults, $4.00 for children.

To return to Philadelphia, head east on Pratt Street to Charles Street; turn right onto Charles and right again at Conway Street. Turn left in front of the ballpark, onto I–395. Stay toward the right; you'll be exiting almost immediately onto I–95 north. Pass through the toll tunnel and take I–95 north all the way back home. The trip should take about two hours.

### THERE'S MORE

**Baltimore Zoo,** Druid Hill Park; (410) 366–5466. Wilderness and farmland habitats are home to more than 2,000 animals from around the world. Open daily 10:00 A.M.–4:00 P.M., extended summer weekend hours. Admission is $8.50 for adults, $5.00 for seniors and children two to fifteen.

**Harborplace and the Gallery,** Inner Harbor; (410) 332–4191. Together, these two complexes connected by a skywalk are home to about 200 national name and one-of-a-kind shops, sit-down restaurants, and takeout eateries. Open Monday–Saturday 10:00 A.M.–9:00 P.M., until 6:00 P.M. Sunday.

**Maryland Historical Society,** 201 West Monument Street; (410) 685–3750. Among the more than 100,000 artifacts pertaining to Maryland's history housed here are Francis Scott Key's original manuscript of "The Star-Spangled Banner" and the nation's largest collection of nineteenth-century silver. Open Tuesday–Friday 10:00 A.M.–5:00 P.M., Sunday 9:00 A.M.–5:00 P.M. Call in advance.

**Baltimore Maritime Museum,** 802 South Caroline Street, Inner Harbor; (410) 396–3543. Three historic ships (including the only one to survive the attack on Pearl Harbor), a lighthouse, and other exhibits and hands-on activities provide a wealth of maritime history. Open daily 10:00 A.M.–6:00 P.M. in summer; call for off-season hours. Admission is $5.50 for adults, $4.50 for seniors; $3.00 for youngsters five to twelve, and free for children under five.

**Baltimore Museum of Art,** 10 Art Museum Drive, North Charles Street at Thirty-first Street; (410) 396–7100. More than 100,000 objets d'art ranging from ancient mosaics to renowned contemporary works, including a whole wing devoted to post-1945 art. Open Wednesday–Friday 11:00 A.M.–5:00 P.M., Saturday and Sunday 11:00 A.M.–6:00 P.M. Admission is $6.00 for adults, $4.00 for seniors and students, children under eighteen free.

**Maryland Science Center,** 601 Light Street at Key Highway, Inner Harbor; (410) 685–5225. Three floors featuring a science arcade filled with hands-on activities, an IMAX theater, a planetarium, and live images from the Hubble telescope. Open 10:00 A.M.–5:00 P.M. Monday–Friday, until 6:00 P.M. Saturday and Sunday. Hours are extended during the summer. Admission is $9.50 for adults, $7.00 for seniors, military personnel, and children. Children under four are admitted free.

**Pimlico Racetrack,** Northern Parkway; (410) 542–9400. Thoroughbred racing at this 140-acre track, famous for being the second jewel in the annual Triple Crown, begins in mid-March and ends in mid-June. Dark days are usually Monday and Tuesday.

**Babe Ruth Birthplace Museum,** 26 Emory Street (2 blocks from Camden Yards); (800) 453–BABE or (410) 727–1539. Exhibits in this 12-foot-wide row house where George Herman Ruth was born chronicle his life and career and feature Orioles memorabilia. Open daily April–October 10:00 A.M.–5:00 P.M. (7:00 P.M. on Orioles home game nights); November–March 10:00 A.M.–4:00 P.M. Admission is $6.00 for adults, $4.00 for children five to sixteen, and free for children under five.

**National Museum of Dentistry,** 31 South Greene Street; (410) 706–0600. If you think a museum devoted to teeth sounds as if it would be about as much fun as a root canal, you haven't seen the feats of an iron jaw performer, a tooth jukebox, and George Washington's not-so-wooden teeth. Open Wednesday–Saturday 10:00 A.M.–4:00 P.M., Sunday 1:00–4:00 P.M. Admission is $4.50 for adults, $2.50 for seniors and students.

### SPECIAL EVENTS

**First Thursday of every month.** First Thursdays on Charles Street; (410) 342–SHOW. Live music, free admission to Mt. Vernon attractions, and lots of other good stuff from 5:00 to 8:00 P.M. Park for $1.50 at Penn Parking on Franklin and Charles Streets with validation from participating merchants and attractions.

**May.** Preakness Celebration and Race, Pimlico Racetrack, Northern Parkway; (410) 542–9400. This weeklong festival leading up to the running of the Preakness Stakes, the middle jewel in the prestigious Triple Crown, features hot air balloons, parades, and lots of other pre-race hoopla.

**Memorial Day Weekend–Labor Day Weekend.** Free Summer Concert Series, Harborplace Amphitheatre; (800) HARBOR–1 or (410) 332–4191. Rock, tropical rhythms, and patriotic tunes every Friday, Saturday, and Sunday.

**September.** A Star-Spangled Weekend, Fort McHenry; (410) 962–4290. This annual commemoration of the bombardment of the fort and the writing of "The Star-Spangled Banner" includes military encampments and reenactments, a concert by the U.S. Army Field Band and Soldiers Chorus, and fireworks.

### OTHER RECOMMENDED RESTAURANTS AND LODGINGS

## *Fell's Point*

Admiral Fell Inn, 888 South Broadway; (800) 522–7377 or (410) 522–7377. You'd never know this elegant European-style inn was once a seaman's hostel and, later, a YMCA. Among the amenities are beautiful Federal period–style furnishings, an on-premise gourmet restaurant, and an English-style pub. Rates in season range from $195 to $225. Off-season rates vary.

Lista's, 1637 Thames Street; (410) 327–0040. An authentic taste of Santa Fe in a waterfront setting. Bountiful dinner combinations are a real bargain at $11–$15.

## *Baltimore*

Abacrombie Badger Bed & Breakfast, 58 Biddle Street; (410) 244–7227. Located in the heart of Baltimore's cultural center, this enchanting 1880s townhouse has an engaging personality all its own. Continental breakfast is included. Rates for double occupancy range from $105 to $145 per night.

Sissons, 36 East Cross Street; (410) 539–2093. Maryland's first brew pub has a spicy past as a saloon/hangout for gamblers. So it's no wonder the moderately priced menu finds its inspiration in the robust Cajun flavors of the American South and seasonings of the Southwest. The brewery also turns out seventeen varieties of handcrafted beer.

## FOR MORE INFORMATION

Baltimore Area Visitors Center, 301 East Pratt Street; (800) 282–6632 or (410) 837–4636. Open daily 9:00 A.M.–5:30 P.M.

Baltimore Area Convention & Visitor Association; (800) 343–3468 or (410) 659–7300; www.baltimore.org.

Maryland Office of Tourism Development; (410) 767–6298; www.mdisfun.org.

# Washington, D.C.

## MONUMENTAL DECISIONS

### 2 NIGHTS

*President's Residence • International Neighborhoods
Smithsonians Galore*

You might not normally think of Washington, D.C., as a free-and-easy kind of town. But it can be if you know where to look . . . and how to get around.

Now that doesn't mean you can leave the credit cards at home. D.C.'s outstanding hospitality of the food-and-lodging variety is far from free. But many of its most outstanding attractions—and hidden treasures—are.

If you're going in peak season and want to avoid standing in lines at the White House, U.S. Capitol, Supreme Court, Bureau of Engraving and Printing, and the Federal Bureau of Investigation, try calling your congressional representative's office to request advance tour tickets. Special guided congressional tours (separate from the regular tours) of most of these sites may also be available. Supplies are limited so your best bet is to call at least several months in advance. With or without advance tickets, all of these attractions are free.

## DAY 1

### Morning

Washington, D.C., is 144 driving miles south of Philadelphia. However, you will be driving on the outskirts of several heavily trafficked cities, so expect to be on the road about three hours. Take the Schuylkill Expressway (I–76) east to I–95 south 88 miles to I–895 south through the Harbor Tunnel to I–295

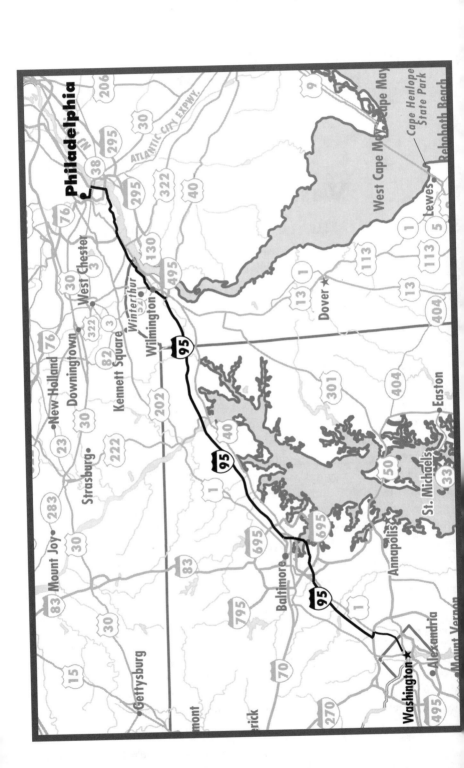

(Baltimore-Washington Expressway). I–295 turns into Route 95 again and continues south to Route I–495 (the Beltway). Go west on 495 to exit 30 and head south on Route 29 for about 15 miles. Route 29 will become Sixteenth Street and will take you to the intersection of Sixteenth and H Streets, 2 blocks from the White House.

Once in the city, your focal point should be the U.S. Capitol.

**IMPORTANT DRIVING TIPS:** Radiating out from the Capitol are four quadrants: northwest, northeast, southwest, and southeast—all addresses should include one of these quadrant designations. The divider streets for the quadrants are North Capitol, South Capitol, and East Capitol Streets, and the National Mall. Numbered streets run north–south with addresses getting higher the farther away you go from the Capitol; east–west streets are named for letters in alphabetical order.

Your best bets for downtown parking are under the bridge in West Potomac Park near the Jefferson Memorial (free, but fills up early) or at Union Station (paid, 50 Massachusetts Avenue NE). Be sure to carefully read all signs—parking can be tricky all over Washington.

## *Afternoon*

**LUNCH: 2 Quail Restaurant,** 320 Massachusetts Avenue NE, about 4 blocks north of the Capitol; (202) 543–8030. Three townhouses on historic **Capitol Hill** have been joined together and furnished with big, overstuffed library chairs, floral drapes, all kinds of pictures, and other homey touches to create a slightly funky, totally charming dining spot. The $8.95 prix fixe lunch is always a good buy with its choice of soup or salad and imaginative variations of chicken, pasta, and fish.

In D.C. the **Smithsonian Institution** operates fourteen art, history, and science museums and galleries in addition to the National Zoo. From the Capitol building it's an easy walk due west on the **National Mall** to nine of them. Each is unique and all of them are wonderful. So how do you make up your mind which one (or ones) you will visit during this brief foray to our nation's capital? Head straight for **The Castle,** the can't-miss-it regal piece of 1855 architecture that graces 1000 Jefferson Drive, SW, about midway between the Capitol and the Washington Monument. The Castle (202–357–2700) is the official visitors center for the Smithsonian where you can pick up brochures, maps, and other information as well as see a twenty-four-minute video overview of all the other museums and galleries in the complex.

All of the Smithsonians are free and open daily 9:00 A.M.–5:30 P.M. unless otherwise noted.

The largest and most visited of the Smithsonians—and, in fact, of all the museums in the world—is the **National Air and Space Museum,** Independence Avenue between Fourth and Seventh Streets SW; (202) 357-1686. You can actually trace the history of aviation just by viewing its star-studded lineup of vehicles, including the Wright Brothers' 1903 *Flyer,* Charles Lindbergh's *Spirit of St. Louis,* the Apollo 11 command modules and rockets, and the Skylab orbital workshop. Other highlights include more than fifty interactive stations, a planetarium, and an IMAX theater (202–357–1686). Museum admission is free; ticket prices for the IMAX theater are $5.00 for adults and $3.00 for children.

By this time you're probably ready for some outdoor fun. But it's hard to tear yourself away from all of the fascinating educational and historical attractions Washington has to offer. No problem! Head to the west end of the Mall to the body of water called the Tidal Basin. Get a rental at **Tidal Basin Pedal Boats** (Ohio Drive and Tidal Basin, NW; 202–484–0206) and have some fun floating in the shadow of the majestic marble-columned rotunda of the **Thomas Jefferson Memorial** (202–426–6841) under the watchful eye of the 19-foot-tall bronze statue of our third president. Pedal boats are available seven days a week, March–September, 10:00 A.M.–6:00 P.M. Rental rates are $7.00 per hour for a one-person boat, $14.00 for a two-person boat. The Jefferson Memorial is open daily, 8:00 A.M.–midnight.

## *Evening*

Get ready for an international evening visiting two of D.C.'s most colorful neighborhoods. Travel west on Massachusetts Avenue until you come to DuPont Circle; about 6 blocks past the circle is **Embassy Row,** where you can take a mini-tour of the world just by taking a stroll down the street. Nearly 150 countries are represented in Washington by embassies and chanceries. The majority of them are located here in these tree-shaded, late-Victorian mansions that can be easily identified by the national flags, coats-of-arms, and other accoutrements they proudly display.

On to **Adams-Morgan,** a little United Nations unto itself with its multi-ethnic sights, sounds, and flavors. To get there take Massachusetts Avenue going east until you intersect with S Street. Make a left onto S, go 3 blocks to Connecticut Avenue and turn left. In 2 blocks Connecticut Avenue will intersect in a V-shape with Columbia Road. Follow Columbia Road about 3 blocks into Adams Morgan.

In this neighborhood of colorful wall murals and eclectic art and music, you will find boutique shops of just about every nationality selling a wide range of wares, from beaten metal jewelry to authentic garb from Africa and other faraway places. Restaurants and sidewalk cafes tempt you with a multitude of accents, including Vietnamese, Brazilian, Hindi, Cajun, Caribbean, French, and Italian.

**DINNER: Red Sea,** 2463 Eighteenth Street NW; (202) 483–5000. One of the most popular cuisines in D.C. is Ethiopian, and this is quite possibly the best of the numerous establishments that offer it. The food is terrific—traditional spicy-hot *wat* (stew) and milder *alecha* dishes made rich and flavorful with a golden butter spiked with herbs, onions, and light spices called *niter kibbeh.* There are lots of options for vegetarians and non. Dining is a communal affair, with everyone tearing off pieces of *injera* (a pancakelike sourdough bread), scooping up the wat and other savory morsels, and popping the delectable packages into their mouths. Even kids will love this Ethiopian finger food. Inexpensive to moderate.

To return to Georgetown, go south on Eighteenth Street to M Street, then west on M Street to Wisconsin.

Top off your evening at **Chelsea's** in Georgetown (1055 Thomas Jefferson Street NW; 202–298–8222) with the wry topical insights of a group of former congressional staffers cum musicians/political satirists called **Capitol Steps.** Cost is $33.50 per person for show and bar credit (dinner and show is $50.00). Performance times are 8:00 P.M. on Saturday and 7:30 P.M. on Sunday.

**LODGING: Latham Hotel,** 3000 M Street NW, Georgetown; (800) 368–5922 or (202) 726–5000. With its elegantly appointed lobby, spacious rooms, and gracious staff, the Latham offers a combination of comfort, luxury, and personal attention that is indicative of the fine European accommodations on which it is modeled. It is also home to one of Washington's most celebrated fine dining restaurants, Citronelle. Rates range from $149 to $190. Special winter discount packages are available.

# BETWEEN AND BEYOND

## DAY 2

## *Morning*

**BREAKFAST: Citronelle,** at the Latham Hotel; (202) 625–2150. Internationally acclaimed chef Michel Richard has made this spot a Washington landmark for lunch and dinner with his personal take on American-French cuisine. This pretty stone and mirror-walled restaurant also serves a great breakfast, including a hearty everything-you-can-think-of buffet ($12.50), or you can sample a bit of signature Richard with an a la carte chicken shiitake sausage, eggs, and potatoes feast or a peasant-style omelette.

Head into downtown D.C. as early as possible to grab a parking space at the Jefferson Memorial or Union Station. Again, be sure to read the signs. To get into the downtown area, go east on M Street to Pennsylvania Avenue. Make a right onto Pennsylvania and follow it to the White House.

If you want to tour the **White House** (1600 Pennsylvania Avenue NW; 800–717–1450 or 202–456–7041), but don't have a prearranged congressional tour or other ticket, make your first stop the **White House Visitor Center** (1450 Pennsylvania Avenue NW; 202–208–1631). During peak spring and summer seasons admission is by timed ticket only and the lines can get excruciatingly long. Your window of opportunity for touring is quite narrow (10:00 A.M.–noon Tuesday–Saturday), so get there as early as you can. (The Visitor Center is open from 7:30 A.M.)

Throughout your tour, you will see many reminders of former first families, particularly in the portraits of presidents and first ladies that hang on the walls of the corridors and hallways and in the China Room's displays of presidential china and glass. In the East Room, you can almost envision the fabulous weddings of White House daughters Nellie Grant, Alice Roosevelt, and Lynda Bird Johnson. (If you feel a sense of déjà vu, it's because this is also the place where the presidential press conferences originate.)

It isn't likely that you will be granted an audience with the president while visiting the White House, but you can make your friends back home believe you did by posing with one of the life-size cardboard cutouts of the president and first lady that enterprising photographers have set up right outside the gates.

If you're one of those people who thinks that making money is what life is all about, take a stroll down by the Tidal Basin to the **Bureau of Engraving and Printing** (Fourteenth and C Streets SW; 202–622–2000) and get a few pointers from the pros. Each year, more than $100 billion in currency is printed here, with new bills (along with postage stamps and other important stuff) being produced at the rate of 7,000 sheets per hour—make sure you warn the kids not to try this at home. Exhibits at the **Visitor Center** trace the history of money from pieces of eight to our present currency. Open for guided tours Monday–Friday 9:00 A.M.–2:00 P.M. Peak season timed tickets are available from 7:30 A.M.

## *Afternoon*

Head back to Georgetown and park at the hotel. Then walk across the street to **Miss Saigon** (3057 M Street NW; 202–333–5545) for a selection of delectable Vietnamese specialties to go. The restaurant is particularly well known for its sweet, yet tongue-tingling, clay pot–cooked caramel meat and seafood. For vegetarians, there's also a faux duck meat and vegetable sauté that could easily pass for the real thing. Inexpensive to moderate.

With lunch in hand, stroll the few blocks to **Washington Harbor** to rent a canoe at **Thompson Boat Center,** 2900 Virginia Avenue NW; (800) 654–6308 or (202) 333–9543. This is the best (and one of the only) means of transportation for getting to **Theodore Roosevelt Island** (703–289–2530), a beautiful eighty-eight-acre wilderness preserve in the Potomac between Georgetown and Virginia dedicated to one of America's most ardent environmentalists. Wandering the 2 miles of footpaths, you may very well find yourself alone (except for the 17-foot bronze statue of our twenty-sixth president) to commune at will with the abundant trees, wildflowers, and wildlife.

**LUNCH:** Picnicking is permitted at Theodore Roosevelt Island if you don't mind eating on a bench or bringing along a blanket to spread out on the grass.

On your return to Georgetown, head north on Rock Creek Parkway until you come to the **Arlington Memorial Bridge.** With the Lincoln Memorial on one side and the Arlington House (also known as the Robert E. Lee Memorial and Custis-Lee Mansion) on the other, this bridge was viewed as a symbolic post–Civil War link between the North and South. Cross to the Virginia side and you'll come to **Arlington National Cemetery,** once the estate where General Robert E. Lee and his family lived. It's now the final resting place for presidents, astronauts, and some 200,000 U.S. soldiers who fought in battles from the American Revolution to the Gulf War. At the main entrance you will see the new **Women in Military Service for America Memorial** and the **Visitor Center,** where you can pick up free maps and

*Inside the National Air & Space Museum.*

information. Parking fees range from $1.25 to $2.00 per hour.

Admission is free if you choose to explore the site on foot, but you also have the option of boarding a **Tourmobile** ($4.75 for adults, $2.25 for children three to eleven) for a narrated highlights tour that includes the **Kennedy Grave Sites,** the ceremonial changing of the guard at the **Tomb of the Unknowns,** the **Shuttle Challenger Memorial,** the **Iwo Jima Statue,** and **Arlington House** (703–557–0613). At the south end of the cemetery is an area known as **Freedman's Village,** once a village for fugitive and liberated slaves, now the burial place of more than 3,800 of those who lived there during and after the Civil War. Arlington National Cemetery is open to visitors 365 days a year 8:00 A.M.–7:00 P.M. April 1–September 30, and until 5:00 P.M. October 1–March 31.

To get back into downtown Washington, cross the bridge to Constitution Avenue, then turn right onto Constitution Street.

By late afternoon the traffic in downtown Washington usually begins to thin out a bit, which means that your chances of finding a parking space increase and the lines at even the most popular monuments dramatically decrease. More than just another 555-foot-tall marble obelisk, the **Washington Monument** (National Mall at Fifteenth Street NW; 202–426–6839) has many stories to tell. Each of its 193 commemorative stones has a history of its own. Once inside, it's only a seventy-second elevator ride to the top and a panoramic view of the city you'll find nowhere else. Admission is free. Open daily 8:00 A.M.–midnight.

At the west end of the Mall at Twenty-third Street NW, the seated marble statue of our sixteenth president looks out over the capital from its columned Greek temple inscribed with the immortal words of his own Gettysburg and Second Inaugural Addresses. The **Lincoln Memorial** (202–426–6839) is open daily 8:00 A.M.–midnight. Free.

## *Evening*

Every evening year-round at 6:00 P.M., you can see a free hour-long live musical and/or dance performance at the **Millennium Center** in the grand foyer of the **John F. Kennedy Center for the Performing Arts,** New Hampshire Avenue NW, at Rock Creek Parkway; (800) 444–1324 or (202) 467–4600. On stage (actually a specially built platform) you might see musicians representing genres from classical to jazz to folk, dancers from toe to tap, or even storytellers. No tickets are required. The Kennedy Center complex features five theaters and is home to the National Symphony Orchestra, the Washington Opera, and the American Film Institute.

**DINNER: Filomena,** 1063 Wisconsin Avenue NW, Georgetown; (202) 33–PASTA. You can't miss Filomena's when you're walking down Wisconsin Avenue—not with its two "pasta mamas" merrily working in the front window. The Italian gardenlike dining room with its statuary, bold displays of flowers, and softly glowing antique gas lamps is romantic. Presidents dine here, in a little area reserved for VIPs who might need a little special protection. But when it comes to service, the same gracious hospitality is extended to all. Resist filling up on the home-baked focaccia with pesto butter because the Italian regional entrees are enormous. Complimentary after-dinner decanters of sambuca and amaretto are accompanied, in the Italian tradition, by three coffee beans—one each for love, wealth, and health. Moderate to expensive.

**LODGING:** Latham Hotel.

## DAY 3

## *Morning*

**BREAKFAST: Martin's Tavern,** 1264 Wisconsin Avenue NW, Georgetown; (202) 333–7370. Weekend brunch here has been a D.C. tradition for generations. Since it opened in 1933, Martin's has been a regular stop for a wide variety of movers and shakers from presidential to media types. There's something for everyone from the basic ham-eggs-potatoes purist to the luxury seekers' lump-meat crab cakes. Inexpensive to moderate.

If you can possibly plan your Washington quick escape for a weekend when historian, author (*The Burning of Washington*), and tour guide extraordinaire **Anthony Pitch** is scheduled to lead one of his Sunday two-hour walks through Georgetown, for heaven's sake do it! And be sure to arrive at the R Street steps to Georgetown Library at the corner of Wisconsin Avenue at 11:00 A.M. sharp because, as Pitch will show you, there's much more to this historic neighborhood than its profusion of great restaurants and glitzy shops. A master storyteller with a huge storehouse of facts at his fingertips, he will regale you with stories of the noted and the notorious who have always populated Georgetown and of the soap operas that continue to play out behind the elegant front doors of its town homes. Among the highlights are residences of past and present literary lights, politicos, suspected spies, even the neighborhood Mata Hari. Cost is $10.00 per person. For a schedule of Pitch's tours, call (301) 294–9514.

## *Afternoon*

Drive back to the National Mall area one last time. A few blocks north of the mall between the Capitol and the White House is **Ford's Theater** (511 Tenth Street NW; 202–638–2941, tickets 800–955–5566 or 703–218–6500), where you can take in a matinee or evening performance of a new musical or original production in the restored setting of one of America's most infamous sites. It's kind of eerie to sit in this theater and look up at the bunting-draped presidential box with its empty chairs. It's even eerier to go down to the basement museum (free admission) where John Wilkes Booth's gun, Abraham Lincoln's bullet-torn coat, and other artifacts from that fateful night in April 1865 sit silently on display. Theater performance prices range from $27 to $40; tours (daily 9:00 A.M.–5:00 P.M.) are free.

After the shooting, Lincoln was carried to the **Petersen House** across the street (516 Tenth Street NW; 202–426–6924) where he died at 7:22 the next morning. Outside the house is a tree that visitors have turned into a makeshift memorial by covering its trunk with pennies. Open daily 9:00 A.M.–5:00 P.M. Modest admission fee.

## *Evening*

**DINNER: Georgia Brown's,** 950 Fifteenth Street NW; 202–393–4499). For some real Southern comfort, don't miss the low country South Carolina fare. Specialties include buttermilk-fried chicken, Carolina gumbo, catfish, and pecan-crusted lamb chops served with such down-home go-withs as fried green tomatoes, dirty rice, hoppin' John, and, of course, grits. Mostly moderately priced. Sunday gospel or jazz brunch, too.

To return to Philadelphia, go north on Route 29 about 15 miles, past Walter Reed Hospital; then get on the Beltway going east at exit 28 AB and stay on until exit 27 (I–495). Take I–495 north to I–95. Take I–95 north all the way to Philadelphia. The trip should take about three hours.

## THERE'S MORE

**Tourmobile Sightseeing Trams,** (888) 868–7707 or (202) 554–5100. For a single ticket price ($14.00 for adults, $7.00 for children three to eleven), you can hop on and off all day at twenty-five stops convenient to more than forty major historic sights and attractions (including Arlington National Cemetery).

**Ticketplace,** Old Post Office Pavilion (ground floor), 1100 Pennsylvania Avenue NW; (202) 842–5387. Selling half-price day-of-show and full-price advance tickets for sixty of Washington's cultural institutions and theaters. Discount tickets for Sunday and Monday are sold on Saturday.

**National Museum of American History,** Fourteenth Street and Constitution Avenue NW; (202) 357–2700. Edison's phonograph, the original star-spangled banner, and Fonzi's jacket—all in one place! And let us not forget that famed statue with the head of George Washington and the body of an Arnold Schwarzenegger look-alike. Free. Open daily 10:00 A.M.–5:30 P.M.

**National Zoological Park,** 3000 block, Connecticut Avenue NW. Home to 5,000 animals from around the world, including Hsing Hsing, the remaining giant panda of the two donated by the People's Republic of China. Be sure to get there in time for his 11:00 A.M. or 3:00 P.M. feeding. Open daily 10:00 A.M.–4:30 P.M.; until 6:00 P.M. May–mid-September.

**Federal Bureau of Investigation,** E Street NW, between Ninth and Tenth Streets; (202) 324–3447. Guided tours, available weekdays from 8:45 A.M. to 4:15 P.M., take you to visit exhibits of weapons used by Capone, Dillinger, and Bonnie and Clyde. You'll also see the inner workings of the DNA lab and watch a sharpshooting demonstration. Free.

**U.S. Capitol,** Capitol Hill, First Street between Constitution and Independence Avenues; (202) 224–3121. Guided tours are offered Monday–Saturday, 9:30 A.M.–7:00 P.M. Free.

### SPECIAL EVENTS

**Late March–mid-April.** Cherry Blossom Festival, various locations; (202) 547–1500. Each year Washington celebrates the blossoming of its 6,000 Japanese cherry trees with a parade, crowning of the Cherry Blossom Festival Queen, sports activities, and arts and crafts shows. Free.

**April.** Annual White House Easter Egg Roll, White House South Lawn and Ellipse; (202) 456–2200. Children of all ages are invited to participate in this day of fun and entertainment.

**December.** National Christmas Tree Lighting Pageant of Peace, the Ellipse; (202) 619–7222. The celebration includes seasonal music and caroling. Nightly choral performances and special programs until New Year's Day. Free.

### OTHER RECOMMENDED RESTAURANTS AND LODGINGS

## Washington, D.C.

Georgetown Inn, 1310 Wisconsin Avenue NW; (202) 333–8900. The first guests when this hotel opened in 1962 were the Duke and Duchess of Windsor, followed by Charles Lindbergh, Pearl Buck, and all of the Apollo astronauts. Colonial warmth, European style. Deluxe rooms range from $175 to $250.

Hay-Adams Hotel, Sixteenth and H Streets NW; (202) 638–6600. Right across Lafayette Square, this small, intimate hotel is a feast of architectural delights. The rooms can run quite high, so be specific and ask for one of the Quaint Rooms (twelve-by-twelve feet, queen-size bed, $205 weekdays, $179 weekends) or an Interior Room Queen ($300 weekdays, $220 weekends).

Kinkead's, 2000 Pennsylvania Avenue NW; (202) 296–7700. Adapting international dishes to American ingredients and taste is the hallmark of this very popular restaurant. Moderate to expensive.

Old Ebbitt Grille, next to the White House; (202) 296–7700. D.C.'s oldest saloon (1856) has fed presidents from Grant to Clinton and is a regular haunt of White House staffers. The menu features good crab cakes, mussels, and an oyster bar paired with oyster-friendly wines. Prices are surprisingly moderate for a legend.

Red Sage, 605 14th Street NW; (202) 638–4444. The creative hand of superchef Mark Miller is evident in menu and decor inspired by the Old and New West where smoked and roasted meat, game, seafood, and poultry are among the house specialties. Prices run the gamut from $5.00 to $13.00 for variations on chilis, tacos, burritos, enchiladas, and the like to $30.00 for more elaborate dinner grub. Sunday jazz brunch.

J. Paul's, 3218 M Street NW; (202) 333–3450. The place to go for burgers, crab cakes, and hickory-and-applewood ribs. Moderately priced menus for lunch, dinner, and brunch.

## FOR MORE INFORMATION

Washington D.C. Convention & Visitors Association; (202) 789–7000; www.washington.org.

D.C. Office of Tourism & Promotion; (202) 727–1576.

# BETWEEN AND BEYOND

# Alexandria and Mount Vernon, Virginia

## GEORGE'S BELOVED

### 2 NIGHTS

*Hometown of Titans • Presidential Party Place*
*Torpedo on Target*

George Washington may have slept in a lot of places, but he always came home to his "beloved Alexandria." Who could blame him? For 2½ centuries this lovely city on the Potomac has been capturing the affections of Americans with its timeless beauty and vibrant personality.

In Old Town Alexandria, today and yesterday happily coexist—sometimes in a single building. On gas-lantern-lit cobblestone streets named for international and American royalty, you can admire three centuries of architecture ranging from the modest to the magnificent. Then only a block or two away, find yourself in a modern mecca of top-shelf shopping and dining.

There has rarely been a dull moment here from its days as a busy seventeenth century seaport to its role as a tinderbox for revolution and a somewhat reluctant defender of the capital during the Civil War. You can immerse yourself in all of that history by day. At night, however, Alexandria becomes a real party town, with an energy reminiscent of New Orleans during Mardi Gras. In fact, the place where George himself used to kick back is still around . . . and it's still a pretty happening spot.

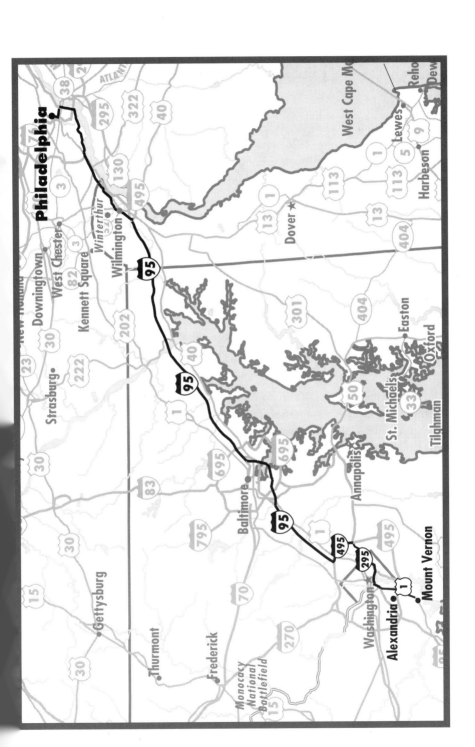

## BETWEEN AND BEYOND

## DAY 1

## *Morning*

It's a 2½-hour (152-mile) drive from Philadelphia to Alexandria. Take the Schuylkill Expressway (I–76) to I–95; go south on 95 for 95 miles to I–895. Take 895 through the Harbor Tunnel and continue for 12 miles until you come to I–295 (the Baltimore-Washington Expressway). Take the Expressway for 29 miles to the Anacosta Freeway and stay on that for 21 miles. Get back on I–495 (the Capital Beltway) and drive south for 2 miles into Alexandria.

## *Afternoon*

Stop at the **Ramsey House Visitor Center** (221 King Street; 800–388–9119 or 703–838–4200; open daily 9:00 A.M.–5:00 P.M.) and ask for a free twenty-four-hour guest pass that will allow you to park for free at any of the two-hour metered spots in Old Town. While you're there, buy a Market Square Block Ticket ($9.00 for adults, $5.00 for children eleven to seventeen) for admission to three of the area's major attractions—Carlyle House, Gadsby's Tavern Museum, and Stabler-Leadbeater Apothecary Museum.

**LUNCH: King Street Blues,** 112 North St. Asaph Street; (703) 836–8800. This real Southern roadhouse tucked away just west of King Street in Old Town is a fun place with its whimsical murals and funky artwork, including a random pair of 3-D legs protruding from one wall. In a position of honor hangs a reverent stained-glass tribute to the restaurant's famous Wet Willie, a giant frankfurter with shredded pork barbecue, cheese, and other stuff. Also in residence (but not yet immortalized in stained glass) are its burger brother, the Wet Wimpy and German sausage cousin, the Wet Wilhelm. The ribs are definitely worth a try, too. Generally moderate prices.

A few blocks east of St. Asaph Street and just north of King Street is **Carlyle House** (212 North Fairfax Street; 703–549–2997), one of the most important yet little-known buildings in American history. Built in 1753 as a personal residence, it became the headquarters for British General Edward Braddock in 1775 and the place where the idea for the Stamp Act, trigger for the Revolution, was born. Open 10:00 A.M.–5:00 P.M. Tuesday–Saturday; noon–5:00 P.M. Sunday.

**Stabler–Leadbeater Apothecary Shop** (105–107 South Fairfax Street; 703–836–3713), opened in 1792, was the place where George and family, Daniel Webster, and Robert E. Lee bought everything from medicine to house paint. When the Depression caused the shop to close in 1933, the doors were simply locked and everything left as it was. Now this amazingly well-preserved collection speaks volumes about the theories and tools that were the basis of medical care in early America. Open Monday–Saturday, 10:00 A.M.–4:00 P.M., Sunday 1:00–5:00 P.M.

George Washington attended many balls and, in fact, held more than one of his own birthnight celebrations at **Gadsby's Tavern,** 134 Royal Street (703–838–4242). Today Gadsby's has been restored to its eighteenth-century splendor and lives on as both a highly regarded restaurant serving authentic Early American fare (more about the food later) and a museum furnished in period tavern style. Open April–September, Tuesday–Saturday 10:00 A.M.–5:00 P.M. (October–March, 11:00 A.M.–4:00 P.M.; Sunday 1:00–5:00 P.M. (October–March until 4:00 P.M.).

A popular spot to river- and boat-watch is **Founders Park** (400 North Union Street; 703–838–4343), particularly at the **City Marina** at the park's southeast tip. The waterfront is also a favorite open-air stage for a variety of colorful street performers. And you never know when one of those magnificent tall ships will happen to dock nearby.

## *Evening*

**DINNER: Bilboe Baggins,** 208 Queen Street; (703) 683–0300. If you are one of the many ardent fans of J.R.R. Tolkien's *The Hobbit* and *Lord of the Rings* trilogy, you have to love this piece of the books' Middle Earth kingdom in Old Town Alexandria. The setting, with its literary-inspired murals and stained-glass windows, has the look of a charming old wood-and-brick cabin in the woods. There's also a lively bar that serves draft beer on tap. The menu shows imagination as well, from the tortellini with salmon, crabmeat, and fresh dill to citrus shrimp. Moderate.

In a town with as tumultuous a history as Alexandria, you can be sure there will still be some restless spirits from the past floating (flying? walking?) around. You can hear some of their stories—and perhaps even experience your own sighting—on the one-hour guided **Doorways to Old Virginia Original Ghost & Graveyard Tour;** (703) 548–0100. The tour departs from the Ramsey House Visitors Center late March through early November (weather permitting) Friday and Saturday at 7:30 and 9:30 P.M. and Sunday at 7:30 P.M. only. Cost is $5.00 for adults, $3.00 for ages seven to seventeen, free for children six and under.

**LODGING: Morrison House,** 116 South Alfred Street; (703) 838–8000. Designed and furnished in the style of a grand manor house of the late eighteenth-early nineteenth century Federal period, this fine hotel reflects the character of Old Town Alexandria in the most charming of ways. Small and intimate, it is a bastion of elegance, from its comfortable parlor (the perfect place for daily afternoon tea and the popular piano sing-alongs that are held here every weekend) to its handsome mahogany-paneled library. Guest room amenities include mahogany poster beds, brass chandeliers and sconces, decorated fireplaces, and Italian marble baths. Morrison House also has two distinctive restaurants—the laid-back, clublike Grille Room with its piano bar and the more upscale Elysium. Room. Rates range from $150 to $295. Parking is an additional $10 per day.

## DAY 2

## *Morning*

**BREAKFAST: Alexandria Farmers' Market,** South Plaza, City Hall (200 block of King Street); (703) 838–4770. When in Alexandria, do as the Colonials did–rise and shine early so you can get the freshest breakfast fixings at this farmers market held every Saturday from 5:00 to 9:00 A.M. George Washington was an early trustee of the market and would regularly send wagon loads of produce from Mount Vernon to be sold. Local farmers still bring their produce, meats, and plants to be sold here, and you can assemble a hearty morning meal from their fruits and fresh-squeezed juices, just-from-the-oven baked goods (including Southern ham biscuits), and tantalizing cinnamon-laced coffee. Look for real homemade crafts here as well.

Although he was born in Stratford, Virginia, 607 Oronoco Street (4 blocks north of King Street) in Old Town Alexandria is remembered as the **Boyhood Home of Robert E. Lee** (703–548–8454). It was to this stately 1795 Federal mansion that Revolutionary War soldier and statesman Henry "Light Horse Harry" Lee brought his family to live before the War of 1812 and where they remained after he died not many years later. It is said that upon his return here after the surrender at Appomattox Courthouse, one of the first things Robert E. Lee did was to climb the garden wall to see if his treasured snowball bush was in bloom. A guided tour of the house reveals rare antiques and family mementos from Lee's early years. Open Monday–Saturday 10:00 A.M.–4:00 P.M., Sunday 1:00–4:00 P.M. Admission.

Less than 4 blocks south on Cameron and North Washington Streets is **Christ Church** (703–549–1450), the house of worship regularly attended by George Washington (his pew has been preserved) and Robert E. Lee. Built between 1767 and 1773, this still active Episcopal church welcomes visitors Monday–Saturday 9:00 A.M.–4:00 P.M., Sunday beginning at 2:00 P.M. Donations are welcome. Among the grave sites in the adjacent cemetery are those of eighteenth-century Yankee seamen and Confederate prisoners of war.

## *Afternoon*

**LUNCH: Firehook Bakery & Coffeehouse** (main commissary), 214 North Fayette Street, corner of Fayette and Cameron Streets; (703) 519–8020. While you're picking up a sandwich and assorted goodies for your afternoon picnic, you can enjoy a great show watching the bakers mix, knead, shape, and bake traditional and exotic artisan breads in huge wood-burning ovens. Inexpensive sandwiches, giant cookies, including the award-winning Presidential Sweet (oatmeal with chocolate chips, dried cherries, pecans, and coconut). Open weekdays. For weekend breads and pastries, Firehook also has a retail outlet at 105 South Union Street by the waterfront; (703) 519–8021.

Take your picnic lunch to **Fort Ward Museum and Historic Site** (4301 Braddock Road; 703–838–4848) located 2½ miles northwest of Old Town. To get there, follow King Street west to T.C. Williams High School. At the traffic light in front of the school, turn right on Kenwood Avenue. At the next block, turn left on West Braddock Road; follow it for ¾ mile. The entrance is on the right.

Immediately after Virginia's official secession in 1861, Union troops occupied Alexandria and nearby Arlington and began building a series of sixty-eight earthenwork forts known as the Defenses of Washington. The best preserved one, the newly restored Fort Ward, sits within a more than forty-five-acre park, which also includes picnic facilities and an open-air amphitheater where free twilight concerts are presented on Thursday evenings at 7:00. Adjacent are a museum (open Tuesday–Saturday, 9:00 A.M.–5:00 P.M., Sunday noon–5:00 P.M.) and a reconstructed officers' hut that interpret the site's history and feature a broad-ranging display of Civil War artifacts. The park is open daily from 9:00 A.M. to sunset. Both the park and museum are free.

One of the things that makes Alexandria's waterfront so exciting is the fabulous art center known as the **Torpedo Factory,** 105 Union Street; (703) 838–4399). Once used for the manufacture of weapons of war—such as the torpedo on display on the first floor—this huge building now houses studios for more than 160 artists. Although not all of the work spaces are active at the same time, you can always find sculptors, painters, photographers, printmakers, jewelers, and other talented residents working in any number of media from paper and fibers to silver and gold. The center also showcases the works of over 1,500 more nonresident artists in its five cooperative galleries. On the third floor is the **Alexandria Archaeology Museum,** a working laboratory where you can watch the pros piece together the city's past through rescued artifacts. The Torpedo Factory is open daily 10:00 A.M.–5:00 P.M.; the Archaeology Museum on Tuesday–Friday, 10:00 A.M.–3:00 P.M., Saturday until 5:00 P.M. and Sunday 1:00–5:00 P.M. Both are free.

## Evening

**DINNER:** **The Fishmarket,** corner of King and Union Streets; (703) 836–5676. The glistening seafood in the front display case should be your first clue that your catch of the day will be fresh. Built in 1765 and family-owned and -operated since 1950, the Fishmarket is indeed just what its name implies, as well as a restaurant where you can have your marine life prepared thirty different ways. Just about everything on the very moderately priced menu is available in lunch and dinner portions.

On weekend evenings when the museums close, Old Town shifts into party mode as the streets fill with revelers, and music from King Street pubs and clubs spills out onto the sidewalks. A number of the shops are open late, too, adding another dimension of entertainment to the evening. One of these is **Bird in the Cage Antiques** (110 King Street; 703–549–5114), which plays old Rudy Vallee records to lure you upstairs into its fantasyland of things past where little girls (and their mothers) have a ball trying on vintage prom dresses and feather boas, and every collectible has a story. For an international sampling of handmade crafts, art, and wearables from around the world, stop in at **Ten Thousand Villages** (824 King Street; 703–684–1435), which represents thirty developing countries, and **Women's Work** (1201 King Street; 703–684–7376), which represents fifty western Pacific islands.

Follow the long line to the **Scoop Grill and Homemade Ice Cream** (110 King Street; 703–549–4527) for a cone of Jack Daniel's, papaya, chocolate raspberry truffle, or other lick of heaven they've concocted today. If you're lucky (or not, depending on your sense of humor), you will be served by Hugh, an actor by day and the frozen confection equivalent of Seinfeld's Soup

Nazi by night. It's all in fun, and, anyway, a little abuse may help assuage your guilt at eating all that ice cream!

**LODGING:** Morrison House.

## DAY 3

*Morning*

**BREAKFAST: Two-Nineteen Restaurant,** 219 King Street (next to the Visitors Center); (703) 549–1141. If the weather is nice, you can sit outside and savor a traditional New Orleans brunch as you watch the weekend people-parade on King Street. You can have your eggs perched atop fried Gulf fish with hollandaise, on artichoke bottoms over creamed spinach, or reclining on sautéed lump crabmeat and cloaked with brandied cream. Other Creole specialties include red beans, sausage, and rice; Louisiana fried oysters; and good old jambalaya. Moderate brunch and lunches, moderate to expensive dinners.

You couldn't possibly leave George Washington country without paying a visit to the place he cherished most, not only in Virginia, but in the world— **Mount Vernon** (703–780–2000). The 8-mile trip south takes only about twenty minutes by car along the scenic George Washington Memorial Parkway, but an even more interesting way to travel there is by boat. On the *Miss Christin* (703–548–9000), which sails daily at 10:00 A.M. and noon, the trip takes fifty minutes each way, but it's a relaxing sail across the Potomac with plenty of beautiful sights to see along the way. Tickets, which include admission to Mount Vernon, are $22 for adults, $10 for children.

During your 2½-hour layover at Mount Vernon, you'll have ample time to tour the mansion that Washington built between 1735 and 1787. Among the original furnishings are the bed where our first president died and his family's coat of arms. Recently opened at Mount Vernon is George Washington's personal study, filled with personal possessions that offer some interesting insight into the human side of this American legend. The more than 500-acre estate also features a working 4-acre Pioneer Farm; the slaves' living quarters, burial ground, and memorial; and the tombs of George, Martha, and other members of the family. Many special programs and exhibitions are held here throughout the year. Open daily April–August 8:00 A.M.–5:00 P.M.; March, September, and October 9:00 A.M.–5:00 P.M.; November–February 9:00 A.M.–4:00 P.M. Admission for adults is $8.00, $7.50 for senior citizens, and $4.00 for children.

*Mount Vernon, where George Washington slept whenever he could.*

**LUNCH: Mount Vernon Inn,** adjacent to the mansion; (703) 780–0011. I am always wary of dining establishments associated with major attractions because all too often they are merely bastions of mediocre food and so-so service hiding behind a stellar name. But this was an extra delightful surprise. The dining rooms, of course, are pure Colonial, complete with wood beams and fireplaces. However, instead of the usual cutesy theme menu (OK, so they do insist on calling one of their offerings a "pye"), the items reflect the chef's creativity as well as a true respect for old-time Southern cooking. You can start with a bowl or mug of Virginia peanut and chestnut soup, then move on to Tidewater jambalaya or salmon corn cakes. If it's just a sandwich you want, you can make it a burger topped with Smithfield ham and cheddar, or Southern barbecue. The prices are surprisingly inexpensive to moderate.

If you took the early boat, you should arrive back in Alexandria at about 4:00 P.M. To return to Philadelphia, reverse route from Day 1. The drive home should take about 2½ hours.

### THERE'S MORE

**Lee-Fendall House Museum,** 614 Oronoco Street, Alexandria; (703) 548–1789. Guided tours of this home to several generations of the Lees of Virginia reveal family furnishings, records, and inventories, as well as wonderfully extensive collections of nineteenth- and twentieth-century dolls and dollhouses. Open Tuesday–Saturday 10:00 A.M.–4:00 P.M., Sunday noon–4:00 P.M. Admission is $4.00 for adults, $2.00 for children eleven and up.

**George Washington Masonic National Memorial,** King Street at Callahan Drive, Alexandria; (703) 683–2007. One of the most outstanding collections of Washington memorabilia in existence. Open daily 9:00 A.M.–5:00 P.M. Free.

**Potomac Mills Mall,** 2700 Potomac Mills Circle, Prince William; (703) 643–1770. A mecca for domestic and international travelers, this monster manufacturers' outlet and name brand discounters' complex features 220 stores. Open year-round. Monday–Saturday 10:00 A.M.–9:30 P.M., Sunday 11:00 A.M.–7:00 P.M.

### SPECIAL EVENTS

**Note for 1999.** There will be many special events throughout 1999 to commemorate Alexandria's 250th anniversary and the bicentennial of George Washington's birth. Call the Visitors Center at (800) 388–9119 or (703) 838–4200 for schedules and information.

**February.** George Washington Birthnight Banquet and Ball, Gadsby's Tavern and Museum. This annual black tie/Colonial costume banquet and ball held each year on the Saturday evening of Washington's Birthday weekend is much like the ones George and Martha attended right here in 1798 and 1799. Reservations are required. Admission.

**February.** Revolutionary War Encampment, Fort Ward Museum and Park. Held the Sunday afternoon of Washington's Birthday weekend, this event features reenactors demonstrating camp life during the Revolution and re-creating a skirmish between British and Colonial troops. Free.

**July.** Annual Virginia Scottish Games and Festival, Episcopal High School, 3901 West Braddock Road; (703) 912–1943. Alexandria celebrates its Scottish roots with the U.S. National Highland Heptathlon, dancing competitions, bagpipe parades, and a British antique automobiles show. Admission.

## OTHER RECOMMENDED RESTAURANTS AND LODGINGS

### *Alexandria*

Princely Bed & Breakfast Ltd.; (800) 470–5588 (Monday–Friday 10:00 A.M.–6:00 P.M.). Offering one-stop shopping, this company features a selection of thirty-one of Old Town's finest eighteenth- and nineteenth-century private residences with guest accommodations. Rates ranging from $75 to $150 per night include private bath and "continental plus" breakfasts.

Ecco, 220 North Lee Street; (703) 684–0321. How could a restaurant that greets you with a life-size Charlie Chaplin shyly holding out a bouquet of silk flowers be anything but fun? This lively Italian spot makes delicious pastas and pizzas (there's even a sauceless white pie loaded with garlic, red peppers, and scallions if romance isn't on your day's menu). Portions are generous and prices quite moderate.

Fin & Hoof Restaurant & Art Gallery, Sheraton Suites Alexandria, 801 North St. Asaph Street; (703) 549–6622. The daily breakfast buffet is a real bargain, featuring fresh fruit, made-to-order omelettes and pancakes; scrambled eggs, and all kinds of breakfast meats; assorted muffins, pastries and cereals; juice and coffee—all for only $7.50! The restaurant also is known for its steak and seafood lunches and dinners.

Ireland's Own, 132 North Royal Street; (703) 549–4535. Tuck into some traditional ham and cabbage, an Irish mixed grill (complete with black and white pudding) or real Irish stew—either O'Flaherty's with lamb or Dublin-style with beef. Moderate. Entertainment nightly.

Gadsby's Tavern, 138 North Royal Street; (703) 548–1288. Quite good Colonial American fare (yes, they serve pye) including George Washington's Favorite Duck served in authentic surroundings. Period-style musical entertainment is offered in the evenings. Moderate lunches, moderate to expensive dinners, great Sunday brunch (rum French toast—yum!).

## FOR MORE INFORMATION

Alexandria Economic Development Partnership; (703) 739–3820.

Alexandria Chamber of Commerce; (703) 739–3810.

Virginia Tourism Corporation; (800) 932–5827 or (804) 786–2051; www.virginia.org.

Alexandria Transit Company's DASH system bus service; (703) 370–DASH.

# Richmond, Virginia

## RISING FROM THE ASHES

### 2 NIGHTS

*Warehouses of Fun • Rafting Through Town*
*The Other White House*

From almost the very beginning of the Civil War in 1861, Richmond was more than just the capital of the Confederate States of America. It was a principal center of manufacturing, supplies, and medical care as well. In short, it was the Confederacy's heart, soul, and major source of strength. After a bloody, four-year-long struggle, the city was burned in 1865 . . . not by invading Union troops, but by the heartsick sons of the South who felt they had to resort to this desperate measure to prevent their remaining supplies from falling into enemy hands.

Today Richmond is still recovering from the ravages of war and the subsequent economic turmoil that continued for many years. But instead of trying to wipe out all memories of this devastating past, the city has tried to preserve as much of its history as possible, while celebrating the present and building toward the future.

The city's diverse neighborhoods provide a colorful mosaic of cultures and a variety of historical perspectives that help to put a human face on the facts we have all read in our history books. From antebellum plantations to the Confederate White House to the post–Civil War "home of black capitalism," Richmond explores the complexities of its—and America's—past.

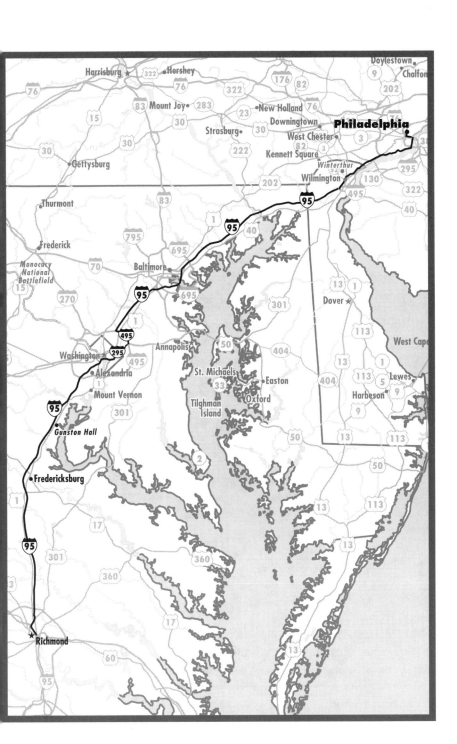

## DAY 1

### Morning

It's 251 driving miles from Philadelphia to Richmond, Virginia, which would take you about 4½ hours of nonstop driving. But quick escapes are supposed to be fun, so add another hour or so for a lovely, relaxing lunch-time stopover in the garden of an eighteenth century Southern plantation located in southern Fairfax County, Virginia, a few miles south of Alexandria. Take the Schuylkill Expressway (I–76) to I–95; travel south on I–95 for 96 miles. Continuing south, take I–895 through the Harbor Tunnel and you'll flow back onto I–95. Stay on 95 for another 76 miles until you come to exit 161; take 161 to Route 1 north.

### Afternoon

**LUNCH:** Along Route 1, within 2 miles either way of your destination, you will have a choice of dining options ranging from authentic Southern barbecue to fast-food burgers. Whatever you choose, get it to go and keep going north on Route 1 until you come to the first light (Gunston Road/SR 242); turn right. About 3.5 miles on the left you will find the entrance to **Gunston Hall** (10709 Gunston Road, 703–550–9220), located in the town of Mason Neck, Virginia. You will have been traveling approximately three hours.

"*That all men are by nature equally free and independent, and have certain inherent rights . . . namely, the enjoyment of life and liberty, with the means of acquiring and possessing property, and pursuing and obtaining Happiness and Safety.*" If these words written by George Mason in his Virginia Declaration of Rights have a somewhat familiar ring to them, that's because they were a major source of inspiration for Thomas Jefferson as he composed the Declaration of Independence. Like many of the major political figures of his time, Mason was a paradox—an unfaltering advocate of human rights who was also an owner of slaves.

Gunston Hall, Mason's circa 1755 home with its reconstructed slave quarters and other outbuildings, gives you a glimpse of plantation life as it was two centuries ago. You can also picnic on the grounds, stroll the restored boxwood gardens, and, for some real leg-stretching, take a walk along the beautiful nature trail on this more than 500-acre (once 5,500) former tobacco and wheat plantation. Open all year, daily 9:30 A.M.–5:00 P.M. Admission is $5.00 for adults, $4.00 for seniors, $1.50 for students in grades one to twelve, and free for preschool children.

Get back on I–95 south and take it 90 more miles (another hour and a half) until it joins with I–64 in Richmond. Get off at exit 78. That will take you to the **Metro Richmond Visitors Center** (1710 Robin Hood Road; 804–358–5511), where you can pick up some brochures, maps, and other useful information. Open daily 9:00 A.M.–5:00 P.M. (until 7:00 P.M. June–August). From there, head north on Boulevard (yes, just Boulevard) past West Broad Street and Monument Avenue and you'll find yourself in the middle of **The Fan,** one of Richmond's most beautiful and historic districts, so named because its streets literally fan out from Virginia Commonwealth University.

The largest intact Victorian neighborhood in the United States, the Fan is an architectural treasure trove where genteel turn-of-the-century brownstones and town houses in pastel candy colors with wrought-iron porches line cobblestone streets. Right in the heart of this district is the **Virginia Historical Society** (428 North Boulevard; 804–358–4901), where the permanent exhibition "The Story of Virginia" will give you an overview of the state's history from prehistoric to present times through interpretive displays and hundreds of artifacts including George Washington's diary and J.E.B. Stuart's uniform. Open Monday–Saturday 10:00 A.M.–5:00 P.M., Sunday 1:00–5:00 P.M. Admission is $4.00 for adults, $3.00 for seniors, $2.00 for students and children.

One of the boundaries of the Fan district is **Monument Avenue,** a magnificent boulevard where graceful eighteenth- and nineteenth-century mansions provide a dramatic backdrop for a series of elaborate and eloquent statues honoring Civil War heroes, including Jefferson Davis, Robert E. Lee, J.E.B. Stuart, and "Stonewall" Jackson. A recently added statue of tennis great Arthur Ashe Jr. recognizes his dedication to children as well as his athletic achievements.

## Evening

To get to your next destination, head east on Monument Avenue, which will turn into Franklin Street, until you come to Eighth Street. Make a right onto Eighth, go 1 block, and make a left onto Main Street; follow Main through the downtown area to the **Church Hill** district.

**DINNER: Millie's,** 2603 East Main Street; (804) 643–5512. In the late 1800s and early 1900s when tobacco was king in Richmond, warehouse workers in the Church Hill district used to frequent a diner that probably looked very much like its modern incarnation, Millie's, does today. Inside they might even recognize the vintage diner decor, from the red-topped stools at the counter/bar to the old-time jukeboxes at each table (two plays for a quarter—and you won't believe the selections). What they wouldn't recognize is the clientele, which seems to cover just about the entire spectrum of Richmond society, or the equally eclectic food, distinguished by all kinds and no particular kinds of local, regional, and international influences. The plating is sheer art and the appetizers and desserts pure magic. Expensive. Get there before 6:30 to avoid the long lines.

**LODGING: Linden Row Inn,** 100 East Franklin Street; (800) 348–7274 or (804) 783–7000). Housed in a row of seven meticulously restored antebellum townhouses built in the mid-1800s, the inn is itself considered a historic attraction. The walled courtyard garden is believed to have been the childhood playground of Edgar Allan Poe. Guest rooms are elegantly furnished with antiques and decorative fireplaces. Continental breakfast is included. Valet parking is available for $7.00 per day. Also on-site is an acclaimed white-tablecloth restaurant. Room rates range from $89 to $189.

If you're up for a little night music, the Linden Row Inn provides a free round-trip shuttle to **Shockoe Slip** (about 15 blocks away), the center of Richmond's glittering nightlife. Here you can choose your favorite style of live entertainment and/or dancing in any number of nightclubs, taverns, and comedy clubs that line the 1200 and 1300 blocks of Cary Street. One of the hottest places for live music every evening is the **Tobacco Company Restaurant & Nightclub** (1201 East Cary Street; 804–782–9431), two turn-of-the-century warehouses that have been transformed into one fabulous dual-level nightspot.

## DAY 2

### *Morning*

**BREAKFAST:** Linden Row Inn. Enjoy your complimentary continental breakfast in the lovely dining room.

Richmond is one of the only places I know where you can go whitewater rafting right through the heart of the downtown business district. **Richmond Raft Company** (4400 East Main Street; 804–222–RAFT) offers 5½-hour ($45 weekends, $40 weekdays) and three-hour ($40 weekends, $25 weekdays) James River rapid-shooting adventures daily from March through November.

*Shopping in historic Shockoe Slip.*

## Afternoon

Follow Main Street west to **Shockoe Bottom** (derived from the Indian name Shocquohocan, which means *flat stone at the mouth of the creek)*, where at 1914–16 East Main you will find the **Edgar Allan Poe Museum** (804–648–5523). The site of Poe's actual Richmond residence is a few blocks from this five-building complex with its centerpiece nineteenth-century stone house, courtyard, and garden. But here is where you'll find the largest collection of Poe first edition works, rarities, editions, manuscripts, and personal belongings. Open Sunday–Monday noon–5:00 P.M., Tuesday–Saturday 10:00 A.M.–5:00 P.M.; call for winter hours. Admission is $6.00 for adults, $5.00 for seniors and students, free for children eight and under.

**LUNCH: Poe's Pub,** 2706 East Main Street; (804) 648–2120. Thus inspired, go back to Church Hill where the pub awaits with "Raven fries," "Raven chili," and other fun lunchtime fare. Actually, the only thing even remotely related to Poe in this Irish tavern is a portrait on the wall, but the fries came highly recommended by the folks at the museum, and they were outstanding—hot, crisp, and spicy ($1.95 for a basket). Among the sandwich and platter offerings are such Southern standards as ribs and farm-raised catfish, which you can have batter-fried, Cajun, broiled, or topped with cheese in a sub. Inexpensive to moderate prices.

Heading back toward the downtown area, stop at the **Farmer's Market** at Seventeenth and Main Streets in the center of Shockoe Bottom, one of the oldest marketplaces in the country. Since the 1740s, Richmonders have been buying just-picked produce and other products at this open-air site, now a block-long facility that houses more than seventy-five local farmers. Be sure to stock up–it's going to be a long ride home tomorrow. Open Monday–Saturday 8:00 A.M. to "whenever" (usually around 4:00 or 5:00 P.M.).

Continue west on Main Street to Second Street, then north to Clay Street in the heart of **Jackson Ward,** a neighborhood that became a focal point for black culture and entrepreneurial enterprise following the Civil War. Tucked into a quiet residential street at the odd, yet true, address 00 Clay Street is the **Black History and Cultural Center of Virginia** (804–780–9093). You can take a self-guided tour through the constantly changing exhibitions chronicling the black experience in the Old and New South. But if Mary Lauderdale is available to walk you through, I can guarantee you one of the most moving and meaningful experiences you have ever had in your life. Every exhibit, photograph, and document has so much more to say than the casual eye could ever see, and Mary's heartfelt interpretations bring it all to life. Open Tuesday–Saturday 11:00 A.M.–4:00 P.M. Admission.

From the early 1600s until the beginning of the Civil War, **Shockoe Slip** was the primary commercial center of Richmond. Just about destroyed at the end of the war, it continued to decline until the early 1970s when the appearance of new and restored restaurants, nightclubs, and shops brought life back into the neighborhood. In fact, the 1300 block of East Cary Street in the Slip has become one of the most fashionable shopping districts for everything from apparel to antiques. At 1307 is **Glass Reunions** (804–643–3233), a cute name for a shop that carries some very pretty things—stained and glass-blown lamps, kaleidoscopes, fountains, and other one-of-a-kind decorative items. At 1314, **Cudahy's Gallery** (804–782–1776) features original arts and fine crafts from local and regional emerging and established artists.

## *Evening*

**DINNER: Frog and the Redneck,** 1423 East Cary Street; (804) 648–FROG. Shockoe Slip is also the home of this terrific whimsically named restaurant. Just to get the explanations out of the way, the Redneck is owner/chef Jimmy Sneed, who earned his nickname by wearing long hair, cowboy boots, and jeans with his chef jacket. The frog is a tribute to his French mentors and their influence on his all-American cooking. The decor makes you smile—cartoon images on the walls, a scribble of neon that reads simply "passion." Chef Jimmy makes up a new menu each day, always with an emphasis on the freshest seafood, pasta, and game. Some recent offerings have included grilled buffalo skirt steak, and saffron pasta with pan-seared fresh scallops. Expensive. A fixed price five-course tasting menu is also available (only by the table) for $45 per person. Dinner is by reservation only.

**LODGING:** Linden Row Inn.

## DAY 3

## *Morning*

**BREAKFAST: Strawberry Street Cafe,** 421 Strawberry Street; (804) 353–6860. The old-fashioned claw-foot bathtub-turned-salad bar that sits in the center of this pretty restaurant is such a well-known Richmond landmark that it was once part of an answer on *Jeopardy!* Another claim to fame is the restaurant's weekend brunch, including its $7.95 bar featuring all kinds of hot and cold selections (including that famous Virginia baked ham) and fresh-baked muffins and pastries. While you're enjoying your meal, take note of the four chalkboards featuring regularly changing art created by staff and local artists, and of the intricate stained-glass and wrought-iron arch suspended across the ceiling.

Designed in 1785 by Thomas Jefferson, the neoclassical, white-columned **Virginia Capitol** building (Ninth and Grace Streets on Capitol Square in the heart of downtown; 804–698–1788) is a true work of art. And in its rotunda stands another one, the world-famous life-size marble statue of George Washington by Jean Antoine Houdon, said to be the only sculpture for which our first president ever agreed to pose. Look closely at the rotunda's floor and you might see the prehistoric fossils in the marble. Open Monday–Saturday year-round, 9:00 A.M.–5:00 P.M.; Sunday April–November 9:00 A.M.–5:00 P.M., December–March from 1:00 P.M. Free.

Only a few blocks away at 1201 East Clay Street, the **Museum and White House of the Confederacy** (804–649–1861) was the nerve center of the Confederate States of America and home to President Jefferson Davis during those years. Now restored and furnished to its original grandeur, it offers a picture of his life as a leader and as a family man. The museum exhibits more than 15,000 items of Confederate artifacts and memorabilia, the largest such collection in the nation, including personal effects of Generals Lee, Jackson, and Stuart. The museum shop offers a selection of related goods; sales help support the museum's exhibitions and programs. The Museum and White House is open Monday–Saturday 10:00 A.M.–5:00 P.M., Sunday from noon. Admission is $8.00 for adults, $7.00 for seniors, $5.00 for students, and free for children under seven.

## *Afternoon*

At 2:00 every Sunday afternoon throughout the summer months, Patrick Henry's stirring "Give me liberty or give me death" speech can be heard ringing throughout **St. John's Church** (the centerpiece of **Church Hill** at 2401 East Broad Street; 804–648–5015) as the scene that took place right here in 1775 before the Second Virginia Convention is dramatically reenacted. Get here by 1:30 if at all possible because this is a popular event and fills up quickly. In addition to getting a seat, you'll also be rewarded for your punctuality with a pre-speech musical program. The speech lasts about thirty-five minutes. Admission is free.

**LUNCH: Julian's Restaurant,** 2617 West Broad Street; (804) 359–1607. For more than sixty years, the warm family welcome and Old World recipes have made Julian's Richmond's favorite spot for authentic northern Italian food. Aside from freshly made sandwiches and pizzas, the lunch menu features appropriately sized portions of the restaurant's famous fare, including baked lasagna, eggplant Parmigiana, and linguine with clam sauce for prices that only go as high as $6.95.

To return to Philadelphia, get on I–95 going north and follow it for 47 miles to Route 1. Take Route 1 north for about 5 miles into **Fredericksburg, Virginia,** and to the **Fredericksburg Battlefield Visitor Center,** 1013 Lafayette Boulevard; (540) 373–6122 (open 9:00 A.M.–5:00 P.M. daily with extended summer hours). If you're hungry or thirsty, there are numerous places to pick up a snack along Route 1.

Located halfway between the opposing capitals of Washington, D.C., and Richmond, this quaint little town was repeatedly shelled, burned, ravaged, and looted as four major Civil War battles—Fredericksburg, Spotsylvania Court House, the Wilderness, and Chancellorsville—raged in and around it from 1862 to 1864. All of these battlefields are close to the visitor center, which is located on Sunken Road, one of the major focal points of the fighting. An audiovisual presentation and museum exhibits recount these tumultuous years. You may also visit the nearby **Fredericksburg and Spotsylvania Military Park,** which encompasses portions of all four battlefields. Open daily from dawn to dusk. Admission is free for the Visitor Center and $3.00 for adults over seventeen for the park.

From Fredericksburg, get back onto I–95 heading north and retrace your steps from Day 1. The remainder of your return trip home should take about 3½ hours.

### THERE'S MORE

**Greater Richmond Transit Authority Trolley** (804–358–GRTC). Continuous service weekdays and Saturdays from 11:00 A.M. to 11:00 P.M. Stops within 2 blocks of most of the city's major attractions, restaurants, and entertainment spots. Cost is an almost unbelievable twenty-five cents per trip, or you can buy an all-day passport for $1.00.

**Golf.** Call (804) 323–6962 for a free guide to Richmond's thirteen public courses and other golfing facilities.

**Virginia Museum of Fine Arts,** 2800 Grove Avenue; (804) 367–0844. The largest art museum in the South offers a truly impressive collection of original masters from Monet to Picasso; priceless treasures from ancient and modern civilizations, including Africa, Japan, China, India, and the Himalayas; art nouveau and deco; Fabergé fantasies from the imperial Russian court; and even a 7-foot golden rabbit. Free. Tuesday, Wednesday, and Friday–Sunday 11:00 A.M.–5:00 P.M., Thursday until 8:00 P.M.

**TheatreVirginia,** at the Virginia Museum of Fine Arts; (804) 353–6161. Central Virginia's premier regional theater performs comedies, musicals, and classic dramas.

**Richmond Battlefield National Park,** 3215 East Broad Street; (804) 226–1981. Start at the Visitors Center (open daily 9:00 A.M.–5:00 P.M.), once the site of Chimborazo General Hospital where more than 76,000 Confederate sick and wounded were brought from the nearby battlefields of Cold Harbor, Drewry's Bluff, and Fort Harrison. In addition to a video and model of the original hospital, the center offers interpretive information and maps covering the 97-mile tour of preserved battlefields. Battlefield sites are open daily dawn to dusk.

**Agecroft Hall,** 4305 Sulgrave Road; (804) 353–4241. If this Tudor manor house looks as if it had been built in the fifteenth century, plucked right off an English estate and transported to Richmond, that's because it was. This painstakingly reconstructed house is furnished with antique art and everyday objects, original sixteenth- and seventeenth-century tapestries, and British military artifacts to offer a rare peek (at least rare on this side of the Atlantic) of life in Tudor and Stuart England. The gardens are not to be missed. Open Tuesday–Saturday 10:00 A.M.–4:00 P.M., Sunday 12:30–5:00 P.M. Combined admission for a guided tour of the house and gardens is $5.00 for adults, $4.50 for seniors, $3.00 for full-time students. Half-price for admission to gardens only.

## SPECIAL EVENTS

**April.** Annual Strawberry Hill Races, fairgrounds on Strawberry Hill; (804) 228–3200. Richmond's biggest steeplechase event sends the city into a celebration frenzy. The races are great, but the party is even better.

**June.** Festival of the Arts, Byrd Park, Boulevard and Idlewood Avenues; (804) 780–5733. An annual summer series of free performances ranging from classical music to modern dance to Shakespeare in the idyllic setting of an outdoor amphitheater.

**September.** Exide NASCAR 400, Richmond International Raceway (by the fairgrounds at Strawberry Hill); (804) 345–RACE. Major names in NASCAR racing.

**September.** State Fair of Virginia, fairground on Strawberry Hill; (804) 228–3200. Running for ten days near the end of the month, this annual event features midway rides, games, pig races, livestock exhibitions, and lots of food.

## OTHER RECOMMENDED RESTAURANTS AND LODGINGS

### *Richmond*

Berkley Hotel, Twelfth and Cary Streets; (804) 780–1300. European-style warmth and amenities with dramatic flair in Shockoe Slip. Rooms range from $145 to $165.

Jefferson Hotel, Franklin and Adams Streets; (804) 788–8000. The marble-columned lobby, sweeping staircase (said to be the inspiration for the one that played such a prominent role in *Gone With the Wind*), and antiques-furnished rooms give this 1890s hotel an unforgettable grandeur. Room rates range from $215 to $265.

Mr. Patrick Henry's Inn, 2300–02 East Broad Street; (804) 644–1322. Located 1 block west of historic St. John's Church, this circa 1855 inn has been restored to its pre–Civil War graciousness with spacious rooms, working fireplaces, and a formal patio garden. The on-site tavern and restaurant are also open to the public for lunch and dinner Monday–Saturday. Room rates range from $95 to $135 for a superior suite. A full breakfast is included.

Sam Miller's Warehouse, 1210 East Cary Street; (804) 644–5465. For almost a century, the freshest Chesapeake Bay seafood (including a to-die-for sherry cream-based lump-meat crab soup) has been served up in this laid-back tobacco warehouse setting. Prices are extremely moderate ($11.95 for a broiled or fried seafood platter).

Havana '59, 16 North Seventeenth Street; (804) 649–2822 or (804) 649–2825. A return to the sensual delights of pre-revolution Cuba with plaintain-encrusted chicken breast stuffed with chorizo and goat cheese, beef pica-dillo (a sort of Cuban chili), and a signature paella. Moderate.

Southern Culture, 2229 West Main Street; (804) 355–6939. At this noisy, lively spot, "Southern" can refer to anything from Virginia to Mexico, Louisiana Cajun to Caribbean. It's a flavorful mix of constantly changing surprises. Moderate.

None Such Place, Franklin Street at Eighteenth; (804) 644–0832. Located in Richmond's oldest commercial building, this lovely restaurant has an elegant—yet generally moderately priced—menu featuring new American cuisine.

### FOR MORE INFORMATION

In addition to the Visitors Center location on Robin Hood Road, there are three others strategically located around town:

- Richmond International Airport, exit 197 off I–64, east of Richmond; (804) 236–3260.

- Historic Downtown, Virginia State Capitol grounds at historic bell tower; (804) 648–3146.

- Metro Richmond Convention and Visitors Bureau, 550 East Marshall Street; (804) 782–2777; www.richmondva.org.

- Virginia Tourism Corporation; (800) 932–5827 or (804) 786–2051; www.virginia.org.

# INDEX

# ABOUT THE AUTHOR

MARILYN ODESSER-TORPEY is a freelance travel and feature writer whose work has appeared in a number of publications, including *Mid-Atlantic Travel* and *Philadelphia Magazine's Elegant Wedding*. She is also editor of the *Pennsylvania Wine Traveler*. A native Philadelphian, Marilyn only leaves home for quick—and sometimes not-so-quick—escapes. She, along with husband, Dan, two daughters, Dana and Kristen, and a spoiled cockatiel named Iago, are happy living at the center of the universe.